Moving to
Free Software

Moving to Free Software

Marcel Gagné

◆▾ Addison-Wesley

Upper Saddle River, NJ • Boston • Indianapolis • San Francisco
New York • Toronto • Montreal • London • Munich • Paris • Madrid
Capetown • Sydney • Tokyo • Singapore • Mexico City

Many of the designations used by manufacturers and sellers to distinguish their products are claimed as trademarks. Where those designations appear in this book, and the publisher was aware of a trademark claim, the designations have been printed with initial capital letters or in all capitals.

The author and publisher have taken care in the preparation of this book, but make no expressed or implied warranty of any kind and assume no responsibility for errors or omissions. No liability is assumed for incidental or consequential damages in connection with or arising out of the use of the information or programs contained herein.

The publisher offers excellent discounts on this book when ordered in quantity for bulk purchases or special sales, which may include electronic versions and/or custom covers and content particular to your business, training goals, marketing focus, and branding interests. For more information, please contact:

U.S. Corporate and Government Sales
(800) 382-3419
corpsales@pearsontechgroup.com

For sales outside the United States, please contact:

International Sales
international@pearsoned.com

This Book Is Safari Enabled

The Safari® Enabled icon on the cover of your favorite technology book means the book is available through Safari Bookshelf. When you buy this book, you get free access to the online edition for 45 days.

Safari Bookshelf is an electronic reference library that lets you easily search thousands of technical books, find code samples, download chapters, and access technical information whenever and wherever you need it.

To gain 45-day Safari Enabled access to this book:

- Go to http://www.awprofessional.com/safarienabled
- Complete the brief registration form
- Enter the coupon code LHJA-3TTK-DWU7-U8KH-UJZW

If you have difficulty registering on Safari Bookshelf or accessing the online edition, please e-mail customer-service@safaribooksonline.com.

Visit us on the Web: www.awprofessional.com

Library of Congress Cataloging-in-Publication Data
Gagné, Marcel.
  Moving to free software / Marcel Gagné.
    p. cm.
  Includes bibliographical references and index.
  ISBN 0-321-42343-7 (pbk. : alk. paper)
 1. Shareware (Computer software) 2. Open source software. I. Title.

QA76.76.S46G64 2007
005.3—dc22

2006029712

ISBN 0-321-42343-7

Text printed in the United States on recycled paper at Courier in Stoughton, Massachusetts.

First printing, November 2006

This book is dedicated to
my friend, Robert J. Sawyer,
who said, "I want you to write a book
titled Kiss the Blue Screen of Death Gooodbye!*",*
thereby getting me into this mess . . .
and to Carolyn Clink, who, as far as I know,
hasn't gotten me into any trouble.

Contents

Acknowledgments

Writing is primarily a solitary exercise, yet many people helped make this book, *Moving to Free Software*, possible. They did so by offering their time, expertise, and support along the way. I would like to take a few moments to thank some of those people.

First and foremost, I want to acknowledge my wonderful son, Sebastian, and my beautiful wife, Sally, the two most important people in my life. I love you both dearly. Sally is my love, my life, my inspiration, and my strength. She is also my best friend and confidante. Sebastian, meanwhile, has given me new eyes with which to see the world. I can't imagine a greater gift.

To my family and friends, thank you for believing in me, for your love, and for your support. I love you all.

Many thanks to Mark Taub, my editor, and to Heather Fox and Andrea Bledsoe, my publicists. Thanks also to Lara Wysong, Kelli Brooks, Michelle Bish, and to everyone at Addison-Wesley and Pearson. Thanks also to my agent, Richard Curtis.

My sincere thanks to those people who reviewed my book along the way. They are (in alphabetical order) Peter Linnell, Charles McColm, Lew Pitcher, and Sally Tomasevic. Your hard work, sharp eyes, and suggestions have helped make this a better book.

Finally, I would like to recognize and thank the free software community: the developers and software designers, the members of Linux user groups (including my own WFTL-LUG), the many who share their experiences on Usenet, and all those unnamed folks who give free advice under pseudonyms in IRC groups.

—Marcel Gagné

1

Introduction to Free Software

Welcome to the world of free software! This is a world where you can run excellent, high-quality software, free of charge. In fact, when you read about and start using some of the software I cover in this book, you'll feel like you are getting paid to use these packages. You could literally save hundreds, perhaps thousands, of dollars. After all, it is free software.

Don't be fooled by the high price tags of commercial software, or the non-existent price tag of this free software. Free software packages can provide the same level of high quality as any equivalent commercial package. Free software programmers are also professionals, sometimes working for large software companies that have chosen to make resources (of both time and money) available so that those same programmers can continue to contribute to free software projects.

Really Free?

When the discussion of what *free* means in relation to software, you'll often see the expressions "*free* as in speech" or "*free* as in beer." Sometimes, free isn't a question of cost. For instance, you can get a free copy (as in *free beer*) of a software package and install it on your system without breaking any laws.

Software can also be free, as in speech, in that you have the right to view the source code and modify it to suit your needs. This is important to understand because with some software packages, including your Windows operating system, looking at or changing the code could get you in legal trouble if you aren't specifically licensed to do so (or employed by the company as a programmer working on that software).

Perhaps this is where a little French helps. You'll also see the delineation free (*libre*) and free (*gratis*). The first, *libre*, means free in the sense that you have freedom of expression, the freedom of speech, and the freedom to think. The second, *gratis*, refers to no cost. Imagine yourself at a friend's party. Your friend walks up and hands you a beer—*gratis*.

All You Need Is . . .

I'm going to cover a lot of ground with the free software packages I tell you about in this book. There are Internet applications for surfing the Web, sending and receiving email, and chatting with your friends on Instant Messaging networks. Anyone who spends time online knows the Internet can be a dangerous place, so I'll be showing you how to protect yourself from viruses and spyware.

Back at the office, the OpenOffice.org package has everything you need for word processing, spreadsheets, presentations, and easy database management. Great looking documents sometimes need a little more, which is why I've included Scribus, a great desktop publishing package. Finally, because the office (or home) telephone bill can be another expense, I'll even teach you how to make free long distance phone calls, anywhere in the world.

Let's not forget multimedia. Create digital collections of all your music, set up a free audio recording and editing studio, and create your own podcasts. Of course, you might just want to download your favorite podcasts automatically; I'll show you how to do that as well.

After you've expressed yourself with your first podcast, you may want to try your hand at a little digital art. I'll tell you about the premier free graphical package or the open source world, the GIMP, an excellent alternative to Photoshop. With it, you can create something fresh or use it to touch up your digital photographs. If you've heard of Corel Draw or Macromedia Freehand, you know about vector art; if you know about vector art, you'll be thrilled to learn Inkscape, a powerful and remarkable package. What you create there might well wind up on the Web site you create using Nvu.

What point is all this work if you can't relax and have some fun with that computer of yours? No book on free software would be complete without some great, free games. Race down a snow-covered slope at high speed. Save the universe from alien invasion. Uncover an underwater mystery. Race other programs to the virtual death inside your computer. Fly the world. Rescue a princess.

As they say on television: but wait, there's more! The free software packages covered in this book may be all you need.

About the Money . . .

Let's face it, we could all use the extra money. That goes for home users, businesses, and public institutions alike. Especially the latter. If you are tired of your government, schools, hospitals, and public institutions always telling you why they don't have any money and why you should learn to do without, walk up to them and hand them a copy of this book.

Those institutions we support through our taxes have a moral obligation, if nothing else, to consider free software alternatives when they are deciding how to spend the millions we pay in taxes every year.

Besides, Bill Gates has enough billions from all the support you and your friends have given him over the years. He won't starve if you don't spend five hundred dollars on the next version of Microsoft Office. I don't just want to pick on Bill though; he's not the only billionaire out there who could do without your support.

They'll do all right. Honest.

Has Marcel Gone Mad?

Those of you who know me from my Linux columns and books, open source articles, and my frequent appearances on television and radio pushing all things Linux and open source might find this book a little strange. You might even find yourself asking this question:

A book about Windows software? Has Marcel gone to the dark side?

The short answer is no, but the long answer is somewhat more interesting. You see, I am a huge proponent of what I call transitional software.

Transitional Software

It has been an exciting time for the talented developers at the Mozilla project. Their Firefox browser (see Chapter 2) has re-ignited the browser wars and done what no one thought possible—taken a substantial market share away from the security-problem-plagued Internet Explorer. All around the Internet (and the world), there is a growing chorus of warnings, advising users to dump Internet Explorer and use alternate browsers such as Firefox. Even US-CERT and the Department of Homeland Security have suggested that users might want to use a different browser to deal with the security issues brought about by Internet Explorer.

Despite a seemingly endless parade of security issues, Microsoft's browser has managed to hold on to its position for an amazingly long time. Time, however, has a habit of chipping away at the sturdiest of empires. As I write this, more than two hundred million copies of Firefox have already been downloaded since version 1.0 was released (this book covers version 1.5). Meanwhile, the Mozilla Thunderbird email package (see Chapter 3) is also making real waves, providing an exciting, safer alternative to Microsoft's email package.

Firefox and Thunderbird represent what I call *transitional applications*, open source programs that run on Linux and Windows (and in some cases, Apple MacIntosh), thereby offering an equivalent for users who haven't yet switched to Linux but would like to keep their options *open*. Let's face it, change is difficult for people. As with any *dangerous addiction*, quitting cold turkey isn't easy, which is why there are products like nicotine gum and the patch. These are a smoker's transitional applications. So it is with moving from Windows desktops to Linux desktops. A move to Linux isn't nearly as difficult as some would have you believe, and most people will find themselves at home very quickly, but sometimes it helps to pave the way by introducing some Linux familiarity to the Windows desktop . . . and saving yourself a small fortune in the process.

Transitional applications can be a wonderful way to ease the transition when the time comes to move entirely to Linux (or to Mac OS, for that matter). Furthermore, applications like Firefox and Thunderbird can do wonders to help those users cut down on the security issues they have to deal with every time they turn their machines on. It's not as good or complete a solution as running Linux, but it is definitely a good start.

Tip Chapter 21 is an introduction to Ubuntu Linux, a copy of which is included on the DVD. This copy of Ubuntu Linux is a live CD, which means you can run it on your PC without having to install Linux or uninstall Windows. Then, if you decide you like running Linux, there is an icon on the desktop that makes installation easy.

The first application I'll cover in this book is Firefox, the Web browser. Another alternative worth considering is Firefox's big brother, the original Mozilla browser. Mozilla comes with an email package, IRC client, and an HTML editor built in. I haven't included Mozilla, but I invite you to check it out for yourself. With tabbed browsing and a pop-up ad blocker, Mozilla (or the leaner, faster, Firefox) should be part of every desktop, regardless of operating system. Then, there's Mozilla Thunderbird. With advanced security features and built-in spam filtering, there's no reason not to use it. You can easily import your old mail messages and be back to work in no time at all.

Perhaps the greatest transitional application of them all is the OpenOffice.org office suite, an excellent and powerful replacement for Microsoft Office. It provides a word processor that can read and write Word documents, an Excel compatible spreadsheet package, and a PowerPoint compatible presentation graphics package. OpenOffice.org is free for the price of a download. Simply using OpenOffice.org instead of purchasing Microsoft Office can save a medium-sized office thousands of dollars. If you have a dozen employees, you could save $5,000 or more. Read Chapters 6 through 9 for an introduction to the core OpenOffice.org applications: Writer, Calc, Impress, and Base.

I'm going to wrap up this discussion of transitional applications by talking about instant messaging (or IM). IM is no longer strictly the playground of teenagers or friends and family looking to keep in touch across the networked world. It is rapidly becoming a serious tool for business as well. Nothing beats being in constant touch with employees and team members, even if those people are scattered in offices around the globe. Gaim is a powerful, multiprotocol IM client that makes it unnecessary to run a package for every service you use. It supports Yahoo!, MSN, Jabber, ICQ, AOL, and others. Gaim, a free, open source application, is also available for Windows. I'll tell you all about Gaim in Chapter 4.

By using these transitional applications, or suggesting them to your friends who are still running Windows, you can reap some of the benefits that people running Linux take for granted. Firefox and Thunderbird decrease the number of viruses and spyware programs their systems are exposed to. OpenOffice.org saves money. Gaim saves operating systems from running six programs to do one job.

Running these transitional applications on Windows still isn't as good as running Linux. Nevertheless, it is a huge improvement over what has become the status quo on most desktops. It's also a start on the road to kicking a bad habit.

Installing Programs

Wherever possible, I've tried to include copies of the software covered in this book. The DVD contains the latest versions of the packages I cover at the time this book was completed. You can either use the package included on the DVD or follow the link to the application's Web site and download the latest version. Keep in mind, however, that the version you download may be slightly different than the version covered in the book. But changes in such a short time frame are usually small, so this shouldn't be a problem.

Whether you choose to download a new version or simply use the package included on the DVD, for the most part, installation is the same regardless of which package you install. Double-click the program's installer and you are on your way. Follow the instructions provided by the installer, click Next a few times, and that's pretty much it. Some programs come in a self-extracting archive (you'll learn about those in the chapter on 7-Zip), which unpacks several files into a temporary location before launching the installer.

Of course, this is a somewhat simplified explanation, so I'll emphasize a few points.

Read the license! I can't stress this enough. Most (but not all) of the packages I cover in this book come with an open source license known as the GNU General Public License (or GPL). This license gives you the freedom to makes copies of the software and redistribute it to others. It does not demand money from you, nor does it require that you provide personal information of any kind.

Not all software is this friendly. It's so easy to click that I Agree button, but unless you read the license, you don't know what you are agreeing to. In fact, you may be saying, "*Yes, please install this spyware on my system.*" I will tell you more about spyware in Chapter 17 when I tell you about SpyBot, a program designed to rid your system of spyware (and yes, you should read the SpyBot license, too).

Shut Down? Some installs ask that you reboot your system after installation is complete. Others ask that you shut down any programs you might be using before installing. The latter is usually a *just in case* measure, but if an install program asks you to shut down the applications you are using and this isn't a good time, just put off the install until you are ready. It's usually better than just going ahead with the install.

Start Now? In many cases, the installer has a couple of final check marks just as the process is wrapping up. These are usually offers to show you the latest documentation (or README) and to automatically start the program. This is probably what you want, but just in case it isn't, pay attention to that last install screen.

Finding Even More Free Software

The software in covered in this book should keep you busy for a while, but eventually your appetite for even more free software will send you looking. But where can you start looking for the next great, free package? How about right here.

The following sites are all great places to discover new free software.

The OpenCD Project: www.theopencd.org

The OpenCD is just what it sounds like: a CD of free software where you download, burn, and install free software.

Winlibre, Free Software for Windows: `www.winlibre.com/en`
In some ways, Winlibre sounds a lot like the OpenCD project, but the site also provides a mini mega-installer front-end from which you select packages, click, and install. Think of it as a specialized browser that only serves up free software.

The OSSwin Project: `osswin.sourceforge.net`
This is a huge, categorized list of free software for Windows. Well worth the visit.

My Open Source: `www.myopensource.org`
Visit My Open Source and you'll discover a huge list of open source software for Windows, categorized as to your needs, sorted alphabetically, and rated under a five-star system.

Another place to check is my own Web site. Click the Moving to Free Software book cover in the left menu and you'll discover a great list of free and, where possible, open source software. You can also head directly to the list by clicking the following address:

```
www.marcelgagne.com/freewinlist.html
```

What About Support?

Using free software doesn't mean you are on your own. Many of these packages are supported, not by a single individual, but by a community. Businesses like IBM, Google, and others also put money into free software development and support.

If you have a question, visit the package's Web site (listed in the Resources section of each chapter) and check its forums. Other sites maintain 24-hour-a-day chat channels on IRC (see Chapter 4) where you can ask questions. In fact, support for the most popular free software package of them all, the Linux operating system, is consistently rated among the best you can get.

"Linux?" you ask. Well . . .

Linux! The Ultimate Free Software

At the end of this book, I'm going to spend a chapter introducing you to the very best in free software, a free software operating system called Linux.

Linux is a powerful, reliable (rock-solid, in fact), expandable, flexible, configurable, multiuser, multitasking, and completely free operating system that runs on many different platforms. These include Intel PCs, DEC Alphas, Macintosh systems, PowerPCs, and a growing number of embedded processors. You can find Linux in PDA organizers, digital watches, golf carts, and cell phones. In fact, Linux has a greater support base (in terms of platforms) than just about any other operating system in the world.

A Truly Free Operating System

Linux is free software that is both free as in speech or free as in beer. In the case of Linux, free isn't a question of cost, although you can get a free copy (as in *free beer*) of Linux and install it on your system without breaking any laws. As Robert A. Heinlein would have said, "There ain't no such thing as a free lunch." A free download will still cost you connection time on the Internet, disk space, time to burn the CDs, and so on. However, in the case of Ubuntu Linux (included on the DVD), you can have a free CD mailed to you, so *free* in this case, starts to feel pretty, well . . . free.

Linux is also free, as in speech, in that you have the right to view the source code and modify it to suit your needs.

Any Other Reasons?

Well, several, actually. These days, Linux is even easier to install than your old operating system, and you don't have to reboot time and again as you load driver disk after driver disk. I won't bore you with everything I consider an advantage but I will give you a few of the more important points.

Say goodbye to your virus checker and stop worrying. Although Linux is not 100 percent immune to viruses, it comes pretty close. In fact, to date, most so-called Linux viruses do not exist *in the wild* (only under tightly controlled environments in *proof-of-concept* labs). It isn't that no one has tried, but the design model behind Linux means that it is built with security in mind. Consequently, viruses are virtually nonexistent in the Linux world, and security issues are dealt with quickly and efficiently by the Linux community. Security flaws are well advertised.

The stability of Linux is almost legendary. Living in a world where people are used to rebooting their PCs one or more times a day, Linux users talk about running weeks and sometimes months without a reboot. *Illegal operations* and the *Blue Screen of Death* are not part of the Linux experience. Sure, programs occasionally crash here, but they don't generally take down your *whole* system with them.

Linux is a multitasking, multiuser operating system. In this book, I concentrate on the desktop features of Ubuntu Linux, but under the hood, Linux is a system designed to provide all the power and flexibility of an enterprise-class server. Linux-powered Web site servers and electronic mail gateways move information along on the Internet and run small to large businesses. Under the friendly face of your graphical desktop, that power is still there.

It is possible to do everything you need to do on a computer without spending any money on software—that means new software and upgrades alike. In fact, free software for Linux is almost an embarrassment of riches. And contrary to what you may have heard, installing software on a modern Linux system is incredibly easy.

When you run Linux, you don't have to worry about whether you've kept a copy of your operating system license. The GNU GPL, which I mentioned earlier, means you are legally entitled to copy and can legally redistribute your Linux CDs if you want. You don't have to worry about giving your friend a copy of Linux because you aren't breaking any laws. Make as many copies as you like and hand them out. It's not only perfectly legal, it's encouraged!

Keep in mind, however, that although Linux itself can be freely distributed, *not all software* that runs on Linux is covered by the same license. If you buy or download software for your system, you should still pay attention to the license that covers that software. Remember what I said about reading before you click *I Agree*.

Full Steam Ahead

Regardless of whether you choose to run Linux, you should take it for a spin. If you do decide that Linux isn't for you, you still have some fantastic free software to use on your Windows system.

So turn the page and take your first step toward *Moving to Free Software*.

Resources

My Open Source

http://www.myopensource.org

The OpenCD Project

http://www.theopencd.org

The OSSwin Project

http://osswin.sourceforge.net

Winlibre, Free Software for Windows

http://www.winlibre.com/en

Chapter

2

Surfing the Web with Firefox

The hottest and coolest browser of the day is called Firefox. Before Firefox made its appearance a short while ago, everyone assumed that the browser world belonged to the browser from Redmond, the security-problem-plagued Internet Explorer. As I write this, Internet Explorer has dipped to below 90 percent of the browser market share in North America and below 80 percent in Europe. This is quite the feat considering that Internet Explorer commanded something around 95 percent of the market before Firefox. Better security and advanced features are drawing millions of users away from Microsoft's browser. Firefox is an exciting program, and I'll show you how it works in this chapter.

Mozilla versus Firefox

Firefox is distributed by the same people who distribute the Mozilla browser. In fact, Firefox is a Mozilla product.

So what's the difference between Mozilla and Firefox? The actual Mozilla browser is more like the Swiss Army knife of browsers. It includes an email package and IRC client, is ideal for reading newsgroups, and comes with an HTML editor. Firefox, on the other hand, is strictly a Web browser (see Figure 2-1). It's smaller, faster, and more geared to its primary job, providing you with a superior surfing experience. To get the equivalent standalone email package, you should download Thunderbird (which I will cover in Chapter 3). Right now, I'd like to concentrate on Firefox, so let's get started.

To start Firefox, click the Start button, navigate to the Mozilla Firefox submenu, and then select Mozilla Firefox. There's also a quick access icon for Firefox on your desktop if you accepted the defaults during installation.

Figure 2–1   Firefox is an excellent and capable browser that is setting the world on fire.

Working from Home

When you first start Firefox, it takes you to its home, an introductory page that is locally installed on your system. The location is identified in the URL/location bar directly below the menu bar. Getting to a Web site and navigating Firefox is much the same as it is in any other browser you have used, particularly if you were using Mozilla. All you do is type the URL of the Web site you want to visit into the location bar, and away you go. If you would like to start each time on a personal home page, this is easily done.

Click Tools in Firefox's menu bar and select Tools, then Options from the submenu. The Options window opens up with a number of icons running along the top, directly under the title bar, from which you select what part of Firefox you want to modify. By default, it opens up to the General category (see Figure 2-2). Directly below, in the Home Page section, there are three buttons. The first button, Use Current Page, enters whatever URL (or page) you are currently visiting into the Location field as your home page. The middle button, Use Bookmark, brings up a dialog with your current bookmarks. Clicking the Use Blank Page button starts Firefox on a blank page. You could, of course, just type the URL into the Location field, click OK, and you would be done.

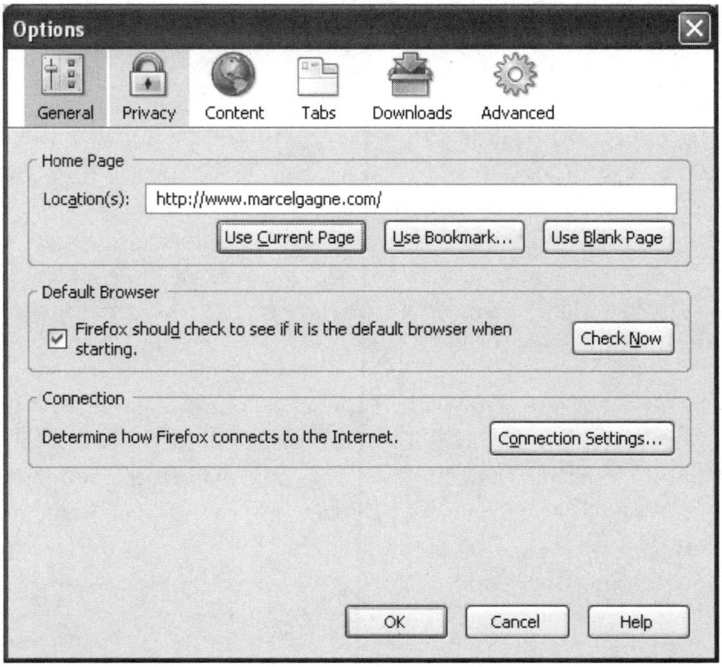

Figure 2–2   Setting your home page in Firefox's Options menu.

Quick Tip   Before closing the Options dialog, did you notice that the Location field actually says Location(s)? That's right, it could be plural. If you have multiple tabs open (which I'll cover next), the Use Current Page button becomes Use Current Pages. When you click the Home icon, Firefox opens tabs to all your favorite pages. If you want to manually enter a list of pages into the location bar, just separate each page with the pipe symbol (|) (usually found above the backslash key on your keyboard).

Keeping Tabs on the Web, Firefox Style

Firefox sports a great feature called *tabbed browsing*. Here's how it works.

Sometimes when you are viewing Web sites, you want to keep a particular site open while moving to another place on the Web. Normally, you click File and select New Window. This is fine, except that if you keep doing this, you wind up with many versions of a browser open on your desktop. Switching from one to the other involves doing a little digital juggling. Tabs make it possible to bring a nice, clean air of sanity to what could otherwise become a very cluttered taskbar (or desktop). With tabbed browsing, you simply open additional Web sites in the same browser window, then move from one to the other by clicking the open site's appropriate tab.

Here's how you do it. Start by visiting a site of your choice. Now click File, select New, and choose New Tab from the drop-down menu. You can also use the <Ctrl+T> keyboard shortcut to do the same thing. Notice that Firefox now identifies your sites with tabs just below the location bar (see Figure 2-3) or if you have it turned on, your Bookmarks toolbar. Add a third or a fourth tab if you like. Switching from site to site is just a matter of clicking the tabs on your single copy of Firefox.

 Tip   Here's a cool trick. There's a right mouse button, a left mouse button, and often a middle mouse button. Even if you don't have a middle mouse button, you can still mimic the action of the middle button by pressing the left and right buttons at the same time. Some applications are written to take advantage of this middle button (or phantom middle button).

So why am I telling you this? Click a link using the middle button and that link automagically opens up in a new tab. Cool? Cool.

Figure 2–3   Firefox showing off its tabs.

While in tab mode (as shown in Figure 2–3), you can right-click on a tab to bring up the tab menu. From there you can close or reload the current tab (or all tabs) and even open new tabs. Another way to close the active tab is to click on the X at the end of the tab list.

Tip When you have several tabs open, you might decide that you would like a particular site in another position. Let's say that you are using one site more than another and you would like it in the first position but it is currently at the end. No problem. Just click the tab and drag it into the new position.

Go for the Big Screen

Just as there's no comparison between your old 20-inch TV and that new 50-inch flat panel HDTV, nothing beats looking at the virtual world through a big screen. As much as I would like to, I can't increase the size of your monitor, but I can help you with the next best thing. When you are busy surfing the Internet and you want as much screen as possible, why not try Firefox's full-screen mode?

At any time while you are viewing a page, you can click View on the menu bar and select Full Screen. The title bar disappears, as does the top and bottom panels, and all other border decorations. Another, quicker way to switch to full-screen mode is to press <F11>. Pay attention to this because this is how you switch back to normal view.

Ban the Pop-Up Ads, Forever!

Honestly, I can't think of a single person who likes to visit a Web site only to have that site throw up annoying pop-up window ads. Firefox lets you stop this easily. Actually, Firefox has pop-ups blocked by default, but you may want to alter that behavior for some sites. Here's how.

Start by bringing up the Options menu again (click Tools on the menu bar and choose Options). From the category list (see Figure 2-4), choose Content. You'll see a check box labeled Block Popup Windows. Next to that label is a button labeled Allowed Sites. Clicking this button allows you to specify sites where pop-ups may be desirable. When you are satisfied with your configuration, click OK to close the Options menu.

When Firefox intercepts a pop-up, it displays a message like the one in Figure 2-5.

Clicking the Options button at the end of the bar offers you three choices. You can allow pop-ups for that particular Web site or edit the pop-up blocker preferences for that particular Web site. You also have the option of choosing never to see the message when pop-ups are blocked. Okay, so there is a fourth choice: You can decide whether to view the pop-up Firefox just blocked.

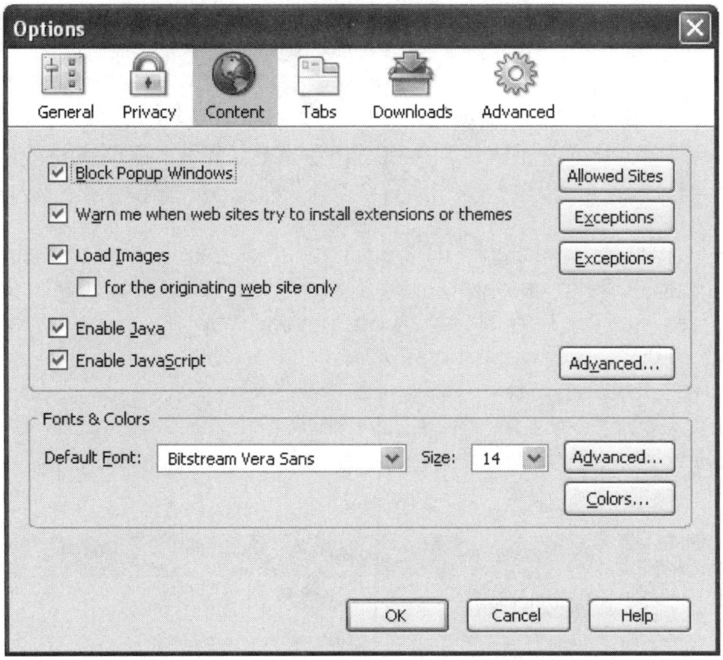

Options

General Privacy Content Tabs Downloads Advanced

☑ Block Popup Windows   Allowed Sites

☑ Warn me when web sites try to install extensions or themes   Exceptions

☑ Load Images   Exceptions
  ☐ for the originating web site only

☑ Enable Java
☑ Enable JavaScript   Advanced...

Fonts & Colors

Default Font: Bitstream Vera Sans ▾   Size: 14 ▾   Advanced...
                                                           Colors...

OK   Cancel   Help

Figure 2–4   Firefox lets you specify sites where pop-ups are okay.

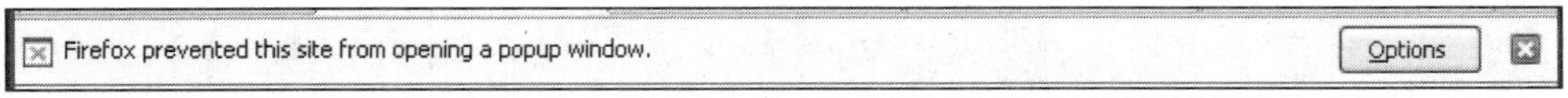

☒ Firefox prevented this site from opening a popup window.   Options ☒

Figure 2–5   Firefox has blocked a pop-up. What would you like to do?

Yummy . . . Cookies

Not that kind of cookie. Cookies are simply small text files transmitted to your browser (or system) when you visit a Web site. The original idea behind cookies was that a server would give you a cookie as a marker to indicate where you had previously visited. That cookie might store a username and password to access a particular Web site or other information related to your visit, such as an online shopping cart. When you next visit the site, the server would ask your browser whether it had served you any cookies, and your browser would reply by sending the cookies from before. In this way, the Web site would recognize you when you next visited, and certain useful defaults would be set up for you. Cookies can be very good.

The problem with cookies is that they can also be shared within larger domains, such as advertising rings. Using these shared cookies, advertisers can build a profile of your likes and dislikes, tailoring and targeting advertising to you specifically. Many people object to this method of building user profiles and consider the use of cookies to be quite unethical, an invasion of privacy. The dilemma then is to find a way to accept the cookies you want and reject the others.

Firefox is quite versatile in its handling of cookies. Before you excitedly turn off all cookies, do remember that they can be useful, particularly with online services such as banks and e-commerce sites. That said, you may very much want to curb cookie traffic as much as possible.

From the Options menu, open up the Privacy category submenu (see Figure 2-6). Along the top, there is a series of tabs, including one labeled Cookies. Click the tab to bring up your cookies Options dialog.

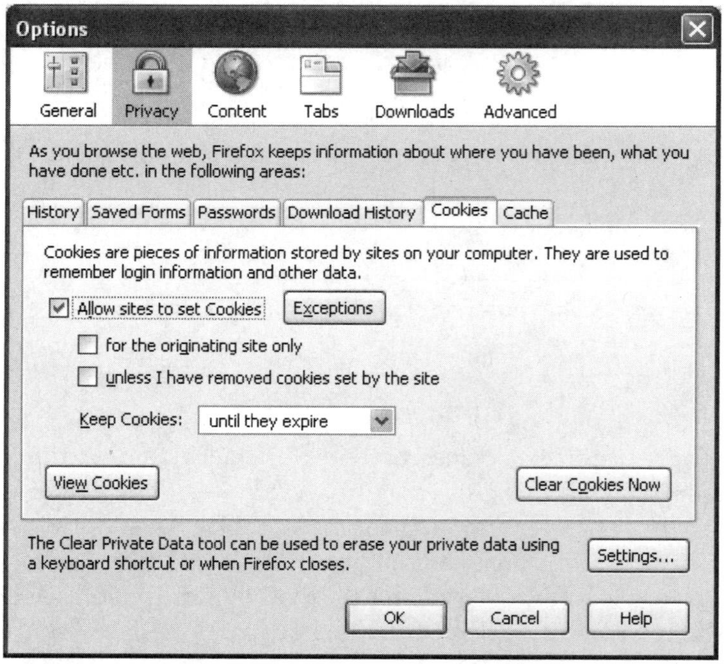

Figure 2–6   Back to Firefox's Options menu to configure cookie policies.

Unless you really want to refuse all cookies, leave the Allow Sites to Set Cookies check box checked. Then, from the Keep Cookies drop-down box, choose Ask Me Every Time. Click Close, and resume your surfing. When you visit a site that tries to set or modify a cookie, an alert pops up, alerting you to the cookie and asking you how to proceed. If you decide to deny a cookie and you never want to see another cookie from that site, check Use My Choice for All Cookies from This Site before clicking Allow or Deny (see Figure 2-7).

Figure 2–7 A pop-up allows you to allow or deny a cookie. This would be a good site to allow all cookies from.

The Firefox Sidebar

The Firefox sidebar is a quick way to get to your information, in this case browsing history and bookmarks. You can have one or the other at your side by clicking View on the menu bar and selecting the sidebar submenu. One quick way to activate the bookmarks sidebar is by pressing <Ctrl+B>. The same keystroke banishes the sidebar.

You may already know that your system keeps a history of Web sites you have visited. By default, that history goes back nine days. The amount of history can be set by clicking Edit on the menu bar and selecting Preferences. You'll find the History settings under Privacy, just as you did with Cookies.

To activate the history sidebar, choose it from the View menu (under Sidebar) or press <Ctrl+H> and the sidebar appears (see Figure 2-8). The sidebar makes searching for a site you visited in the last few days easy. At the top of the sidebar, you see a search field. Just type your search keywords in the location bar and press <Enter>. Click any link displayed and you instantly are transported to that site.

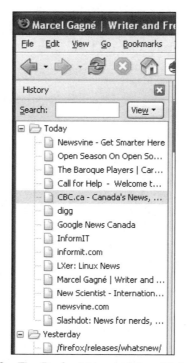

Figure 2–8   The Firefox history sidebar. It's just a jump to the past.

Addicted to News: Firefox Does RSS

I love watching those old movies where something important happens, something momentous even, and suddenly everyone knows about it pretty much instantly. How, you ask, is this possible? The news kid, that's how. One scene change later, some kid with a dirty face appears brandishing a large bag filled with newspapers, waving copies in his equally dirty hands while yelling, *"Extra! Extra! Read all about it!"* Even in this age of networked systems and high-speed Internet access, it's pretty hard to compete with that kind of service. At least, it used to be.

Imagine for a moment that your favorite news source releases a new story, something you definitely want to keep on top of. You don't have time to go looking at all those news sources, blogs, and other dynamic information sites. How do you get that dirty-faced kid to make an appearance with a copy?

That's the function of a news aggregator program. You give the program a list of sites that you want monitored for changes, and it does the collecting for you. No need to visit all those sites looking for the latest information—just look in the list and you'll find it there waiting for you, like that little kid waving the paper in his hand. Aggregators do this by subscribing to RSS or Atom newsfeeds. RSS stands for Real Simple Syndication, the actual feed language. Atom is another XML-based feed language, created to deal with incompatibilities in RSS where multiple, incompatible, versions exist.

Firefox, Collect My News, Please

You may not know it, but with Firefox, you already have a news aggregator and using it to subscribe to newsfeeds is a piece of cake. Visit a page where an RSS or Atom newsfeed exists. This could be your favorite tech news Web site or blog (you can use my Web site at `www.marcelgagne.com` for a test, if you'd like). You'll know that a feed is available by looking at the end of the location field, past the page's URL. You'll see a small orange-colored icon there. Hover your mouse pointer over it, and a tooltip appears with the words Add Live Bookmark (see Figure 2-9).

Figure 2–9 It's easy to monitor a feed inside Firefox. Just click the Add Live Bookmark icon.

Click the icon to see a small pop-up message window offering you the option of subscribing to that feed. Click the message window to accept the subscription; the Firefox Add Live Bookmark dialog box appears (see Figure 2-10). The Name field has the feed's name as provided by the site, but you can override that by entering whatever you would like. Below that is a drop-down list labeled Create In; the default is your Bookmarks folder. You can accept the default, add it to your toolbar, or create a new folder specifically for your newsfeeds.

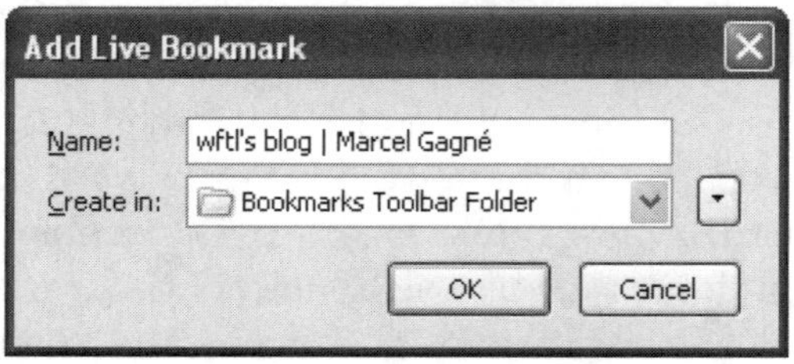

Add Live Bookmark   ☒

Name: wftl's blog | Marcel Gagné

Create in: 📁 Bookmarks Toolbar Folder   ⌄   ▾

OK   Cancel

Figure 2–10   Your next step is to tell Firefox
where to store the bookmark.

That's it. When you click that bookmark, a list of the current postings
relating to that feed appears. Two options are open to you at this point. The
first is simple: You can click the story that interests you, and it opens in your
browser (the number of items in the list varies, depending on the site).
There's also a second option at the bottom of the list, labeled Open in Tabs.
Choosing this option opens one Firefox browsing tab for each of the stories.

 Tip If you don't see your bookmarks toolbar, you can turn it on
by clicking View on the menu bar, navigating to the Toolbars submenu, and selecting Bookmarks Toolbar. A check mark appears
beside the menu entry and your bookmark toolbar appears
below the navigation toolbar.

Extending Firefox

Firefox is an excellent browser on many counts, but one if its coolest features
is its potential to add features and capabilities through a system of extensions.
Extensions are program enhancements that can dramatically change how
you work with your browser. This framework of extensions makes Firefox
not just a great browser, but a superior browser.

To experience Firefox extensions, click Tools on the menu bar and select
Extensions. A window appears with a list of the extensions already in your system. On a fresh install, there is usually nothing here other than the language
pack. Along the bottom of this window is a button labeled Find Updates (see
Figure 2-11). You use this to keep the extensions you use up to date. Next to it
is a Get More Extensions link, which is where we start our journey.

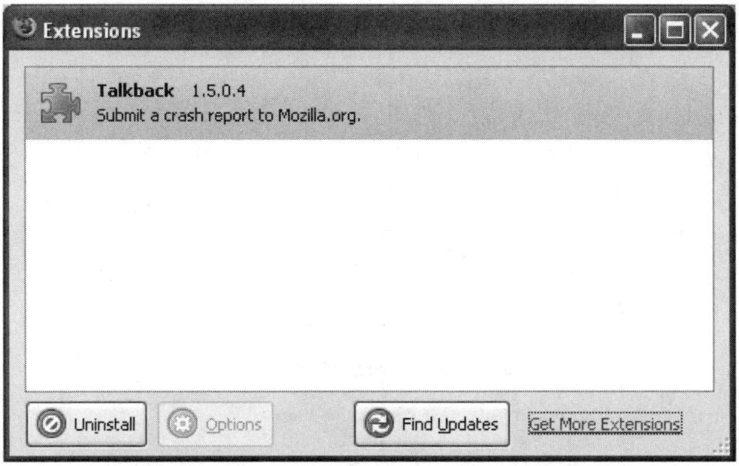

Figure 2–11 The Firefox extensions window not only gives you access to installed extensions, but provides a link to many others.

When you click that link, a new browser opens to the Firefox Add-ons site. You can also visit the site directly, without going through the extension dialog, by visiting `https://addons.mozilla.org/firefox`. The Extensions tab is already selected with some of the latest and most popular extensions front and center. You can also search based on categories from blogging to humor, navigation, search tools, news reading, and more. Some are extremely useful and designed to make your browsing more efficient. Some are just plain silly. Each extension has a description and a link to install it. If this is your first visit, click the We Recommend button for some great suggestions.

Let me show you an example by installing a totally silly extension, Anthony Howe's Bork Bork Bork!, an extension that makes your Web pages look as though they were written by *The Muppet Show's* Swedish Chef. After I click the Install link on the extension's description page, a window appears asking for confirmation before going ahead and installing the extension (see Figure 2-12). There's also a warning about installing malicious software. To continue, click the Install Now button.

That's it. You must restart Firefox to have the new extensions loaded. When I next surf to a site, I can right-click the page and select View Bork Text from the menu; in a few seconds, my page is translated into something only the Swedish Chef could understand (see Figure 2-13).

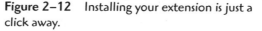

Figure 2–12   Installing your extension is just a click away.

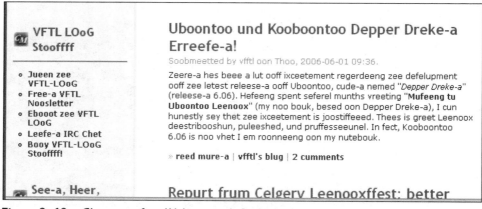

Figure 2–13   Close-up of my Web site with *Borked* text.

My silly example aside, there are some that *must have* extensions. Some of the more popular extensions include AdBlock, BugMeNot, ForecastFox, Fasterfox (soup up your browser), StumbleUpon, VideoDownloader, and FoxyTunes. Browse the Firefox extensions page, try a few, and come up with your own favorites. Of course, not all extensions are on the Firefox site. One of my personal favorites is Tab Preview (see Figure 2-14) from Ted's Mozilla Page (see "Resources" section). This handy little extension provides a thumbnail view of your tabbed pages when you pause your mouse cursor over the tab.

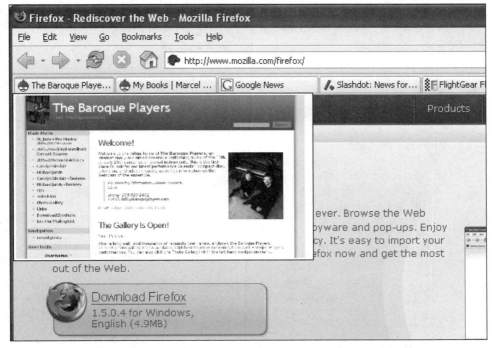

Figure 2–14 Tab Preview provides a handy thumbnail view of your tabbed pages.

Firefox extensions are hugely popular and numerous programmers have contributed their own. Several sites have also appeared to review and discuss the latest extensions. Enter **favorite Firefox extensions** in your Google search bar and enjoy.

Resources

Firefox

http://www.mozilla.com/firefox

Firefox Add-ons

https://addons.mozilla.org/firefox

Mozilla

http://www.mozilla.org

Tab Preview Extension

http://ted.mielczarek.org/code/mozilla/tabpreview/index.html

3

Thunderbird: A Safer Email Client

These days, it seems that when we think about the Internet, we think about Web browsers first. To those of us who have been on the Net for more years than we care to admit, that always seems a bit strange. The chief medium of information exchange on the Internet has always been electronic mail, or email. Although our perception has changed, email is probably still the number one application in the connected world.

In this chapter, I will introduce you to a powerful, graphical email client that is safer, faster, and more flexible than the default client on your PC. It's called Thunderbird and it comes from the same group that brought you Firefox, the Mozilla foundation. Thunderbird also features great spam filtering, a built-in newsreader, and more. In just a few keystrokes, I'll have you sending and receiving mail like a Thunderbird pro. I will also show you how to make Thunderbird do things your old email client never dreamed of.

Be Prepared! Before we start, you need to have some information handy. This includes your email username and password, as well as the SMTP and POP3 server addresses for sending and receiving your email. All of this information is provided for you by your Internet service provider (ISP) or your company's systems administrator.

Thunderbird

Getting started with Thunderbird is easy. The program features a clean, easy-to-use interface that you are going to love (see Figure 3-1). Beneath that friendly face, however, is one of the most powerful email packages available. Let me get you introduced. To start Thunderbird, double-click the desktop icon created when you installed the package. You can also click Start, navigate to the Programs menu, and then the Mozilla Thunderbird submenu. From there, click Mozilla Thunderbird.

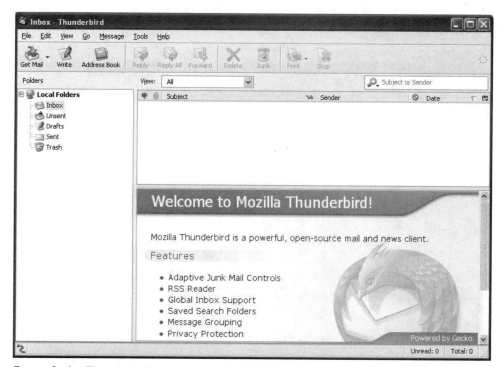

Figure 3–1   Thunderbird has a clean, friendly, easy-to-use interface.

When the program starts up for the first time, you find yourself looking at the Import Wizard (see Figure 3-2). The wizard provides you with a means of importing your settings and mail folders from your old email package. This includes old email messages, address books, and so on.

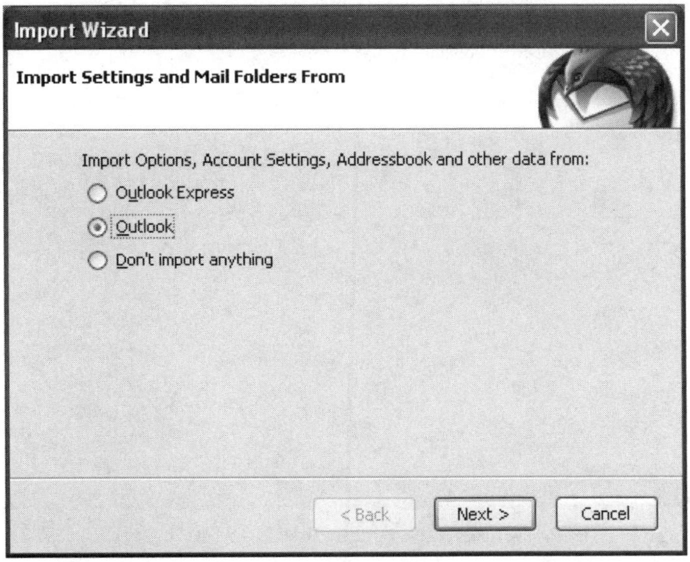

Figure 3–2 The Import Wizard takes care of your old mail folders, settings, and address books.

Select the package you are importing from, and then click Next. As soon as you do, the wizard pulls your data in. As soon as the process completes, a window appears asking you if you want to use Mozilla Thunderbird as your default mail application. The correct answer, assuming you are going to use Thunderbird from here on in, is Yes.

If you would rather skip this step and start clean, select Don't Import Anything. I'm going to continue as though we are starting from scratch and you need to configure Thunderbird completely. In this scenario, the next thing you see is the Account Wizard. You may use it to set up your email account, your RSS feeds, or blogs, or to configure an email account. Email account is selected by default, so click Next to enter your personal information or Identity (see Figure 3-3). Yes, you can have multiple identities, secret or otherwise.

Figure 3–3   Thunderbird's Account Wizard starts by asking you to set up your default identity.

When you are finished, click Next and you can enter information for receiving mail (see Figure 3-4). You start by selecting a server type, whether POP or IMAP, by clicking the appropriate radio button. Now, enter the host name of the POP3 or IMAP host (as provided by your ISP or system administrator).

Click Next to enter your username (the password comes later), then Next again to give the account a name. Thunderbird assigns a default name that is, in fact, your email address. Because this is strictly for display purposes, most people enter a friendlier name here. It could be your name in full or something descriptive like **My home account**. The latter makes sense when you consider that you can have multiple identities.

Click Next one more time and you get one final confirmation screen before you click Finish and commit all these details. A check box on this final screen asks whether you want to download your email now. To fine-tune your account details (e.g., setting an interval to automatically check for messages) or to add another account, click Tools on the menu bar and select Account Settings.

Account Wizard ✕

Server Information

Select the type of incoming server you are using.

⦿ POP ○ IMAP

Enter the name of your incoming server (for example,
"mail.example.net").

Incoming Server: `pop.yourmailserver.dom`

Uncheck this checkbox to store mail for this account in its own
directory. That will make this account appear as a top-level account.
Otherwise, it will be part of the Local Folders Global Inbox account.

☑ Use Global Inbox (store mail in Local Folders)

Enter the name of your outgoing server (SMTP) (for example,
"smtp.example.net").

Outgoing Server: `smtp.yourmailserver.dom`

< Back | Next > | Cancel

Figure 3–4   You need to let Thunderbird know where to pick
up and send your email.

Tip The account wizard sets up your incoming and outgoing
server in the simplest possible way. For instance, the outgoing
SMTP server is set to use the default port 25 and to transmit plain
text. Some servers, however, may use an alternate port or force the
use of a secure connection. Click Tools on the menu bar and select
Account Settings. Then, from the left sidebar, click Outgoing Server
to adjust your settings. The same applies to the incoming Server
Settings (directly below your account information).

Sending and Receiving Mail

Thunderbird starts up with a list of folders in the left sidebar. These folders
are named Inbox, Unsent, Drafts, Sent, and Trash (see Figure 3-5). Now that
you have set up your accounts and Thunderbird is ready to go, click the Get
Mail icon on the left side of the main icon bar.

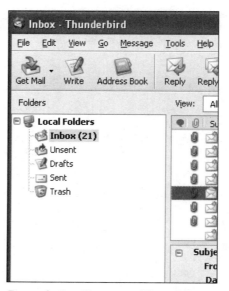

Figure 3–5   Close-up of Thunderbird's main window with its default list of folders.

The first thing you are likely to do, even before sending an email message, is to pick up your mail. Thunderbird pauses and asks for the password (see Figure 3-6). You have an interesting choice to make here. To the left of the words Use Password Manager to Remember This Password is a check box that lets you lock in the information. If you choose not to record your password with Thunderbird, you have to enter your password each time you check for mail.

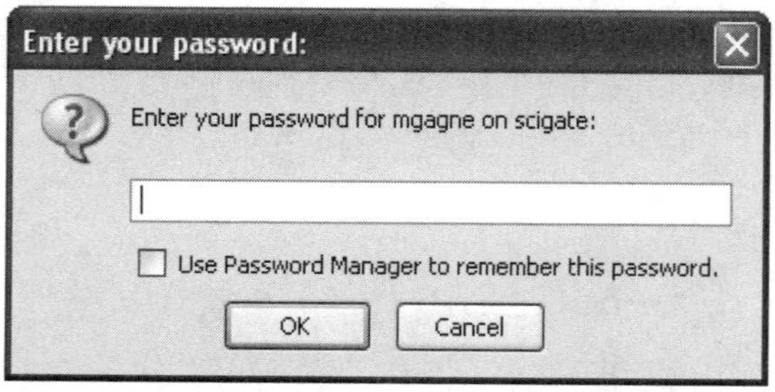

Figure 3–6   Would you like Thunderbird to automatically remember your password?

To send a message, click the Write button, directly to the right of the Get Mail button. To create a new mail message, you can also click File on the menu bar and select New, Message from there. Thunderbird's Compose window appears (see Figure 3-7).

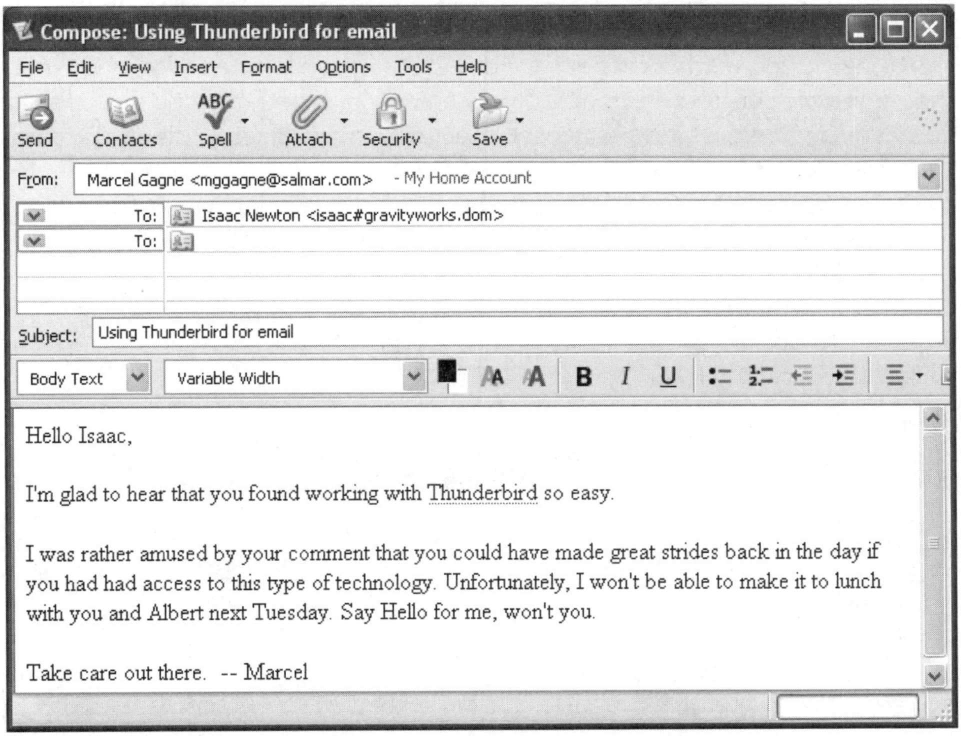

Figure 3–7 Sending a message with Thunderbird—the Compose window.

If you have ever sent an email message, this is pretty standard stuff. Fill in the person's email address in the To: field, enter a Subject, and type your message. When you have completed your message, click the Send button on the Compose window (or click File on the Compose window's menu bar, and then select Send Now).

Tip Click File from the menu bar and you also see an option to Send Later. If you would rather queue up messages and send them at a later time, use this option instead. This is particularly useful for people who are on a dial-up line.

Your Little Black Book

The ladies and gentlemen reading this book have by now wondered when I was going to talk about address books. After all, email implies some kind of socializing, whether business or personal. When composing an email message (as in Figure 3-7), you must enter at least one recipient. If you don't remember the email address of the person you are sending to, it's handy to be able to look them up in your address book. To find a name in your address book, click the Contacts button in the Compose window and a simplified list of addresses from your address book opens up in a left sidebar inside the same Compose window.

You are just pulling contacts, but you aren't actually looking at the address book. The best way to do that is from the main Thunderbird window. Click Address Book on the icon bar, just below the menu bar. The Thunderbird address book appears (see Figure 3-8). If you are going to manage a lot of email addresses or you want to start filling your address book, this is the place to start.

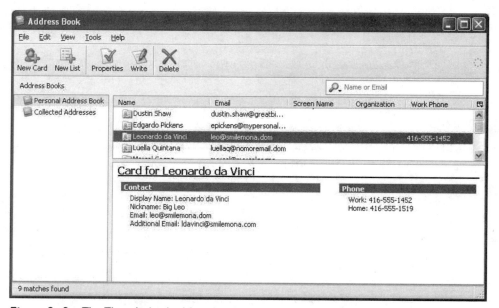

Figure 3–8   The Thunderbird address book is an application on its own and the best place to manage your email addresses.

The address book is an application on its own and provides a place to manage individual addresses, contact information such as telephone numbers, cellphones, home and work mailing addresses, and more. The address book is also useful for creating mailing lists (more on that shortly). When Thunderbird's address book opens up, click the New Card icon at the top left of the address book window. Or, you keyboard wizards can press <Ctrl+N>. You can see the dialog box shown in Figure 3-9.

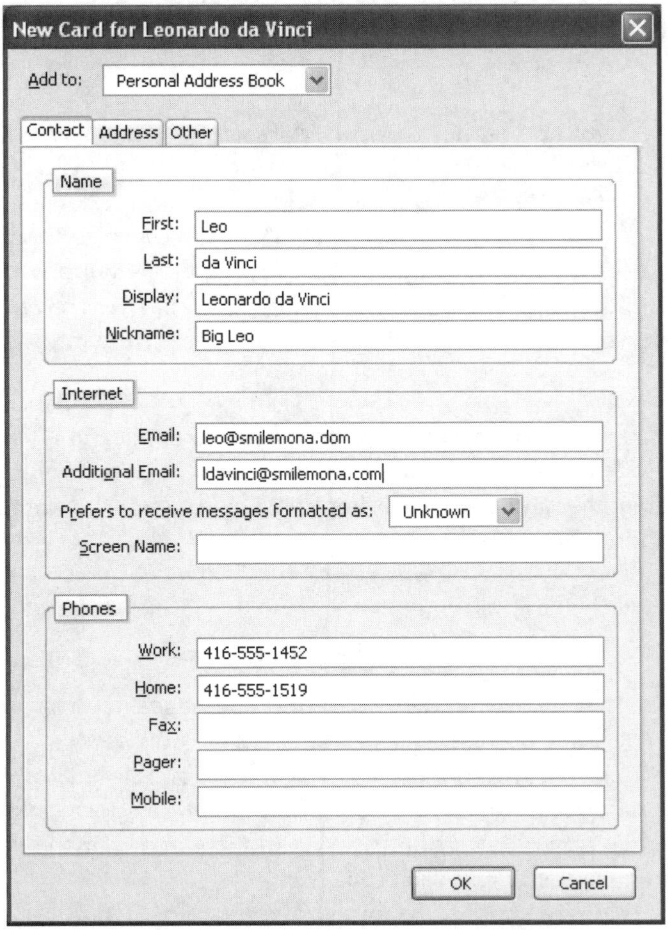

Figure 3-9 When creating a new contact card in your address book, you can add a lot of information beyond a simple email address.

When the New Card window appears, add whatever information is appropriate for the contact. The person's name and his or her email address are sufficient, if these are all you need. When you are done entering information, click OK. You can add as many names as you want in one sitting.

 Tip It's smart: Thunderbird automatically adds the recipient's email address to your address book. You may want to periodically check your address book to include additional information for those addresses.

Another way to add names to your address book (and by far the *easiest*) is to take the address from a message that has been sent to you. While you are viewing someone's email to you, right-click the email address in the From field. A small pop-up menu appears. Click Add to Address Book, and a New Card For appears. This is the same contact information window you saw earlier (refer to Figure 3-9). Enter as much information as you have or would like to have in your address book; then click OK to close the window.

Tip If you have an address from another application, you can use Thunderbird's address book to import it. Click Tools on the menu bar and then select Import to choose from a handful of address book files.

Mailing Lists

Sometimes, it is more convenient to send messages to a group of people rather than entering a number of individual email addresses.

Click New List on the menu bar and the Mailing List dialog appears (see Figure 3-10). Choose a list name (e.g., The Family), a short nickname for the list, and a description. Then, one by one, add the name of the people in that list. When you are done, just click OK.

Next time you are sending an email message, you can just type the short nickname for your list—in my case, family—and the rest is done for you.

Mailing List

Add to: Personal Address Book

List Name: The Family

List Nickname: family

Description: The gang's all here.

Type email addresses to add them to the mailing list:

marcel@mydomain.dom
sally@mydomain.dom
christine@ourdomain.dom
guylaine@ourdomain.dom
Lynda@anotherdomain.dom
michael@hisdomain.dom
sebastian@hisdomain.dom
momdad@theirdomain.dom

OK   Cancel

Figure 3–10   Create mailing lists to simplify sending email to large groups of people.

Attached to You . . .

As you sit there writing a letter to your old high-school friend, it occurs to you that it might be fun to include a recent picture of yourself (with your spouse and new baby). After all, you haven't seen each other in 20 years. To attach a file, click the paper clip icon, labeled Attach, directly below the menu bar. If you have Windows Explorer file manager window open, you can also drag an icon from the file manager into your composer window. In fact, if you have an icon on your desktop, you can drag that into your composer as well, and the images (or documents) are automatically attached.

 Tip You can actually drag images from just about anywhere, including your Firefox Web browser.

If you prefer the menu bar, select File, Attach, File(s). The Attach Files(s) dialog window appears, giving you the opportunity to navigate your directories to find the appropriate file. Figure 3-11 shows this dialog in use.

Figure 3–11   Browsing for an email attachment.

After you have attached a file, it shows up in a separate attachments section of your composer window (see Figure 3-12 for a close-up). You'll see that attachments pane over on the top right. It is here that you can drag and drop files.

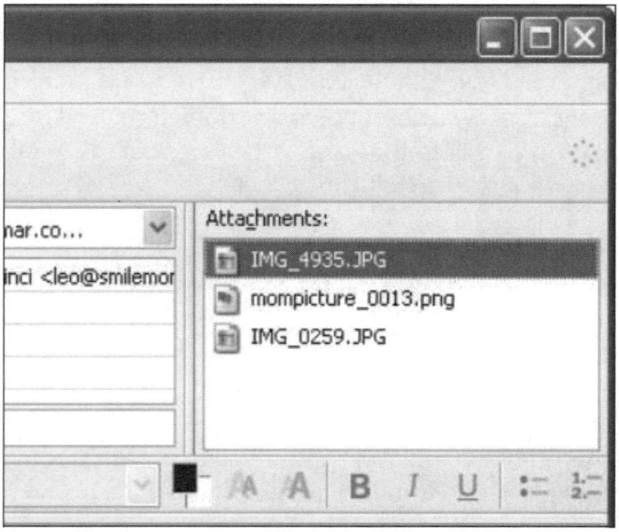

Figure 3–12   Close-up of the Thunderbird attachments are in the Composer window.

From there, you can select those attachments and change your mind. Right-click the attachment and select Delete.

No More Junk Mail!

Thunderbird comes with its own adaptive junk mail recognition software. Junk mail—unsolicited commercial email (UCE), or spam, as it is commonly known—has transformed one of the greatest achievements in personal communication into a minefield of unwanted crap (and perhaps worse, malware). Thunderbird can help you tame this monster, but you need to participate in its education.

Start by clicking Tools on the menu bar and selecting Junk Mail Controls. The first time you do this, Thunderbird tells you about its needs with an informational message about junk mail and how Thunderbird deals with it (see Figure 3-13).

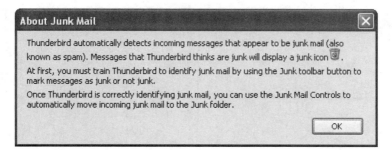

Figure 3–13 Before Thunderbird can filter junk mail, it needs you to set up some controls.

After you acknowledge this message, you are taken to the Junk Mail Controls window (see Figure 3-14). There are two tabs in this window. One is labeled Settings and the other Adaptive Filter. The second tab is the easiest to deal with, so I'll cover it first. Simply said, this tab has a check box that allows you to turn on the adaptive mail filter. Just make sure the box is checked and go back to the Settings tab.

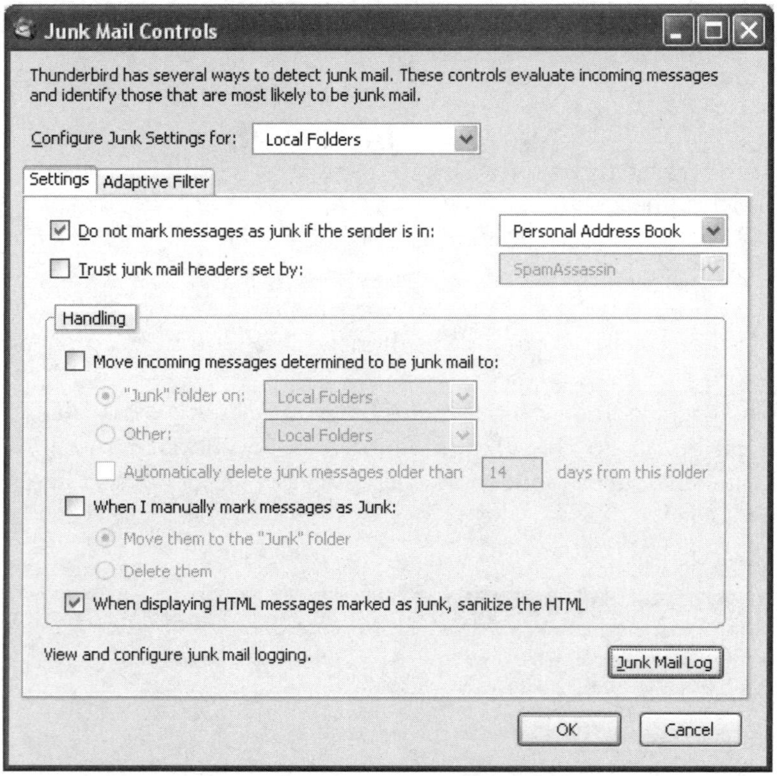

Figure 3–14   Configuring junk mail controls in Thunderbird.

There are a handful of options, checked off by default, that I recommend you set at this point. Most are under the Handling section. Because you don't want all these junk messages to clutter up your inbox, start by checking Move Incoming Messages Determined to Be Junk Mail to. Three grayed sections appear, the first two having to do with the folder in which these messages get stored. Thunderbird creates a folder called Junk for this stuff. For most, that's usually just fine, but you can use a different folder name. Below this is another check box, When I Manually Make Messages as Junk. Check this one as well and another set of options appears with the same intention: to identify a folder into which the junk gets moved. This is another good place to accept the default.

Before you click OK to get things going, look just below the Settings tab where another check box, Trust Junk Mail Headers Set by, can be found. If you are like me and you have an external junk mail flagging program (such as SpamAssassin) running, you can let Thunderbird know that you agree with its decisions so that all messages marked by this package also get filtered into the Junk folder. Click OK and a new folder, Junk, appears in your folder list on the left.

So, How Do You Train Thunderbird?

The whole point of the adaptive junk mail filter is that you help it learn what constitutes junk mail. When you read your email messages, and you judge a message to be junk mail, click the Junk button on the icon bar to mark the message as junk. Another, quicker way to achieve the same result is to press <> on your keyboard. Alternatively, you can right-click the message, select Mark from the pop-up menu, and then select As Junk.

As time goes on, Thunderbird gets better and better at identifying junk messages. This helps to keep your inbox cleaner, with less junk, and more real messages.

Because Thunderbird is making decisions as to what is junk and what isn't, you should occasionally check the contents of your Junk folder before you delete the messages. If something gets trapped that shouldn't have, click the Not Junk icon and make sure you add the sender's name to your address book. By default, Thunderbird's junk mail filter trusts messages coming from people in your address book.

Revisiting RSS

All the news that is news across the nation and the world . . . at least, as much of it as you care to subscribe to. In the previous chapter on Firefox, I told you about RSS news feeds. Thunderbird can also be used to track news and information sites, including your favorite blogs.

To use this feature, you need to create an RSS news feed account. Luckily, this is very easy to do. Click File in the menu bar, then New, and then Account. The Account Wizard appears. Select RSS News & Blogs from the list, and then click Next. The wizard suggests an account name of News & Blogs. You can either change that here or just click Next. Click Finish and you are done. At the top of your folder list, there is now another entry labeled News & Blogs (or whatever name you chose).

To add a news feed, click the News & Blogs group. In the main window to the right, you see a number of options for managing news groups, accounts, and so on. Click Manage Subscriptions to bring up a list of subscriptions (currently empty). You can also right-click the News & Blogs group and select Manage Subscriptions from the pop-up menu. A window listing your RSS Subscriptions appears. Click the Add button and you can enter the RSS information using the Feed Properties dialog (see Figure 3-15).

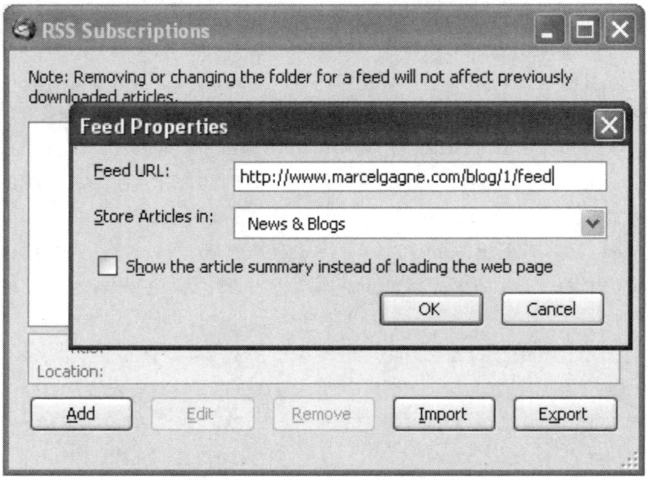

Figure 3–15   Adding RSS news feeds and blogs is easy.

You might just want to click the Show the Article Summary Instead of Loading the Web Page check box regardless of whether you use broadband or dial-up. The default of showing the entire Web page in Thunderbird's reader window kind of defeats the point of RSS. I grant you that this is a personal opinion. You may want to experiment with both ways of displaying content and decide for yourself.

Click OK to finish. You are returned to the subscriptions window. After you close the RSS Subscriptions window, you'll notice that your new news feed, be it a news source or someone's blog, appears in your folder list. You can then select individual postings and read them as you would any other message.

Resources

Mozilla Thunderbird

http://www.mozilla.com/thunderbird/

4

Gaim: Multiprotocol Instant Messaging, and IRC, Too!

Words, words, words . . . and then a whole lot more words, all of them flowing from one person to another. Whatever cool content exists on the world's Web sites, the Internet is still all about communication.

These days, a new kind of communication has evolved—call it mini-email. The one-liner. The short and sweet message. The instant message. The Net-connected society has grown to love those quick, always-on means of sending each other information. My own parents (who live in another province) send me a daily one-line weather report via their Jabber instant messaging client. If you are coming from the Windows world, there's a good chance you already have one of these accounts, either with Yahoo!, AOL, MSN, or Jabber.

Why Jabber?

Because Jabber is an open protocol, it doesn't belong to any one in particular, so there is no single company driving its destiny (although there are companies using Jabber). Jabber uses a decentralized approach, so the system is more robust. In fact, anyone can run a Jabber server. This is a boon to companies that may want to run a *private, secure* instant messaging network.

 Trivia Time Never heard of Jabber? Maybe you've heard of Google. Google Talk, an increasingly popular instant messaging service, uses the Jabber protocol.

Whether you choose to run Jabber, Yahoo!, MSN, or something else, the ideal instant messaging client is a multiprotocol client, one that lets you talk to all these services without having to run a client for Jabber, one for AOL, one for Yahoo!, one for . . . well, you get the idea. In this chapter, I'm going to cover two superb Linux instant messaging clients. One is a great multiprotocol client that handles all your favorite chat services. The second is a powerful IRC client.

What's IRC, you ask? IRC is Internet Relay Chat, and next to your telephone, it is possibly the greatest real-time communication system in the world, and I'll tell you all about it shortly.

Instant Messaging with Gaim

Gaim is one of the best multiprotocol instant messaging systems out there, period. Furthermore, this is one you can share with the people you know who are still running that other operating system. This is one favor they will thank you for. With Gaim, they no longer need a client for Yahoo!, another for MSN, and *yet another* for AOL because Gaim (`Gaim.sourceforge.net`) is available for Windows as well. It even looks and works the same under both operating systems.

To start Gaim, look under the Applications menu, and then select Internet. You'll see an entry there for Gaim Internet Messenger. The actual command name is gaim, in case you would rather start it from the shell or via the <Alt+F2> Run Program dialog.

The first time you start up Gaim (see Figure 4-1), you get a simple window labeled Buddy List, a decidedly empty list. At the bottom of the window is a drop-down box with the word New, although it might say Available, Away, or Invisible. This is your online status; the word *New* is to create alternate status messages to alert your buddies.

Figure 4–1 First time out with Gaim.

Before we start using instant messaging through Gaim, we are going to need at least one account. When you start Gaim for the first time, you are reminded of this because Gaim also pops up the Accounts window (see Figure 4-2). You can have multiple accounts for different types of instant messaging services, but at this stage of the game there is nothing in the window.

Click Add, and the Add Account window appears. At the top of that window, you should see a drop-down list labeled Protocol. By default, it says AIM/ICQ. Click the Protocol button and you see a number of possibilities, including AIM/ICQ, Gadu-Gadu, GroupWise, IRC, Jabber, MSN, Napster, and Yahoo (see Figure 4-3).

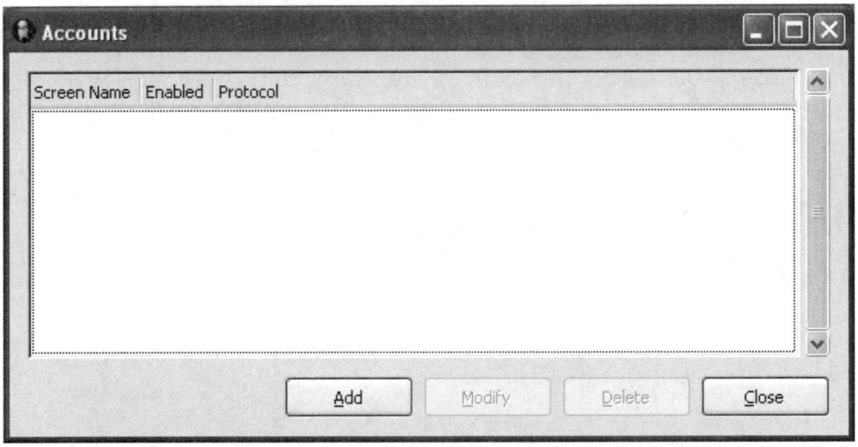

Figure 4–2   The Accounts management screen.

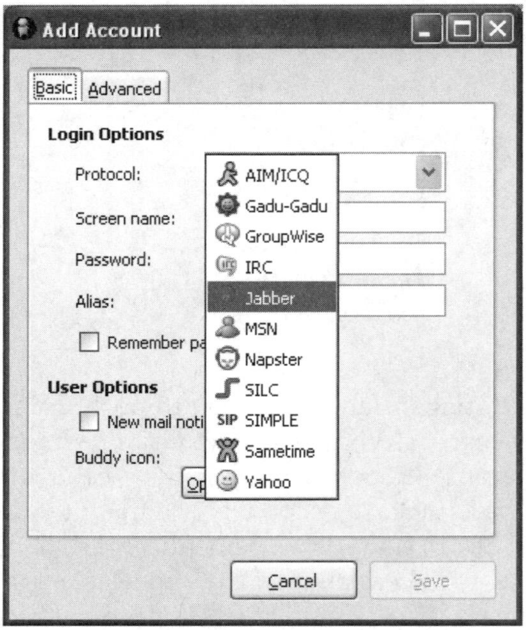

Figure 4–3   Gaim supports a number of different IM protocols.

Select Jabber from the list and watch as the window changes from AIM/ICQ to reflect the requirements of setting up a Jabber account (see Figure 4-4). The number of fields and the information you may need to provide change depending on the account type, whether that is MSN, Jabber, AOL, or any of the other protocols.

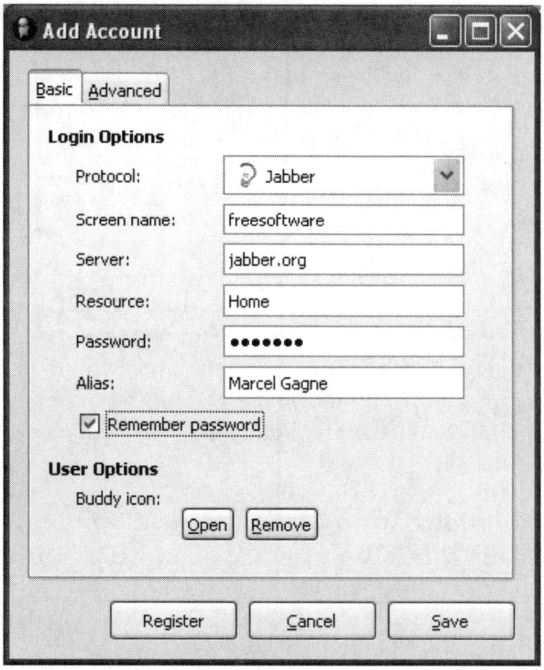

Figure 4–4 Creating a Jabber account.

Enter your Screen Name (this doesn't have to be your real name), Password (don't use an important password), and Alias. To get a free account with Jabber.org, you can leave the Server name as is. The Resource name can also be safely left as Home. Unless you want to be asked for your password each time you log in, click the Remember Password check box. Don't do that yet though. If you are setting up a new account, you need to register your account first.

When you are happy with the information you have entered, click the Register button. The Jabber.org server should respond with a Register New Jabber Account confirmation window, which gives you the opportunity to enter your password (see Figure 4-5). Depending on the server you register with, you may also be offered the opportunity to enter additional information, such as an email address.

Register New Jabber Account

Register New Jabber Account

Please fill out the information below to register your new account.

Username: freesoftware

Password: ●●●●●●●

Name: Marcel Gagne

E-Mail:

Cancel   Register

Figure 4–5   Before you confirm your registration with the server, you may have the opportunity to enter additional information.

Just click the Register button to confirm and you are good to go. Your Accounts window now shows your new account (see Figure 4-6).

Tip The Jabber.org server provides space and resources for people to get free instant messaging accounts; and you may choose to take advantage of this service. Some companies, however, will use their own instant messaging server for security and audit reasons. In this case, you would change Server (refer to Figure 4-4) to something other than Jabber.org, such as chat.yourcompany.dom.

You can either sign on here (by clicking the Enabled check box) or click Close and sign on from the main Gaim window. With your first time in, you'll get a welcome message from the Jabber.org server. You can close this window or visit the site (as indicated in the message) for additional information.

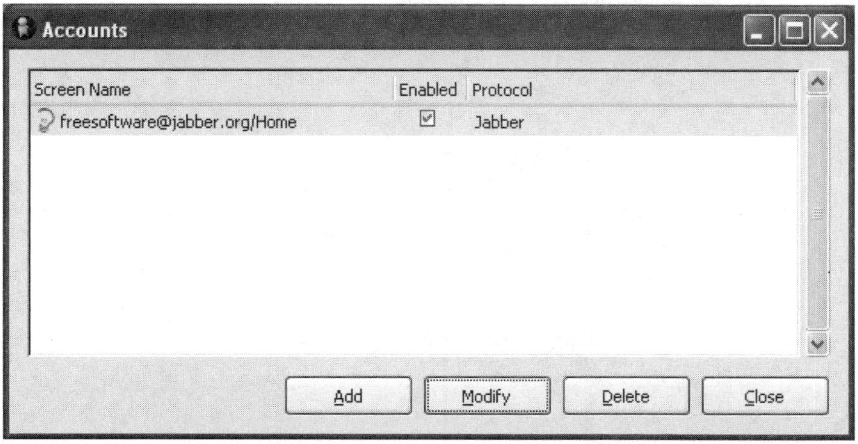

Figure 4–6 The Accounts dialog now reflects the newly added account.

Now that you have your very own Jabber instant messaging account, you need some people to talk to. There are online chats that you can join by clicking Buddies on the menu bar and selecting Join a Chat. You can also use the keyboard shortcut by pressing <Ctrl+C> instead. You can add friends to your Buddy List by selecting Add a Buddy from the menu. Your friends have to give your their screen names, of course.

After you have added your buddies to the list, they will get messages letting them know that you want to add them. When they see the pop-up (see Figure 4-7), they must click Accept, at which point you can begin conversations with them.

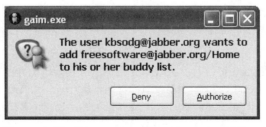

Figure 4–7 Do you accept your new buddy?

This accepting of buddies has to happen at both sides of the connection. The buddy has to accept you, after which you accept the buddy. Think of it as saying, "*I do*," but to a more casual, dare I say, *virtual* relationship.

After all this accepting has taken place, your buddies appear in your buddy list (see Figure 4-8). The icons beside their names in your buddy list indicate whether your friends are on.

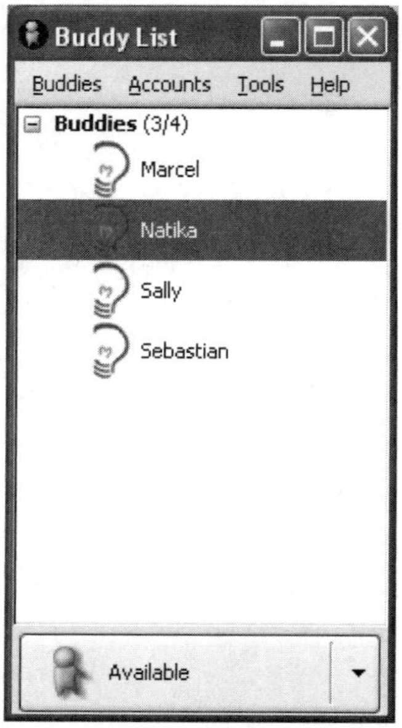

Figure 4–8 An active Gaim buddy list.

If your friend is online, double-click his name and start chatting (see Figure 4-9). Enter text in the bottom part of the chat window and press <Enter> (or click the Send button) to send your message. It is that easy.

Grouping Your Buddies

When your list of contacts (of buddies, if you prefer) becomes long enough, you'll want to organize them into groups. For example, you may have a group called Friends, another called Family, and yet another called Business Contacts. You can then collapse some groups and leave others expanded as you see fit.

To add a group, click Buddies on the Gaim menu bar, and select Add Group. A small dialog appears asking you for the name of the group you want to create (see Figure 4-10). Enter it, and then click Add.

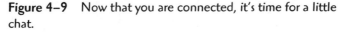

Figure 4–9 Now that you are connected, it's time for a little chat.

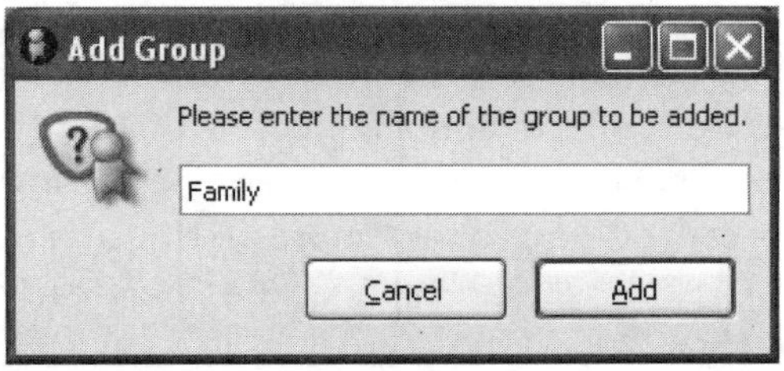

Figure 4–10 Creating groups for your users is an excellent way to organize a large contact list.

By default, empty groups are not shown, so if you want to move existing buddies into new groups, you'll want to make those visible. Click Buddies on the menu bar and make sure Show Empty Groups is selected. Organizing your contacts is now as easy as dragging and dropping them into the group of your choice.

IRC: Internet Relay Chat

Internet Relay Chat, better known as IRC, is a distributed client-server system in which users can communicate with any number of other users in real time. IRC servers host channels that are dedicated to discussion forums on specific topics. These topics aren't fixed other than by convention and the whims of the IRC operators (more on that). If you are old enough to remember CB radio (i.e., you are in your mid-30s and up), you pretty much understand IRC—at least in the human sense of the experience.

A number of IRC servers exist around the world, some with thousands of channels. IRC servers can also peer with other servers. IRC channels cover a plethora of topics, from purely social to politics to business or to high technology. In the Linux world, there are channels devoted to programming in most of the popular languages, as well as your favorite Linux distribution, office applications, games, and so on. IRC channels are great places to meet and exchange information, ask questions, answer questions, or just plain chat. All this chatting takes place via an IRC client. As it turns out, Gaim is also an excellent IRC client. Let me show you how it works.

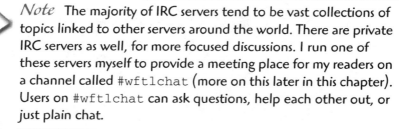

Note The majority of IRC servers tend to be vast collections of topics linked to other servers around the world. There are private IRC servers as well, for more focused discussions. I run one of these servers myself to provide a meeting place for my readers on a channel called #wftlchat (more on this later in this chapter). Users on #wftlchat can ask questions, help each other out, or just plain chat.

Using Gaim for IRC

Gaim, that amazing, multiprotocol, messaging client, is also a superb IRC client. The first step to chatting on IRC is to create an account for one of the many servers that exists out there. You do that by clicking Accounts on the Gaim menu bar and selecting Add/Edit. This first part is going to look very familiar because it is essentially the same step you used to create your Jabber account. When the Accounts window appears (refer to Figure 4-6), click Add to create your IRC account.

A moment later, the Add Account window appears. There are two tabs on this window: Basic and Advanced. The Basic tab should be selected. Click the arrow to the right of the Protocol label and select IRC from the drop-down list. By default, you'll see a Server name of irc.freenode.net filled in (see Figure 4-11).

Figure 4–11   Adding an IRC account is similar to other protocols (e.g., Jabber, MSN, etc.), but you need to specify a server.

Note   Freenode is one of several hundred IRC networks on the planet. Its focus is on discussions relating to free and open source software.

The Screen Name (or nickname, as it is commonly referred to) field is empty at this point, so make up some kind of nickname, keeping in mind that someone else might be using that name already. You can choose whatever you like here. In fact, most people on IRC have some nickname other than their own names. On IRC, you'll see me logged in as *wftl*. That is my nickname.

For most IRC servers, that's all you really need to enter at this point. The Advanced tab lets you set an alternate port; the default is 6667. You can also set additional user information or specify a connection using encryption (if the server requires it). If your home or office requires that you use a proxy, you can also set that here. When you are finished entering information, click Save. You'll find yourself back at the Accounts window. Make sure the Enabled check box for your IRC account is checked on, and then click Close.

Tip I run my own IRC server where readers can ask questions, chat with other readers, and discuss free software, Linux, and a variety of other topics. If you want, you can add this as one of your IRC accounts. Enter your chosen nickname on the Basic tab, and then enter `chat.marcelgagne.com` as the server. Click Save and you are ready to add your channel. The main channel on that server is `#wftlchat`.

Joining IRC Channels

To get in on a conversation, you need to join a channel, what Gaim calls a *chat*. To do that, click Buddies on the Gaim menu bar and select Add Chat. When the Add Chat window appears, you may find yourself looking at a different account. From the Account drop-down list near the top of the window, select your IRC account. The window changes to reflect the correct fields for an IRC chat. Next, enter a channel name in the appropriate field (see Figure 4-12).

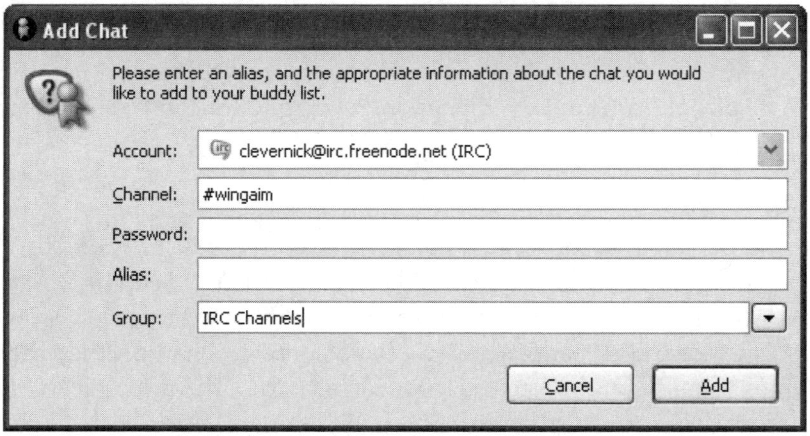

Figure 4–12 To add an IRC channel to your chat list, enter the channel name prefixed by a # sign.

Some servers require a password to join a chat, but this is generally not the case. If you would prefer to see the IRC channel listed in your buddy list as something other than #somename, enter an Alias to describe it. If you have gone ahead and created groups to organize your contacts, you can specify that here as well. When everything is to your liking, click Add. The IRC channel now appears in your buddy list.

> *Tip* To chat with people about Gaim on irc.freenode.net, you can join the #gaim channel; or for Windows specific issues related to Gaim, you can join the #wingaim channel.

To start a conversation, double-click the IRC channel name in your buddy list. The Gaim IRC conversation window appears with your nickname logged in to the appropriate channel (see Figure 4-13). You can even chat on multiple channels at the same time, if you want. Double-click another channel and that channel opens in another tab in the same chat window.

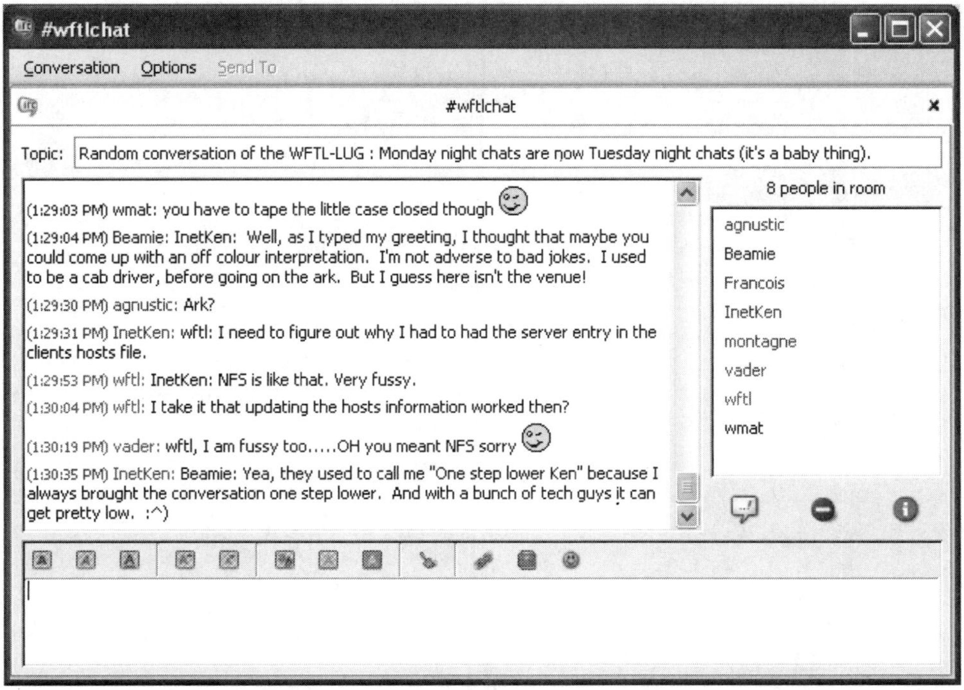

Figure 4–13 Chatting in IRC. To the right is a list of people currently logged in to the channel.

To ask a question or talk to the group, just type your message in the text field at the bottom of the chat window, and then press <Enter>. Congratulations! You are chatting on IRC.

Tip To find IRC networks and channels on those networks, the best place to start is probably the Web site at Netsplit.de (`http://irc.netsplit.de`). The site even has an IRC channel search engine. Enter a topic, click the search button, and the site returns a list of networks, servers, and channels.

Learning More About IRC

IRC has some interesting commands that you might want to know about. IRC commands are fronted by a slash character (/), followed by the command name. Some commands can be used by all users, whereas others are for channel administrators only. To find out what commands are available to you, type **/help** in the text field and press <Enter>. The list of commands appears in the chat window itself. Here are a few of the more common and useful commands.

`/help`	Lists IRC commands
`/help command_name`	Gets help on a particular command
`/nick new_name`	Changes your nickname
`/join #channel`	Joins a specified channel
`/part`	Leaves the channel
`/list`	Lists the available channels
`/me Some_action`	Prints your nickname followed by text of your action and highlights the message in a different color. Try it. It's fun.

Tip Beware the `/list` command. On some servers, this can return a massive list of channels.

IRC is a fantastic resource and one I recommend highly, but with a cautionary suggestion. This vast, distributed network of real-time discussion groups has evolved a culture all its own, with its own rules of etiquette—rules that should be respected. Channels have operators who monitor traffic and requests from users. Operators can also send you packing if you don't behave. There may also be *bots*, small programs designed to handle simple administrative requests, so not every user you see is necessarily human.

It's easy to get hooked on IRC when there is so much at your disposal, but it's also good to take some time and read a little primer on what it's all about. Check out the IRC primer in the "Resources" section for a great introduction to the world of IRC.

Before I close, I feel I should mention the `irc.netsplit.de` IRC information site, one more time. On that site, you'll find a search engine for channels and topics, as well as a comprehensive list of IRC servers and networks.

I'll see you online.

Resources

Gaim Instant Messaging

http://gaim.sourceforge.net

Google Talk

http://talk.google.com

Jabber Software Foundation

http://www.jabber.org

A Short IRC Primer

http://www.irchelp.org/irchelp/ircprimer.html

Netsplit.de IRC Information Site

http://irc.netsplit.de

Netsplit.de List of Channels for Freenode

http://irc.netsplit.de/channels/?net=freenode

5

Skype: Free Long Distance, Anyone?

How does free long distance, to anyone, anywhere in the world, sound?

Skype is a program that allows you to make voice over IP (VoIP) telephone calls. More importantly, from the perspective of the millions of users who love this program, Skype is also a great way to make free long distance telephone calls to any other Skype user worldwide. Skype delivers great voice quality, instant messaging, conference calls, and even video conversations. Skype even works behind firewalls.

The magic behind Skype comes from its use of peer-to-peer (P2P) technology. When you log on to Skype, you and millions of others share a percentage of your network bandwidth to make the high-quality communications possible. Yes, this is the same technology used by people who swap songs on the Internet. Skype, however, is completely legal.

> *Note* Even businesses are getting in on the action. Free long distance is an attractive proposition for a business that spends a lot of time on the phone. Add to that free conference calls, and it makes for an attractive business proposition.

Installing Skype is easy. Download the latest version of Skype for your system, and then double-click the SkypeSetup file on your desktop. The installation wizard is primarily a question of accepting the license agreement. Click Next a couple of times and Skype is ready to run. After the install is complete, you have the option of launching Skype immediately.

Creating a Skype Account

If you haven't already done so, start the Skype program. Unless you chose otherwise during the installation, there should be an icon on your desktop. When Skype starts, it displays a Sign into Skype window (see Figure 5-1). Enter your Skype Name and Password, and then click the Sign In button. If this is your first time using Skype, you need to get yourself an account. Luckily, this is very easy to do.

Directly below the Skype Name field, there is a blue label that looks like a Web link. It says, Don't have a Skype Name? Click that link and the Skype Create Account dialog appears (see Figure 5-2).

After you have finished entering the information, click the Sign In button. The wizard attempts to register your account with Skype. If the account you have chosen is already in use, another dialog appears with some suggestions for an alternate name. Click the radio button beside the name to accept the suggestion or click the bottom radio button and try a different name.

Figure 5–1   When using Skype for the first time, you have the opportunity to create a new account.

After you do successfully create an account, another window, Help Your Friends Find You, appears (see Figure 5-3). This is where you enter your real name as well as the country and city you live in. Because your account has been created at this point, most of this is strictly optional, but it is designed to make it easier for people to search on your name and call you. Click Next to continue.

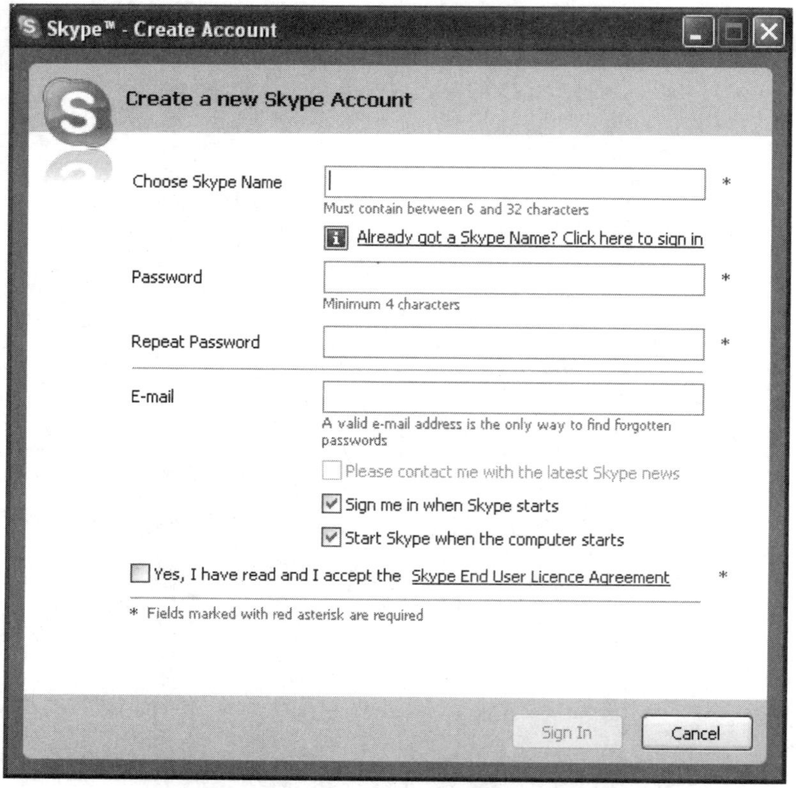

Figure 5–2   It's easy to create an account from the Skype Create Account dialog.

You've got all your information entered. Skype starts the Getting Started Wizard. Its purpose is to give you a very quick overview of how Skype works and how you use it. Think of it as a drastically shortened version of what you are reading now. Every time you start Skype, the wizard also starts. You can stop this behavior by clicking the Do Not Show This Wizard at Startup check box on the wizard's lower left.

 Tip You can start the Getting Started Wizard at any time by clicking Help on the Skype menu bar and selecting Getting Started.

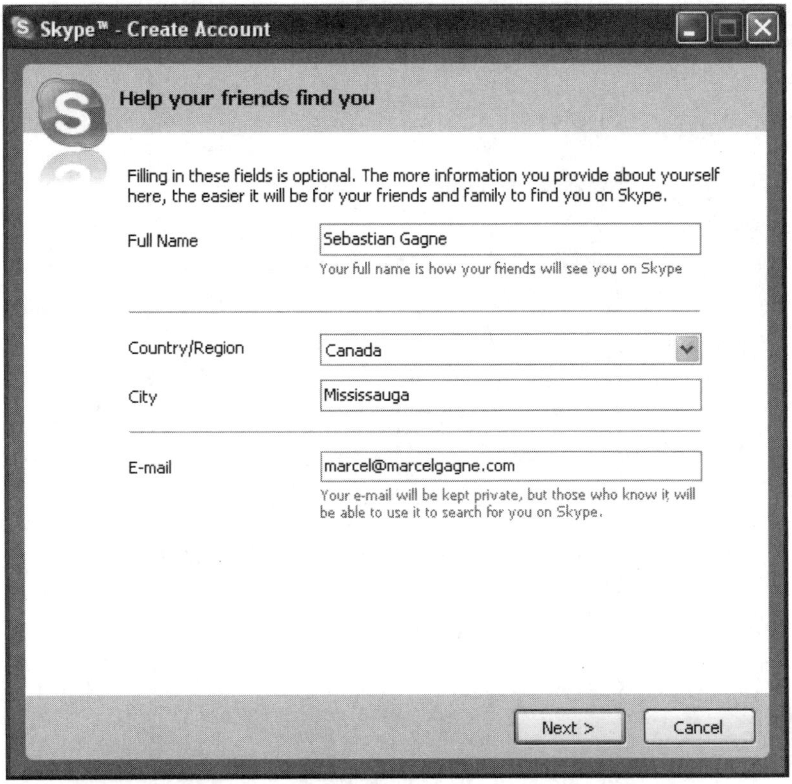

Figure 5-3 Additional personal information, such as your full name or your email address, is entirely optional at this point.

"Is this thing working?" Testing Your Connection

Before you run off and start calling the world, take a moment to make sure your microphone and headset are all working properly. You do this by calling the contact listed as Skype Test Call. Start by making sure that your microphone and headset are plugged in and that your volume level is not muted. To initiate the call, click the green call button at the bottom of the Skype window. When the call begins (see Figure 5-4), listen carefully to the recorded voice and follow the instructions.

You are asked to record 10 seconds of audio, after which the service plays it back for you. Wait for the prompt, and then speak where indicated. If you can hear yourself as well as the recorded test message, your setup is complete.

Figure 5–4   Skype provides an automated system for testing your connection.

Search Me! Adding Friends to Your Contact List

Now that we have a working Skype installation, it's time to build your contact list. Start by clicking the green Add Contact button just below the menu bar of the Skype window. The Add a Contact window appears (see Figure 5-5). If you know the Skype name of the person you are looking for, enter it here. You can also use this form to search for someone if you don't have her Skype address. Enter an email address, her first or last name, and click the Search button.

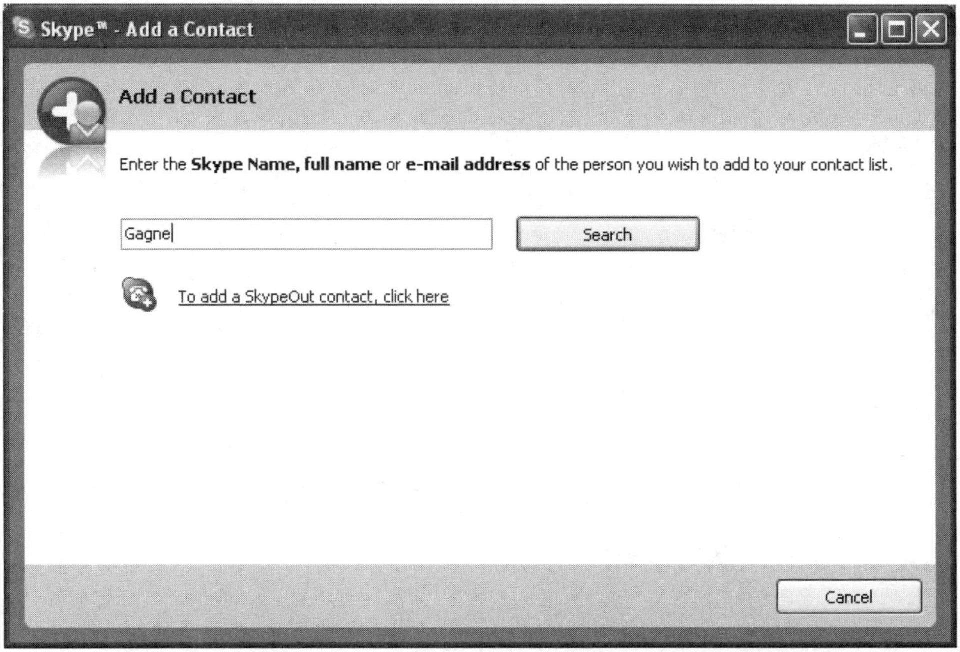

Figure 5–5   Use the Add a Contact search form to locate other Skype users.

Any contacts matching the name you searched for will appear in the list. The listing shows the users' names, Skype name, country, city, and language. If you need more information, highlight the person's name and click the View Profile button. When you are satisfied with the name you have located, click Add Selected Contact to include that person in your contacts list.

Depending on the name you enter in your search field, the return list can be enormous and it may take some time to scroll down and find the person you want. To simplify your search, you can use Skype's extended search. Just click the Search button directly below the menu bar. The extended search function lets you specify a country of origin, state, city, or language (see Figure 5-6). You can also select by gender and age range as well. On a whim, I decided to search for Leonardo da Vinci and discovered that he is alive and well and Skyping!

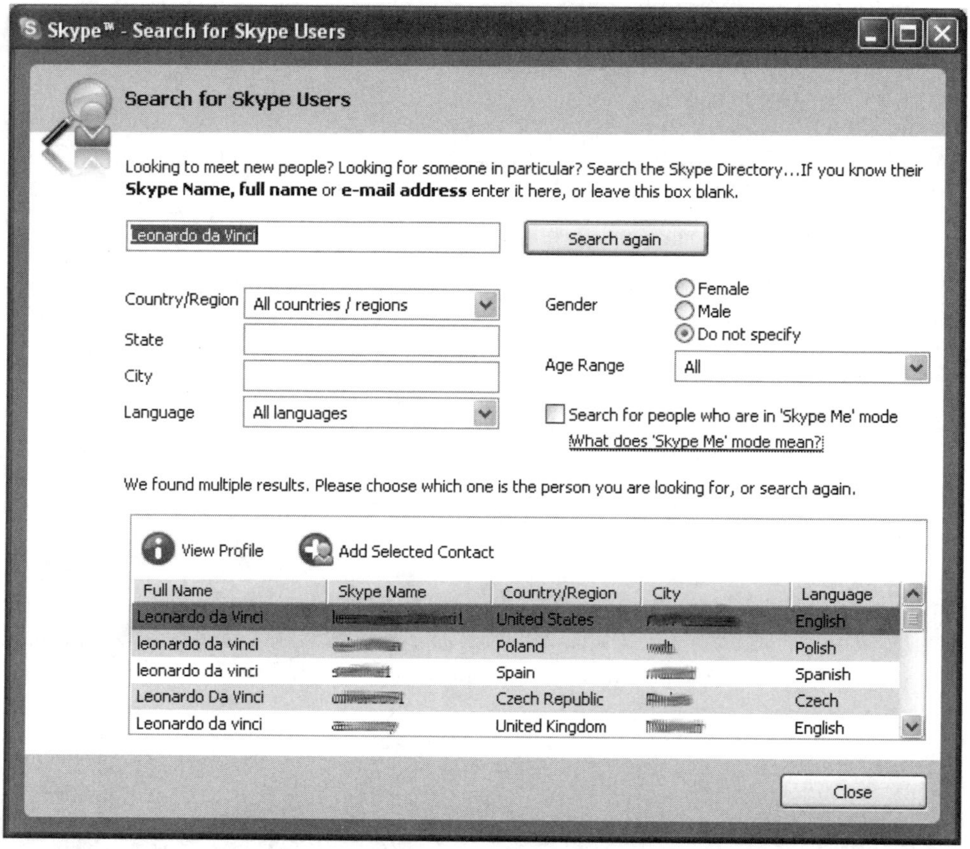

Figure 5–6   Skype's extended search function tells me that Leonardo da Vinci is alive and well and Skyping!

At the bottom of that search window are the search results. If you aren't sure whether you've found the right person, click to select his name, then click the View Profile button at the top of the results list. A small information window appears with any extra information that person has provided. To add a contact, click the Add Selected Contact button. Your contact receives a request to add your name to his list, which appears in a pop-up window (see Figure 5-7). The same applies in the reverse scenario when somebody is adding you as a contact.

Little by little, you build up your list of contacts. The whole point of this is, of course, to make calls.

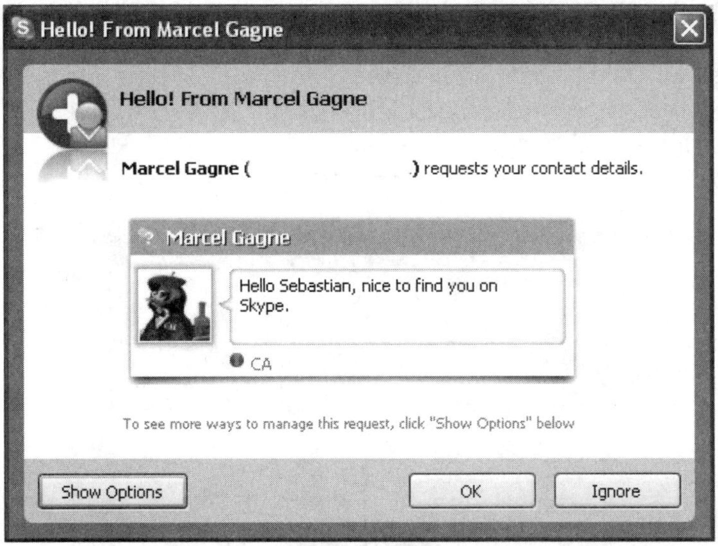

Hello! From Marcel Gagne

Hello! From Marcel Gagne

Marcel Gagne ( ) requests your contact details.

Marcel Gagne

Hello Sebastian, nice to find you on Skype.

● CA

To see more ways to manage this request, click "Show Options" below

| Show Options | | OK | Ignore |

Figure 5–7 A request to add a contact appears in a pop-up window.

Come Here, Watson! Making Calls on Skype

Making a call is very simple and, in a sense, you already did this when you made your test call. If you haven't already done so, click the Contacts tab. From the drop-down list, select the name of the person you want to call. Then, click on the green telephone call button at the bottom of the screen (see Figure 5-8).

Type Skype Name or number with country code

▼ Online   6,416,696 Users Online

Figure 5–8 The call button is a green telephone icon near the bottom left.

If you prefer to do a little typing, you can initiate a call by typing in the person's Skype name in the field labeled Type Skype Name or Number with Country Code located just above the call button.

Yet another way to achieve the same result is to right-click the contact name. A small pop-up menu appears, from which you can select Start Call. When the call starts, a window appears with a Ringing message below that person's representative icon (see Figure 5-9). On the receiver's side, a telephone-like ring sounds from his speaker.

Figure 5–9   After a call has been initiated, a Ringing message appears below that person's representative icon.

After your contact answers the call, by clicking that person's green phone icon, the same window remains, but the Ringing message is replaced with a time duration message so that you know how long the call lasts.

Conference Calls

One of Skype's great features is the capability to easily create a conference call. Three or more users can be invited to a conversation, including people on regular home and cell phones. (I'll cover regular phones shortly when I cover SkypeOut.)

To start a conference call, click the Conference button in the icon bar just below the menu bar. Alternatively, you can click Tools on the menu bar and select Create a Conference Call. A window labeled Start a Skype Conference Call appears with a list of your contacts on the left and a Conference Participants window on the right (see Figure 5-10).

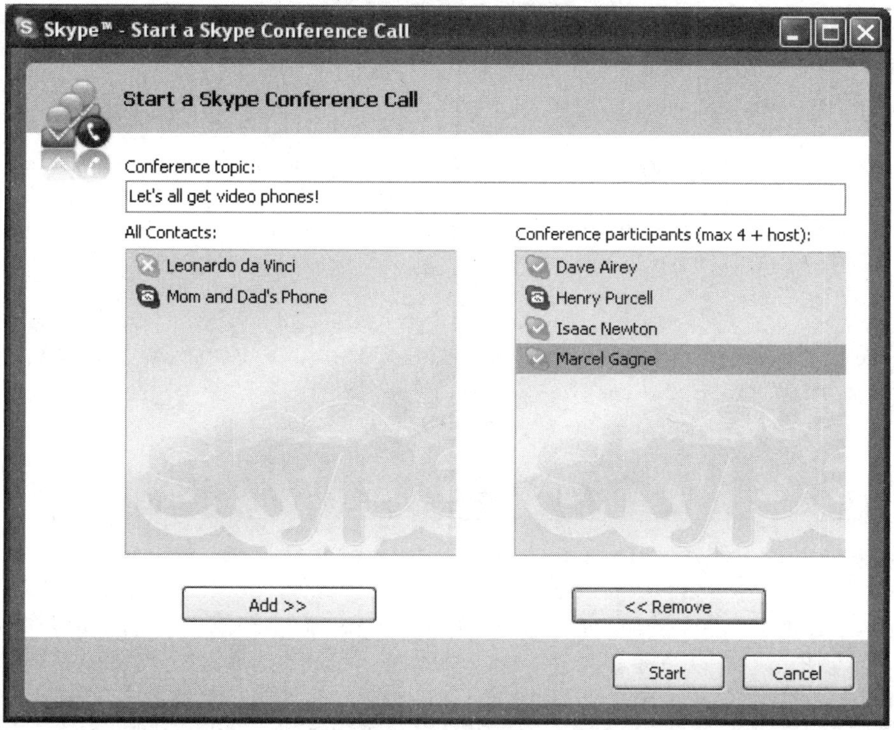

Figure 5–10 Conference calls are easy. Just select your participants and click Add.

After you have selected your participants, click the Start button in the create conference window to begin. Your chat window shows your participants in the various stages of connecting or chatting, including call duration.

Instant Messaging with Skype

In the previous chapter, I told you about Gaim, a great, multiprotocol instant messaging client. Skype, as it turns out, can also be used for text-only instant messaging. Unlike Gaim, Skype instant messaging only works with other Skype users. You might choose to use the chat when a few words typed at the keyboard are sufficient, if one of the parties is having problems with her microphone, or if the other party isn't there.

To start a Skype text chat, select your contact from the list, and then click the Chat icon at the top right of the Skype window (see Figure 5-11).

Figure 5–11   To initiate a text chat, as you
would with your instant messaging software,
just click the Chat button.

A chat window opens, from which you can start typing your messages. There's also a button on the lower right of the chat window that makes it easy to add more people in the chat window.

SkypeOut and SkypeIn

What makes Skype attractive is its promise of free long distance. The only catch is that the person you call must also be on Skype. If you are willing to part with a little money, Skype can also be used to call regular telephones and cell phones. Skype offers a service called SkypeOut, which makes this possible. Making the call is simple; just type in the person's home phone number in the Skype call field, the one just above the call button (see Figure 5-8). Just make sure you prefix it with a plus sign (+) and the country code you are calling.

SkypeOut may not be a free service, but it is very inexpensive. For example, calling Italy from the United States is 2.1 cents per minute (at the time of this writing). A call to Japan isn't a whole lot more at 2.3 cents per minute. Rates for other countries are available from the Skype Web site. Just click the SkypeOut link to get there.

To make a SkypeOut call, you first need to buy some credit. SkypeOut credits are sold in Euros in increments of 10 Euros. That translates to an average of 10 hours of talk time.

What About SkypeIn?

Skype offers another service called SkypeIn, which gives you a phone number that people can call from a normal telephone. This number rings on your computer and, if you are unavailable, also provides a voicemail service so callers can leave messages.

Your SkyeIn phone number isn't necessarily a local number and can be in a handful of different countries. That means you could be living in the United States and have a phone number in Switzerland.

This service is currently in beta, so check the Skype Web site for details.

Face to Face with Skype: Using a Webcam

When I was but a child, it seemed that every television science-fiction program was promising a video phone. Years passed, and my video phone remained as distant as the faraway studios themselves. From my home office in the summer of 2006, video telephones do exist but are hard to come by from your local provider. Luckily, there are programs that fill the gap, and the latest Skype just happens to be one of them. With your handy webcam, the video phone is at your disposal now.

To configure Skype for video calling, click Tools on the menu bar and select Options. When the Skype Options window appears (see Figure 5-12), you see a sidebar on the left side with several categories that let you customize Skype's operation. Click the Video entry in the sidebar. Start by checking the box labeled Enable Skype Video, and then select your webcam from the drop-down list directly below.

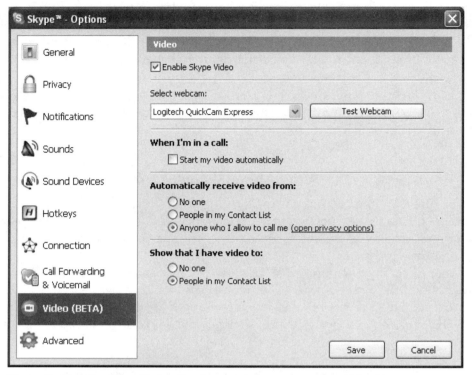

Figure 5–12   To place video calls using a webcam, you must enable video support under Skype's Options dialog.

To make sure you can initiate video calls with Skype, click the Test Webcam button. Another window appears showing the output of your webcam (see Figure 5-13). Even though you may find yourself with working video, the image may require a little tweaking. Click the Webcam Settings button and you can adjust brightness, contract, color, and so on.

When you are content that things are working properly, click Close, and then click the Save button from the Skype Options dialog. You are ready to transmit video.

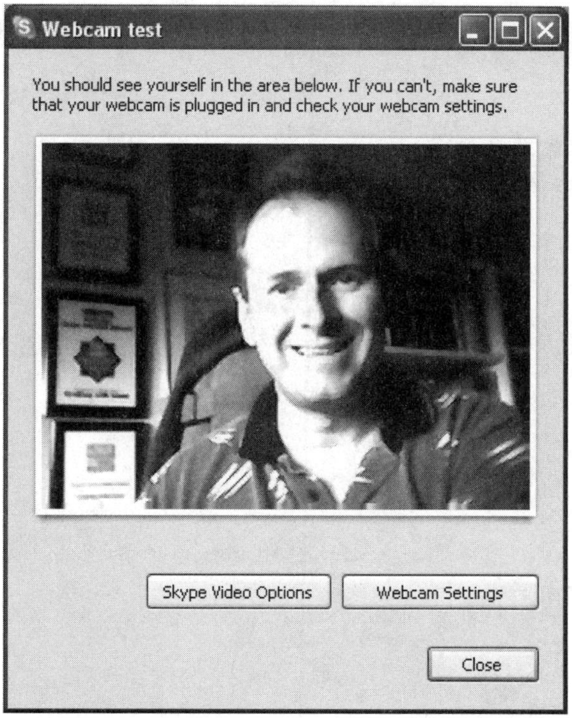

Figure 5–13 After you have selected your webcam, a small window lets you make sure things are working properly.

Getting a Little Privacy

Having access to free long distance is great, but being available for the entire world to call may not be quite as exciting. When you set up your Skype account, you are, by default, available to everyone. On the one hand, this makes it easy to find you, but on the other hand, it makes it easy to find you.

Click Tools on the menu bar and select Options. When the Options dialog appears, select Privacy from the left sidebar (see Figure 5-14).

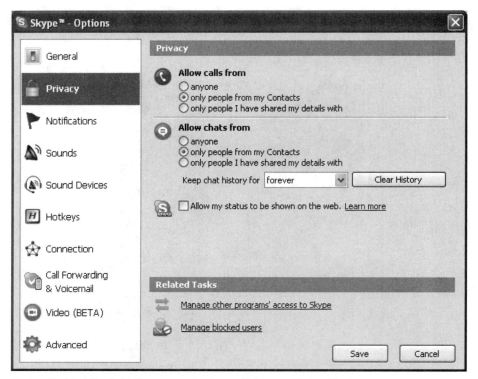

Figure 5–14   By default, anyone in the world can call you. You may want to configure a little privacy.

On the right side, there are two important settings you may want to change. The first has to do with incoming calls. Change the setting from Anyone to Only People from My Contacts by clicking the appropriate radio button. Directly below this section is a similar section; however, this one is dedicated to IM-style chats. Once again, you may want to allow only those people in your contact list to contact you.

Resources

Skype

http://www.skype.com

6

Creating Documents with OpenOffice.org Writer
(It Was a Dark and Stormy Night . . .)

I just love using this infamous opening from Edward George Bulwer-Lytton's "Paul Clifford" (written in 1830) to introduce a chapter on word processing. Those famous words, "It was a dark and stormy night," were made even more famous (infamous?) by Charles M. Schulz's Snoopy, that barnstorming, literary beagle. It just seems fitting considering this chapter's topic—word processors.

Word processors run the gamut in terms of complexity, from simple programs that aren't much more than text editors to full-blown desktop publishing systems. Users coming from the Microsoft world are most likely to use OpenOffice Writer, part of the OpenOffice.org suite.

OpenOffice.org is actually the free sibling of the commercial StarOffice suite. When Sun Microsystems decided to open the source to StarOffice, it became another boon for the open source community, not to mention the average user. OpenOffice became the free version of this powerful word processor, spreadsheet, and presentation graphics package, and StarOffice became the corporate choice. Both of these are full-featured office suites, and users familiar with Microsoft Office will feel right at home with the similarities.

You might well be wondering what differences exist between these two sibling suites. The great difference is the price. For anyone with a reasonably fast Internet connection (or a helpful friend), OpenOffice is *free*. StarOffice, on the other hand, will cost you something for the boxed set. Included with StarOffice are documentation and support, as well as additional fonts and cli-part. That said, you'll find that it is still *far less expensive* than the Windows alternative.

Trivia Time It may interest you to know that this book was written using OpenOffice.org Writer 2.0.

OpenOffice.org Writer

Start OpenOffice.org Writer by clicking the Start button and looking under Programs. Navigate to the OpenOffice.org 2.0 submenu and select Open-Office.org Writer. If you are starting OpenOffice.org Writer for the first time, a startup wizard asks you to accept the license (which is very easy to take). It then asks you to enter your name and initials. This is used for document creation to identify your personal documents. Finally, the wizard provides you with an opportunity to register your installation of Openoffice.org (see Figure 6-1). Registration is entirely optional.

OpenOffice.org Writer starts up with a blank page, ready for you to release that inner creative genius (see Figure 6-2). At the top of the screen, you'll find a menu bar where commands are organized based on their categories, including the friendly sounding Help submenu (more on that shortly).

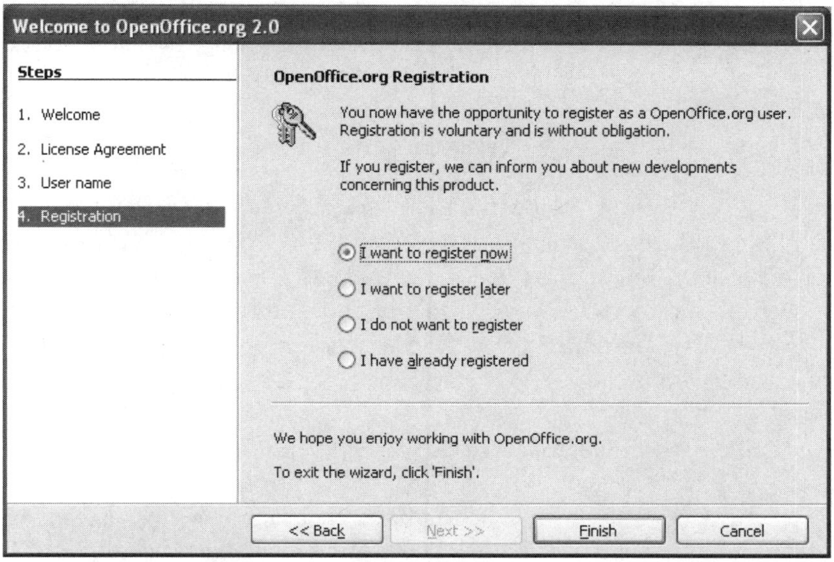

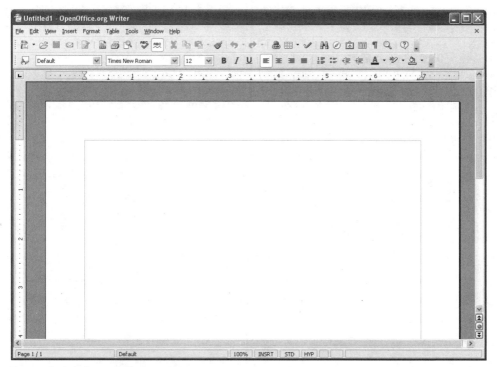

Figure 6–1 In the final part of the installation wizard, OpenOffice.org presents you with an opportunity to register as a user.

Figure 6–2 OpenOffice.org Writer on startup.

At this point, Writer is open and you are looking at a blank screen. Let's write something.

Write Now!

As any writer will tell you, nothing is more *intimidating* than a blank page. Because I opened this chapter with a reference to the famous phrase, "It was a dark and stormy night," why don't we continue along that theme? That phrase is often pointed to as an example of bad writing, but the phrase in itself is only so bad. The paragraph that follows is even worse. Type this into your blank Writer page, as shown in Figure 6-3.

Paul Clifford, by Edward George Bulwer-Lytton

It was a dark and stormy night; the rain fell in torrents—except at occasional intervals, when it was checked by a violent gust of wind which swept up the streets (for it is in London that our scene lies), rattling along the house-tops, and fiercely agitating the scanty flame of the lamps that struggled against the darkness. Through one of the obscurest quarters of London, and among haunts little loved by the gentlemen of the police, a man, evidently of the lowest orders, was wending his solitary way. He stopped twice or thrice at different shops and houses of a description correspondent with the appearance of the quartier in which they were situated—and tended inquiry for some article or another which did not seem easily to be met with. All the answers he received were couched in the negative; and as he turned from each door he muttered to himself, in no very elegant phraseology, his disappointment and discontent.

Okay, you can stop there. Isn't that wonderful stuff? If you feel the need to read more, I've got links to the story and the famous Bulwer-Lytton fiction contest at the end of this chapter.

The Hunt for Typos

For years, I've been including the tag line, "This massagee wos nat speel or gramer-checkered," in the signature section of my emails. Given that I continue to use this line, I am obviously amused by it, but never running a spell check is far from good practice when your intention is to turn in a professional document.

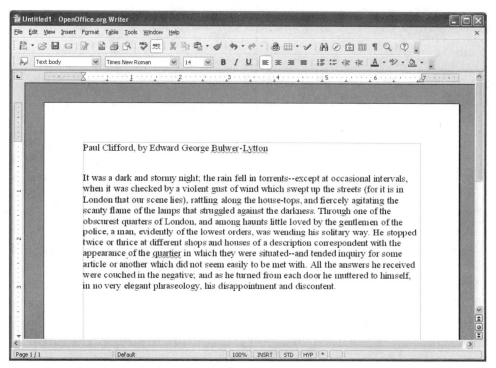

Figure 6–3   Your first document, dark and stormy.

OpenOffice.org Writer can do a spell check as you type without actually correcting errors. With this feature, words that don't appear in the dictionary show up with a squiggly red line underneath them, which signals the possible need for correction. Many people find this a useful feature, but some, like me, prefer to just check the whole document at the end of writing. This feature is activated by default but you can deactivate it if you prefer. Here's how.

Click Tools on the menu bar, and then select Options. This is a multipurpose dialog that allows you to configure many of OpenOffice.org's features (see Figure 6-4). For the moment, we'll concentrate on the auto spell check. To the left of the dialog is a sidebar with many categories. You want Language Settings. Click the plus sign beside it. This drops down a submenu from which you choose Writing Aids. Now look to the right and you'll see a section called Options; at the top of that, you'll see a check box, Check Spelling as You Type. To turn off the auto spell check feature, uncheck this box, and then click OK to close the dialog.

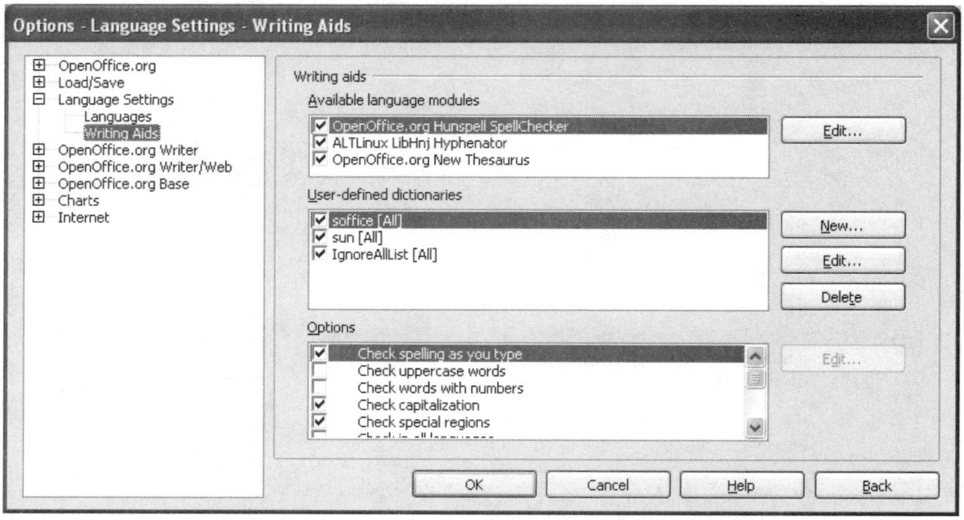

Figure 6–4   *Turning off the spelling-as-you-type feature.*

To start a full document spell check, click Tools on the menu bar, and then Spellcheck. You can also just press <F7> at any time to start a spell check.

What Language Is That?

OpenOffice.org supports many different languages, and depending on where you picked up your copy, it may be set for a different language than your own. To change the default language, click Tools on the menu bar, then Options, Language Settings, and Writing Aids. Look familiar?

The dialog box that appears (refer to Figure 6-4) should have Open-Office.org HunSpell SpellChecker checked on. You can then click the Edit button next to it and select your language of choice under the Default Languages for Documents drop-down box. When you have made your choice, click OK to exit the various dialogs.

Saving Your Work

Now that you have created a document, it is time to save it. Click File on the menu bar and select Save (or Save As). When the Save As window appears (see Figure 6-5), select a folder, type in a file name, and click Save. When you save, you can also specify the File Type to be OpenOffice.org's default Open-Document Text format (.odt), RTF, straight text, Microsoft Word format, and a number of others. You can even save in Palm DOC format so you can take it with you on your Palm device.

If you want to create a new directory under your home directory, you can do it here as well. Click the icon that looks like a folder with a star or globe in front of it (the middle icon near the right-hand corner), and then enter your new directory name in the Create New Folder pop-up window.

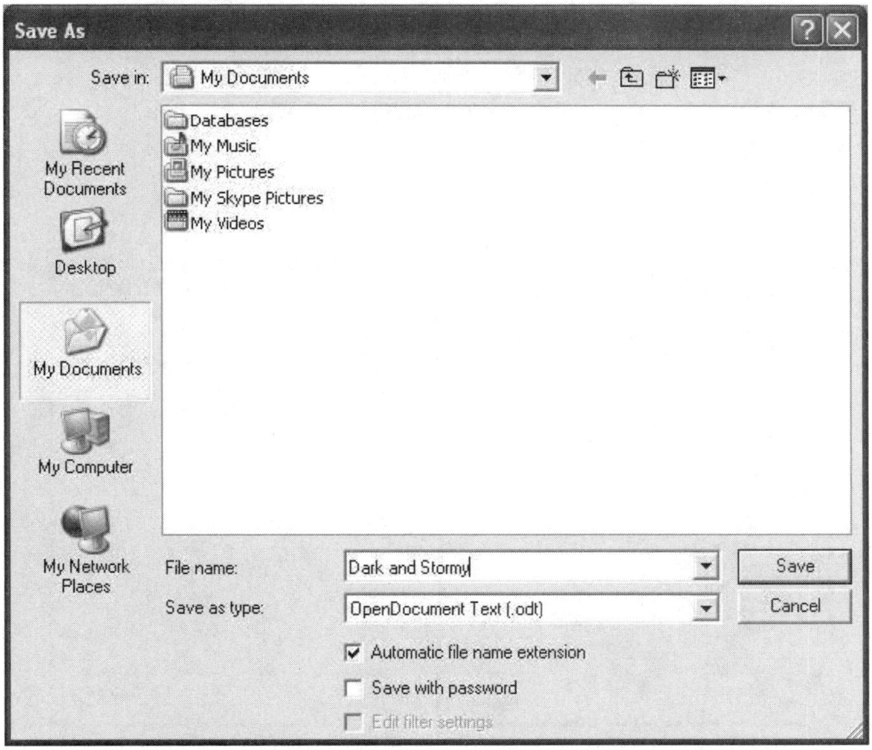

Figure 6–5   It is always good to save your work.

Should you decide to close OpenOffice.org Writer at this point, you can always return to your document at a later time by clicking File on the menu bar and selecting Open. The Open File dialog appears, and you can browse your directories to select the file you want. You can specify a file type via a fairly substantial drop-down list of available formats. This gives you a chance to narrow the search to include only text documents, spreadsheets, or pre-sentations. You can also specify a particular document extension (i.e., only * .doc files) or a particular pattern.

Printing Your Document

The whole point of typing something in a word processor is often to produce a printed document. When you are finished with your document, click File on the menu bar and select Print.

The Print dialog has several options (see Figure 6-6). The easiest thing to do after selecting your printer is just to click OK. The print job is directed to your printer of choice and, in a few seconds, you have a nice, crisp version of your document. You can select a page range, increase the number of copies (one to all your friends), or modify the printer properties (paper size, land-scape print, etc.).

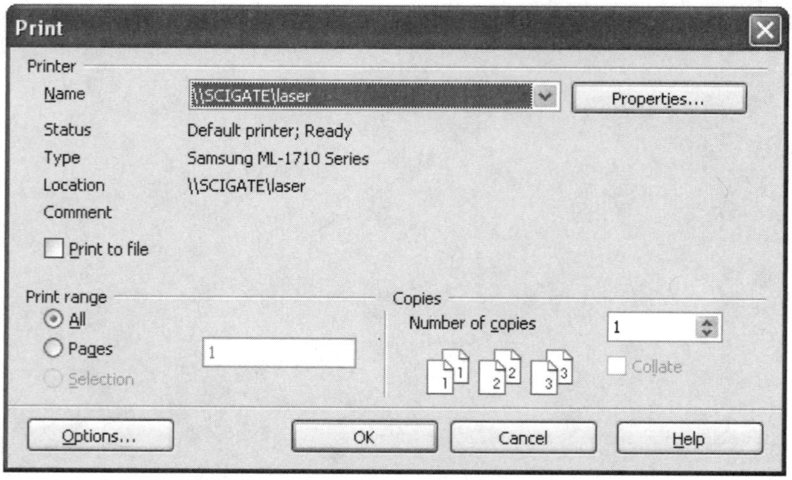

Figure 6–6   Printing your Writer document.

You can also print to a file. By default, this generates a PostScript document, a kind of universal printer language. Because PostScript is an open standard, there are numerous programs that can view and otherwise interpret PostScript documents.

You can also save to PDF, something I'll cover a little later in the chapter.

Toolbars of Every Kind . . .

Now that you are feeling comfortable with your new word processor, let's take a quick tour of the various toolbars, icons, and menus in Writer.

The icon bar directly below the menu bar is called the *Standard bar*, and it contains icons for opening and creating documents, cutting and pasting, printing, and other tasks. The Standard bar is common to all the OpenOffice.org applications (Writer, Calc, Impress, etc.).

Below the Function bar is the *Formatting bar*. It provides common editing options, such as font selection, bolding, italics, centering, and so on. Select words or phrases in your document with the mouse (hold, click, and drag across the desired text), then click *B* for bold or *I* for italics. This bar changes from application to application, depending on what type of formatting is most needed.

At the bottom of the editing screen is the *Status bar*. There, you see the current page number, current template, zoom percentage, insert (or overwrite) mode, selection mode, hyperlink mode, and the current save status of the document. (If the document has been modified and not saved, an asterisk appears.)

In all cases, pausing over each of the icons with your mouse cursor makes a tooltip appear, describing the functions of the individual icons.

Help!

Under the Help heading on the menu bar, you find plenty of information. By default, tooltips are activated so that when you pause your mouse cursor over an item, a small tooltip is shown. These tips are terse, usually no more than a couple of words. It's also possible to get a little more information by turning on Extended Tips. Before I tell you how to do that, have a look at Figure 6-7 for a sample of the difference. The top image shows the default tip for the Paste icon, whereas the bottom image shows the extended tip for the same function.

For that little extra help, click Tools and select Options. Under the OpenOffice.org menu on the right, you find a subsection labeled General. Click there and then look over on the right. You see a check box for Extended Tips near the top. Turning this on gives you slightly more detailed tooltips.

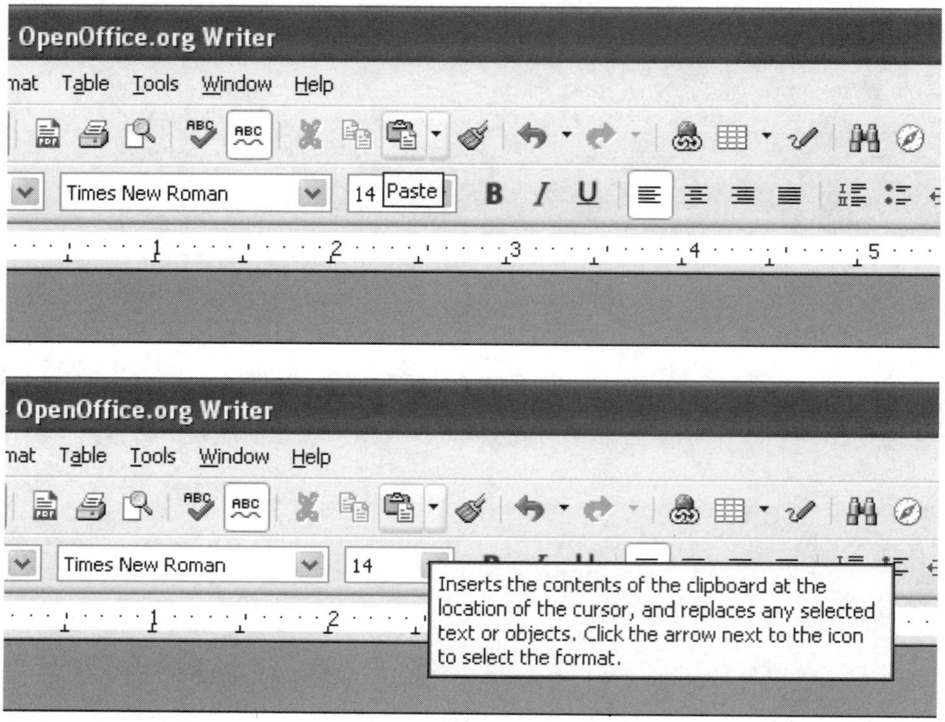

Figure 6–7   What a difference extended tips makes.

If you are looking for help on a specific topic, there's always the included manual. Click Help on the menu bar and select OpenOffice.org Help (you can also press <F1>). The various tabs at the top left of the help screen let you search for topics by application with the Contents tab, alphabetically using the Index tab, and by keyword using the Find tab. You can even set bookmarks under the Bookmarks tab for those topics you regularly access.

To Word or Not to Word?

Ah, that is the question indeed. OpenOffice.org's default document format is the OASIS OpenDocument XML (eXtensible Markup Language) format, an open standard for document formats (it is saved with an .odt extension). The OpenDocument format is the closest thing to document freedom you will get (short of plain text). The format is vendor and application neutral. You are guaranteed support and portability because it is an open standard.

Many organizations such as the European Commission and the State of Massachusetts are starting to recommend the OASIS OpenDocument format for the very reasons I've mentioned. For more on this emerging standard, check the "Resources" section at the end of this chapter.

Alternatively, the main reason for sticking with Word format is, *quite frankly*, that Word is everywhere. The sheer number of Word installations is the very reason that OpenOffice.org was designed to support Microsoft Office format as thoroughly as it does. That said, if you do want to switch to the OASIS OpenDocument format, Writer provides an easy way to do that. Rather than converting documents one by one, the Document Converter speeds up the process by allowing you to run all the documents in a specific directory in one pass. It also works in both directions, meaning that you can convert from Word to OpenOffice.org format, and vice versa. The conversion creates a new file but leaves the original as it is.

From the menu bar, select File, move your mouse to Wizards, and then select Document Converter from the submenu. To convert your Microsoft Office documents (you can do the Excel and PowerPoint documents at the same time), click Microsoft Office on the menu, and then check off the types of documents you want. The next screen asks you whether you want both documents and templates or just one or the other. You then type in the name of the directory you want to import from and save to (this can be the same directory). After you've entered your information and gone to the next screen, the program confirms your choices and gives you a final chance to change your mind. Click Convert to continue. As the converter does its job, it lists the various files that it encounters and keeps track of the process.

When the job is complete, you have a number of files with an .odt extension in your directory. If you change your mind, don't worry. Your original files are still there, so you've lost nothing.

If working with Word documents in Word format is important, then read on. Ah, heck. Even if it isn't, you should read on.

Personalizing Your Environment

Every application you use comes with defaults that may or may not reflect the way you want to work, and this is true here, as well.

Click Tools on the menu bar and select Options. There are a lot of options here, including OpenOffice.org, Load/Save, Language Settings, OpenOffice.org Writer (including HTML/Web documents), OpenOffice.org Base (the built in database), Charts, and Internet. Each of these sections has a submenu of further options. Because there are so many options here, I certainly can't cover them all, and besides, I don't want to bore you. Instead, I'll mention a few things that I *think* are important and let you discover the rest.

The main OpenOffice.org dialog covers a lot of general options regarding the look and feel of the applications. Take a moment to look at the Paths settings. If you keep your documents in a specific directory, you want to set that here. Under Type, choose My Documents, click Edit, and then enter the new path to your directory of choice.

Let's move on to the very important Load/Save settings menu (see Figure 6-8). If you are constantly going to move documents back and forth between systems running Microsoft Word and your own, you want to pay special attention here. Click the plus sign next to the Load/Save label in the Options menu's left hand sidebar, and then click Microsoft Office.

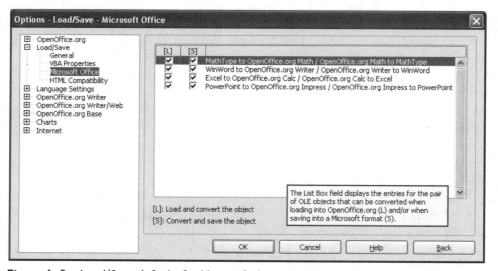

Figure 6–8   Load/Save defaults for Microsoft documents.

Click the convert on Save ([S]) and convert on Load ([L]) check boxes on, and your OpenOffice.org Writer documents are saved in Word format by default, whereas your Calc sheets wind up in Excel format. We're almost there. Although the conversion is pretty automatic here, when you try to resave a document that you have been working on, Writer may still disturb you with the occasional pop-up message informing you of the *minuses* of saving in Word format.

You get around this with one other change. In the same menu section, click General. Notice Default File Format section (see Figure 6-9). For the Document Type of Text Document, select Microsoft Word 97/2000/XP from the Always Save As drop-down list to the right. While you are here (assuming you are making these changes, of course), you probably want to change the Always Save As format for Spreadsheet to be Microsoft Excel, and so on.

Click OK, and you are finished.

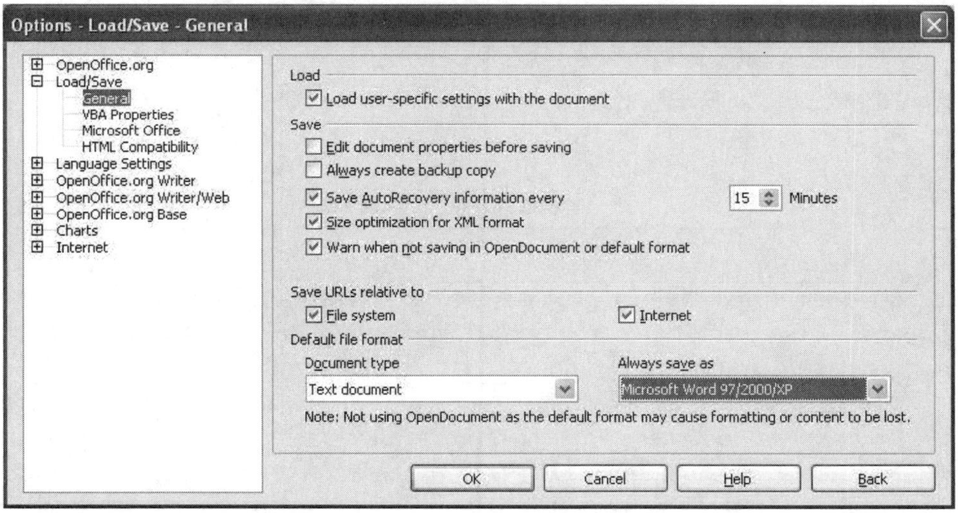

Figure 6–9 Defining the standard file format to be Microsoft Word.

Note I'm not saying that Microsoft's document format is in any way superior. It is not superior, and you are trapped in a proprietary standard that may make it difficult to import your data in the future. Although there's no guarantee that any document format is going to be *the standard* in the future, it's nice to know that you can always load and read your old documents; the OpenDocument format provides you with that kind of comfort. That said, if you have to move back and forth from the open document format to Microsoft's proprietary format all the time, you don't want to be bothered with doing a Save As every time. It just gets tedious.

OpenOffice.org 2.0 can also save in Microsoft's new XML format, which debuted in Microsoft Office 2003.

Let's move on to the OpenOffice.org Writer category (in the left sidebar menu) for changes related specifically to the Writer application. When you start a new document, OpenOffice.org assigns a default font when you start typing. This may not be your ideal choice, and you don't have to accept it. Sure, you can change the font when you are writing, but why do this with every document when you can change it once? Click Basic Fonts, and you have the opportunity to change the default fonts your system uses.

When you are finished with the Options menu, click OK to return to the OpenOffice.org application.

A Wizard of Words

OpenOffice.org comes with a number of templates that are available throughout the suite. The document Wizards feature helps you choose and walk through the setup of some basic documents. The easiest way to understand what these wizards can do for you is to dive right in and try one.

On the menu bar, click File, and move your mouse over to Wizards. You see a number of document types here, from letters to faxes to presentations. We use Letter as an example. When the Letter Wizard starts up, it offers three kinds of letters: business, formal, and personal (see Figure 6-10). Each of these may have different styles depending on the letter type. As you progress through the various steps, you are asked to enter some basic information related to the type of document that you chose. In the case of a letter, this involves an opening and closing greeting, a sender and recipient name and address, and so on. The wizard also lets you save the document as a template so you can use it at a later date.

The wizard also displays a graphical preview of what the document looks like directly behind the design selection window. You shouldn't look at this as a perfect example of what you will wind up with, but it does help in visualizing the final product.

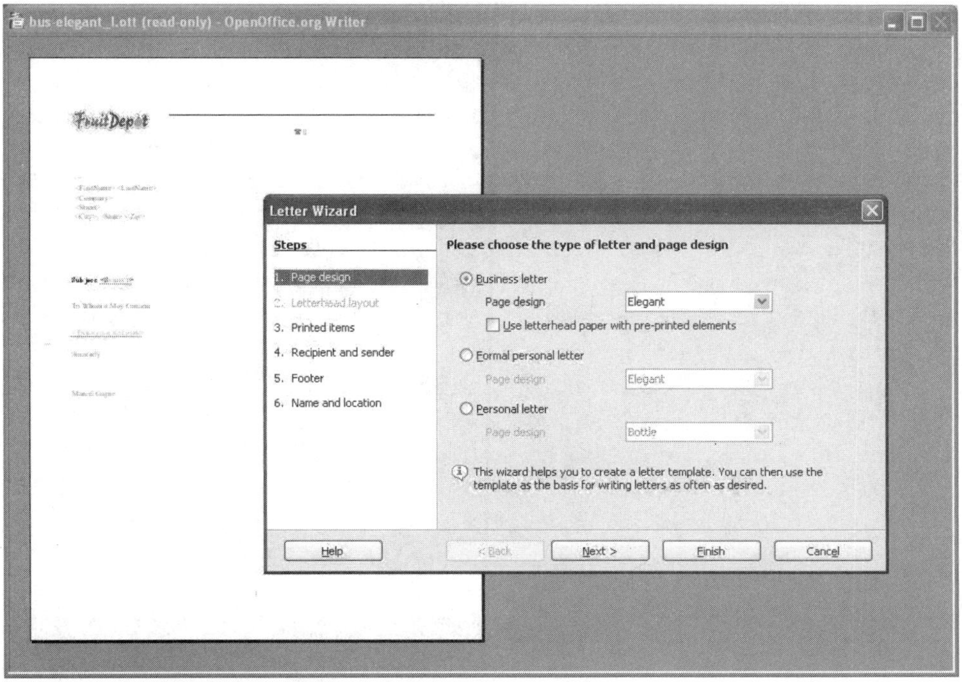

Figure 6–10   Writing using the Letter Wizard.

Navigating Style

With Writer open, click Format on the menu bar, select Styles and Formatting, and a window labeled Styles and Formatting appears, floating above your document. Pressing <F11> also brings up the Stylist. Clicking the X in the corner of the window banishes it. I'd like to give you some idea of how useful this little tool can be in formatting your documents. If you've banished the Stylist, bring it back by clicking its icon or pressing <F11>.

Great Time-Saving Tip   Here's a good trick you might want to keep in mind if you start using styles in a big way. Click the Stylist's title bar with your left mouse button and slowly drag the Stylist window over to the right edge (or the left) of your Writer window. As the Stylist starts to go beyond the edge of the Writer window, you should see a gray vertical outline appear under the Stylist. Release the mouse button and the Stylist docks into the main writer Window (see Figure 6-11).

Whenever you start a new document, it loads with a default style. That style is actually a collection of formatting presets that define how various paragraphs will look. These include headings, lists, text boxes, and so on. All you have to do is select a paragraph, double-click a style, and your paragraph's look—including font style and size—is magically updated. As an example of how to use this, try the following.

Start by reloading your dark and stormy document, and then highlight your title text to select it. The bottom of your Stylist says Automatic. With your title highlighted, double-click Heading 1. The heading changes to a large, bold, sans serif font. Now, click the arrow at the bottom of the list and change from Automatic to Chapter Styles. Double-click Title, and your title is suddenly centered with the appropriate font applied (see Figure 6-11).

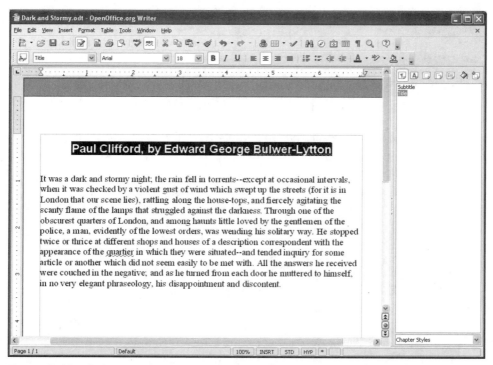

Figure 6–11   Styles make paragraph formatting easy and consistent. Note that the Stylist is docked on the right.

The Stylist is pretty smart, really. Look back to the bottom of the list at those categories—HTML Styles, Custom Styles, List Styles, and so on. Depending on the document type that you are working on, the Stylist comes up with a pretty sane list for that Automatic selection. If you call up an HTML document, HTML formatting shows up in the Automatic list.

Quick Undo Tip To remove a docked Stylist, just drag it out of its dock and drop it above the document itself. It turns back into a floating window. You can also press <F11> and it promptly vanishes from the dock. The great thing about removing it with the function key is that the Stylist remembers where it was. If it was docked when you pressed <F11>, it will be when you press it again.

Navigating the Rivers of Text

The second floating window is called the Navigator. This is a great tool for the power user or anyone who is creating long, complex documents. When you start up the Navigator by selecting Edit, Navigator (or by pressing <F5>), you see a window listing the various elements in your document (see Figure 6-12). These are organized in terms of headings, tables, graphics, and so on.

Figure 6–12 The Navigator: access to all your document elements.

Quick Tip You guessed it! Just like the Stylist, the Navigator can be dragged to either edge of the document and docked into the main writer window. Just make sure you drag it far enough so that it isn't another vertical window next to the Stylist, but is above or below it.

This is a great tool because you can use it to navigate a document quickly. Let's say that (as in this chapter) there are a number of section headings. Click the plus sign beside Headings (the plus sign will only be there if you have headings defined in the document), and a treed list of all the headings in the document is displayed. Double-click a heading, and you instantly jump to that point in the document. The same goes for graphics, tables, and other such elements in your document.

Speaking of Document Elements . . .

Take a look over at the far right of the Standard bar. See the little icon that looks like a picture hanging on a wall? That's the *gallery* of graphics and sounds, decorative elements that can be inserted into your document. When you click the picture (or select Gallery from Tools on the menu bar), the gallery opens up with a sidebar on the left, listing the various themes.

Wander through the collection until you see something that suits your document, then simply drag it into your document, just as I did with that rather bright ruler below the "Paul Clifford" title in Figure 6-13. To banish the gallery, just click the icon again.

While you were using the Gallery, did you notice the words New Theme . . . at the top of the category sidebar? Click those words (which is really a button), and you can create a new category of images, clipart, or sounds. If you have a directory of images you've collected, enter the path to that directory, pick a name for this collection, and you are done. Next time you bring up the Gallery, you can select from your own custom collection.

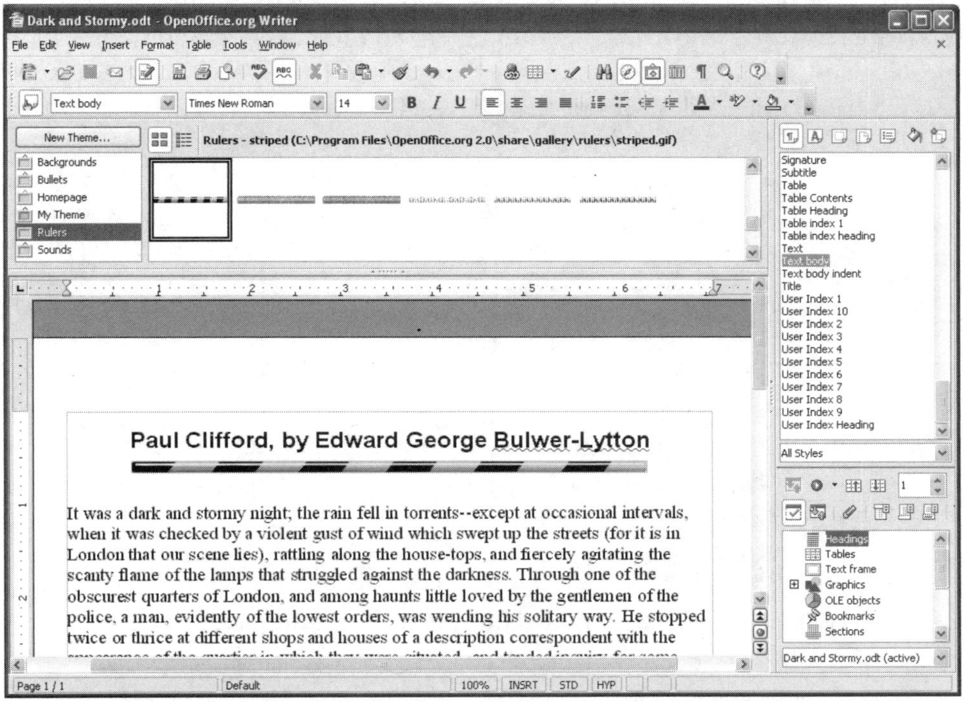

Figure 6–13   Writer with the Gallery open above the document, and with a docked Stylist and Navigator to the right.

> *Tip* How would you like tons and tons of great, license-free, royalty-free, and just plain free, high-quality clipart? Check out www.openclipart.org.

More! Give Me More!

OpenOffice.org comes with a limited number of templates, graphics, and icons. That's one of the advantages of its commercial (non-free) cousin, StarOffice from Sun Microsystems. However, if you find yourself in need of more templates than you already have or a richer gallery, take careful note of the following Web sites.

The first is called OO Extras, and it contains more than two hundred templates for OpenOffice.org Writer, Calc, and Impress. In addition to individual macros, icons, and templates, the goal of this Web site (created by Travis Bauer) aims to provide downloadable packages to enhance OpenOffice.org's suite.

You should also pay a visit to the OpenOffice Documentation Project site (run by Scott Carr), which offers much more than extra templates and macros. There are also tutorials, setup guides, user guides, and even some video presentations.

Links for both projects follow in the "Resources" section.

Resources

Bulwer-Lytton Fiction Contest

http://www.bulwer-lytton.com

OASIS OpenDocument Format

http://www.oasis-open.org/committees/office/faq.php

OOExtras

http://ooextras.sourceforge.net

Open Clip Art Library

http://www.openclipart.org

OpenOffice.org

http://www.openoffice.org/

OpenOffice.org Documentation Project

http://documentation.openoffice.org

Sun Microsystems StarOffice

http://www.sun.com/software/star/staroffice/

Using OpenOffice.org Calc for Spreadsheets (Tables You Can Count On)

A spreadsheet, for those who might be curious, allows an individual to organize data onto a table comprised of rows and columns. The intersection of a row and a column is called a cell, and each cell can be given specific attributes, such as a value or a formula. In the case of a formula, changes in the data of other cells can automatically update the results. This makes a spreadsheet ideal for financial applications. Change the interest rate in the appropriate cell, and the monthly payment changes without you having to do anything else.

The idea of a computerized spreadsheet probably existed before 1978, but it was in that year that Daniel Bricklin, a Harvard Business School student, came up with the first real spreadsheet program. He called his program a visible calculator, then later enlisted Bob Frankston of MIT (Bricklin names him as co-creator) to help him develop the program further. This program would come to be known as VisiCalc. Some argue that with VisiCalc, the first so-called killer app was born.

Now that we have the definitions and history out of the way, let's get back to our exploration of the amazing, yet free, OpenOffice.org and its very own spreadsheet program. It is called *Calc*, an appropriate name given what spreadsheets tend to be used for.

Starting a New Spreadsheet and Entering Data

There are a few ways to start a new spreadsheet using OpenOffice.org. If you are already working in OpenOffice.org Writer (as I am right now), you can click File on the menu bar, move your mouse to the New submenu, and select Spreadsheet from the drop-down list. Another way is to click the Start button, then look under Programs. Navigate to the OpenOffice.org 2.0 submenu and select OpenOffice.org Calc. When Calc starts up, you see a blank sheet of cells, as in Figure 7-1.

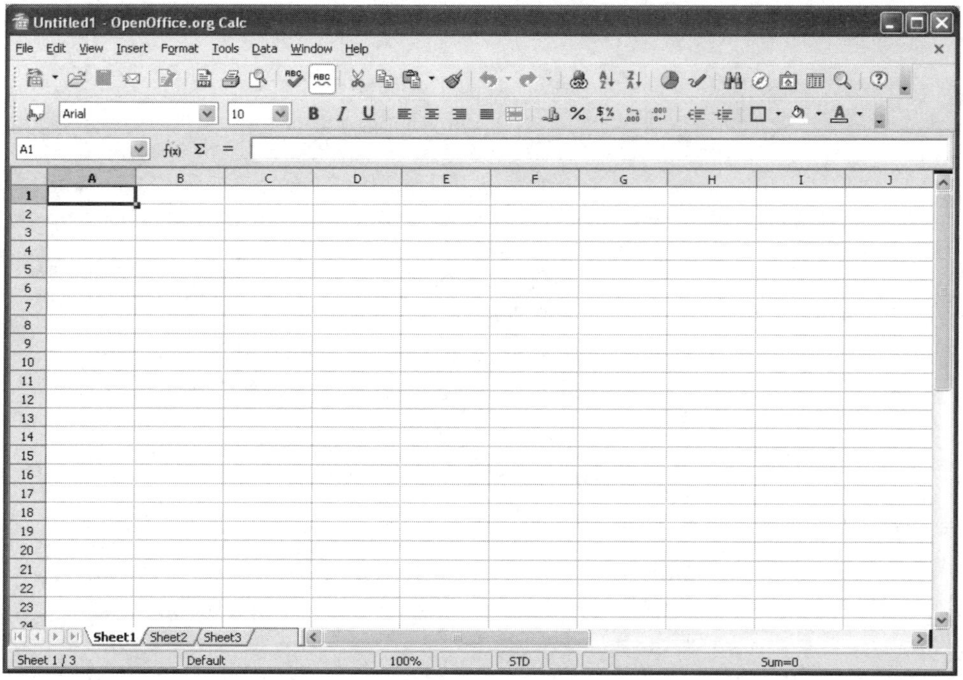

Figure 7–1 Starting with a clean sheet.

Directly below the menu bar is the *Standard bar*. As with Writer, the icons here give you access to the common functions found throughout OpenOffice.org, such as cut, paste, open, save, and so on. Below the Standard bar is the *Formatting bar*. Some features here are similar to those in Writer, such as font style and size, but others are specific to formatting content in a spreadsheet (percentage, decimal places, frame border, etc.).

Finally, below the Formatting bar, you'll find the *Formula bar*. The first field here displays the current cell, but you can also enter a cell number to jump to that cell. You can move around from cell to cell by using your cursor keys, <Tab> (and <Shift+Tab>) key, or simply by clicking a particular cell. The current cell you are working on has a bold black outline around it.

Basic Math

Let's try something simple, shall we? If you haven't already done so, open a new spreadsheet. In cell A1, type **Course Average**. Select the text in the field, change the font style or size (by clicking the font selector in the Formatting bar), then press <Enter>. As you can see, the text is larger than the field. No problem. Place your mouse cursor on the line between the A and B cells (directly below the Formula bar). Click and hold, then stretch the A cell to fit the text. You can do the same for the height of any given row of cells by clicking the line between the row numbers (over to the left) and stretching these to an appropriate size.

Now move to cell A3 and type in a hypothetical number somewhere in the range of 1–100 to represent a course mark. Press <Enter> or cursor down to move to the next cell. Enter seven course marks so that cells A3 through A9 are filled. In my example, I entered 95, 67, 100, 89, 84, 79, and 93. (It seems to me that the 67 is an aberration.)

Now, we will enter a formula in cell A11 to provide us with an average of all seven course scores. In cell A11, enter the following text.

=(A3+A4+A5+A6+A7+A8+A9)/7

When you press <Enter>, the text you entered disappears; instead, you see an average for your course scores (see Figure 7-2).

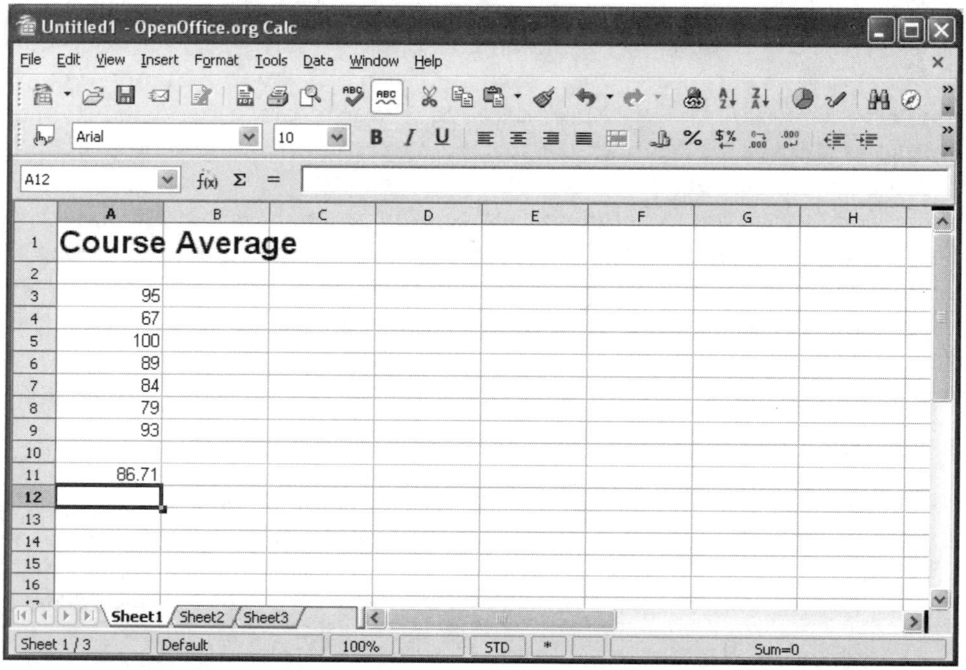

Figure 7–2   Setting up a simple table to determine class averages.

An average of 86.71 isn't a bad score (it is an A, after all), but if that 67 really was an aberration, you can easily go back to that cell, type in a different number, and press <Enter>. When you do so, the average automagically changes for you.

Calculating an average is a simple enough formula, but if I were to add seventy rows instead of seven, the resulting formula could get *ugly*. The beauty of spreadsheets is that they include formulas to make this whole process somewhat cleaner. For instance, I can specify a range of cells by putting a colon between the first and last cells (A3:A9) and using a built-in function to return the average of that range. My new, improved, and cleaner formula looks like this.

=AVERAGE (A3:A9)

Incidentally, you can also select the cell and enter the information in the input line on the Formula bar. I mention the Formula bar for a couple of reasons. One is that you can obviously enter the information in the field, as well as in the cell itself.

The second reason has to do with those little icons to the left of the input field. If you click into that input field, you notice that a little green check mark appears (to accept any changes you make to the formula), and to its left there is a red X (to cancel the changes). Now look to the icon furthest on the left. If you hold your mouse over it, it should pop up a little tooltip, Function Wizard. Try it. Go back to cell A11, and then click your mouse into the input field on the Formula bar. Now, click the Function Wizard icon (you can also click Insert on the menu bar and select Function).

On the left side, you see a list of functions with descriptions of those functions off to the right. For the function called AVERAGE, the description is Returns the Average of a Sample. Because this is what we want, click the Next button at the bottom of the window, after which you see a window much like the one in Figure 7-3. This is where the wizard starts to do its real work.

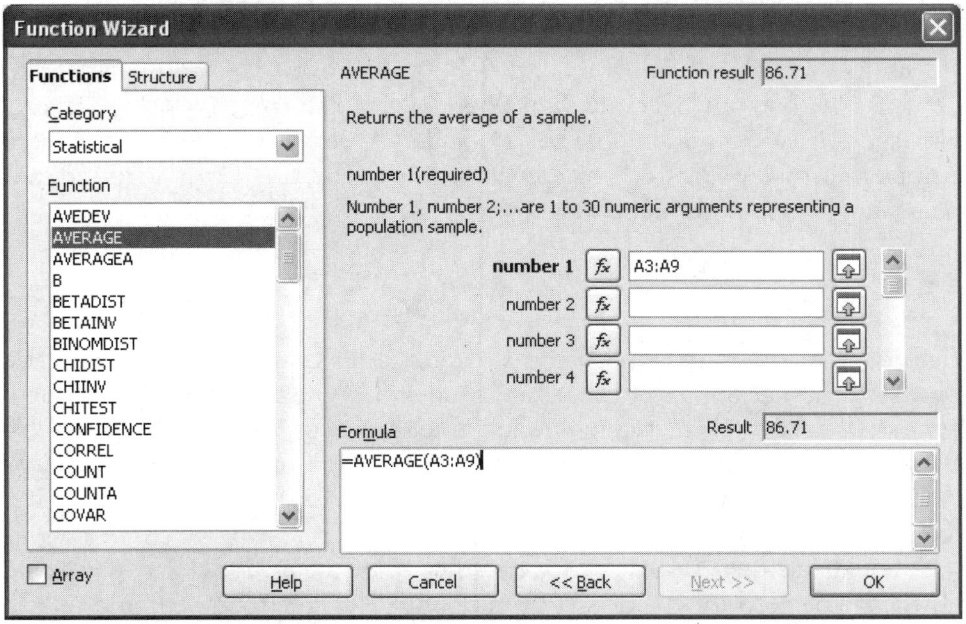

Figure 7–3 Using the Function Wizard to generate a function.

Look at the Formula window at the bottom of your screen. You'll see that the formula is starting to be built. At this point, it says =AVERAGE() and nothing else. Near the middle of the screen on the right side are four data fields labeled Number 1 through Number 4. The first field is required, whereas the others are optional. You could at this point enter **A3:A9**, click Next, and be done. (Notice, while you are here, that the result of the formula is already displayed just above the Formula field.) Alternatively, you could click the button to the right of the number field (the Shrink tooltip), and the Function Wizard shrinks to a small bar floating above your spreadsheet (see Figure 7-4).

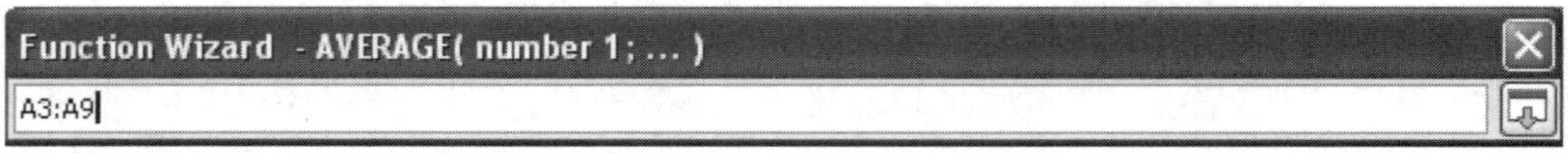

Figure 7–4   The Function Wizard formula bar.

On your spreadsheet, select a group of fields by clicking the first field and dragging the mouse to include all seven fields. When you let go of the mouse, the field range has been entered for you. On the left side of the shrunken Function Wizard, there is a maximize button (move your mouse over it to activate the tooltip). Click it, and your wizard returns to its original size. Unless you have an additional set of fields (or you want to create a more complex formula), click OK to complete this operation. The window disappears, and the spreadsheet updates.

Saving Your Work

Before we move on to something else, you should save your work. Click File on the menu bar and select Save (or Save As). When the Save As window appears, select a folder, type in a file name, and click Save (see Figure 7-5). When you save, you can also specify the file type to be OpenOffice.org's default format, OpenDocument, DIF, DBASE, Microsoft Excel, and other formats.

Should you decide to close OpenOffice.org Calc at this point, you could always go back to the document by clicking File on the menu bar and selecting Open.

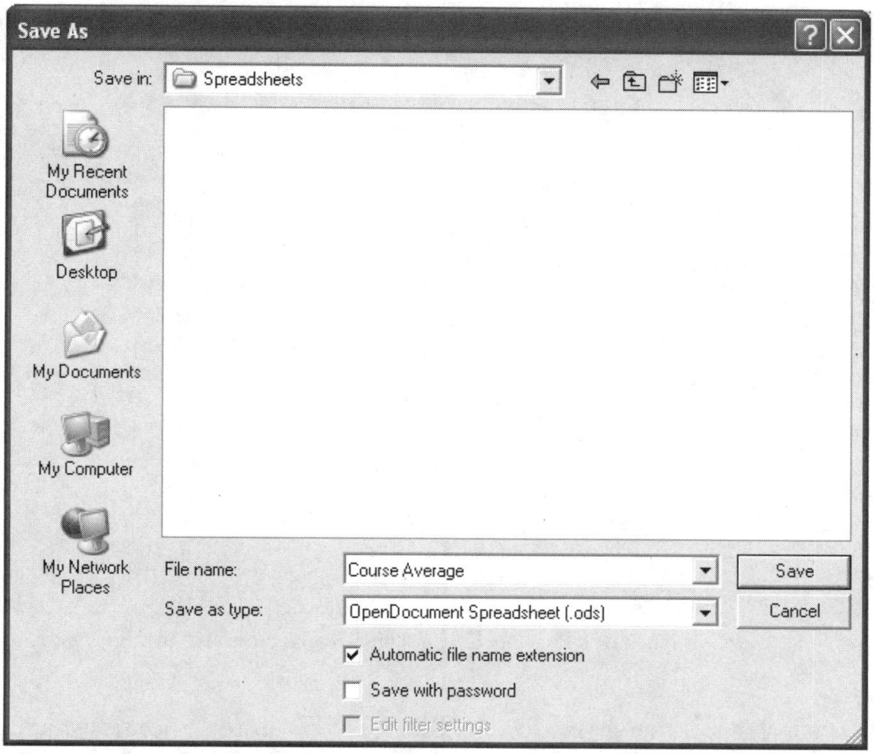

Figure 7–5   Don't forget to save your work.

Complex Charts and Graphs, Oh My!

This time, I'll show you how you can take the data that you enter into your spreadsheets and transform it into a slick little chart. These charts can be linear, pie, bar, and a number of other choices. They can also be two- or three-dimensional, with various effects applied for that professional look.

To start, create another spreadsheet. We'll call this one Quarterly Sales Reports. With it, we will track the performance of a hypothetical company (see Figure 7-6).

In cell A1, write the title (**Quarterly Sales Reports**) and in cell A2, write the description of the data (in thousands of dollars). In cell A4, write the heading (**Period**), and then enter **Q1** in cell A6, **Q2** in cell A7, **Q3** in cell A8, and **Q4** in cell A9. Finally, enter some headings for the years. In cell B4, enter **2001**, then enter **2002** in cell C4, and continue on in row 4 right up to **2005**. You should have five years running across row 4, with four quarters listed.

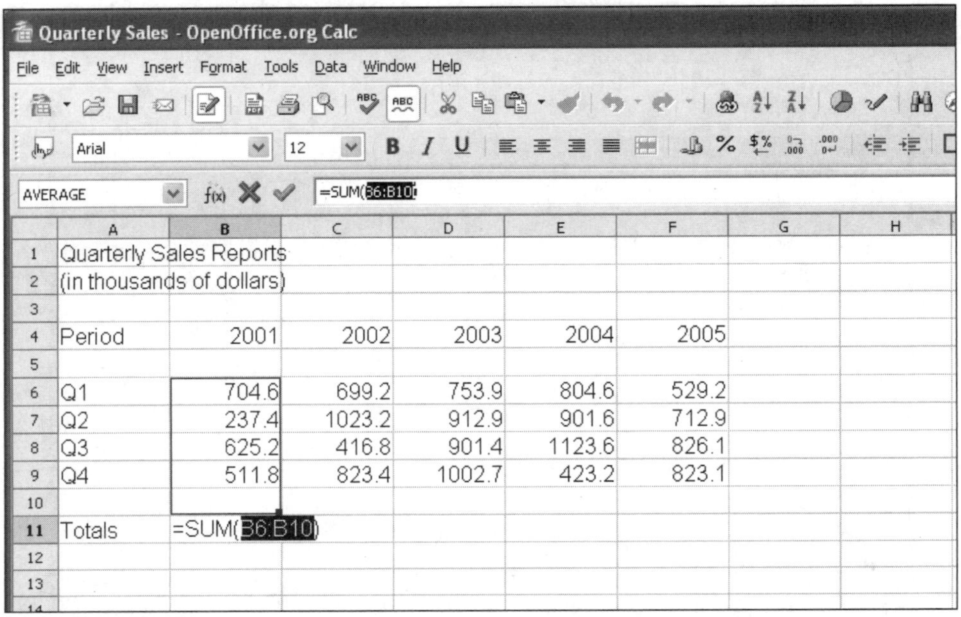

Figure 7-6   Select a series of cells, and Calc automatically generates totals for you.

Time to have some virtual fun. For each period, enter a fictitious sales figure (or a real one if you are serious about this). For example, the data for 2002, Q2, would be entered in cell C7, and the sales figure for 2004, Q3, would be in cell E8. If you are still with me, finish entering the data, and we'll do a few things.

Magical Totals

Let's start with a quick and easy total of each column.

If you used the same layout as I did, you should have a 2001 column that ends at B9. Click cell B11. Now look at the icon in the middle of the sheet area and the input line on the Formula bar. It looks like the Greek letter Epsilon. Hold your mouse pointer over it, and you see a Sum tooltip. Are you excited yet? Click the icon, and the formula to sum up the totals of that line, =SUM(B6:B10), automatically appears (see Figure 7-6). To finalize the totals, all you need to do is click the green check mark that appears next to the input line (or just press <Enter>).

Because a sum calculation is the most common function used, it is kept handy. You can now do the same thing for each of the other yearly columns to get your totals. Click the sum icon, then click your beginning column and drag the mouse to include the cells you want. Click the green check mark, and move on to the next yearly column.

Nice, Colorful, Impressive, and Dynamic Graphs

Creating a chart from the data you have just entered is really pretty easy. Start by selecting the cells that represent the information you want to see on your finished chart, including the headings. You can start with one corner of the chart and simply drag your mouse across to select all that you want. Using the spreadsheet we've created, select the area that includes cell A4 right through to F9. Note that I did not include the Totals line.

 Warning If there are some empty cells in your table (in my example, row 5), you need to deselect them. You can do this by holding down the <Ctrl> key and clicking those cells with the mouse.

After you have all the cells you want selected, click Insert on the menu bar, and select Chart. This window gives you the opportunity of assigning certain rows and columns as labels (see Figure 7-7). This is perfect because we have the quarter numbers running down the left side and the year labels running across the top. Check these boxes.

Before you move on, notice the Chart Results in Worksheet drop-down list. By default, Calc creates three tabbed pages for every new worksheet, even though you are working on only one at this time. If you leave things as they are, your chart is embedded into your current page, though you can always move it to different locations. You have a choice at this point to have the chart appear on a separate page (those tabs at the bottom of your work-sheet). For my example, I'm going to leave the chart on the first page. Make your selection, and then click Next.

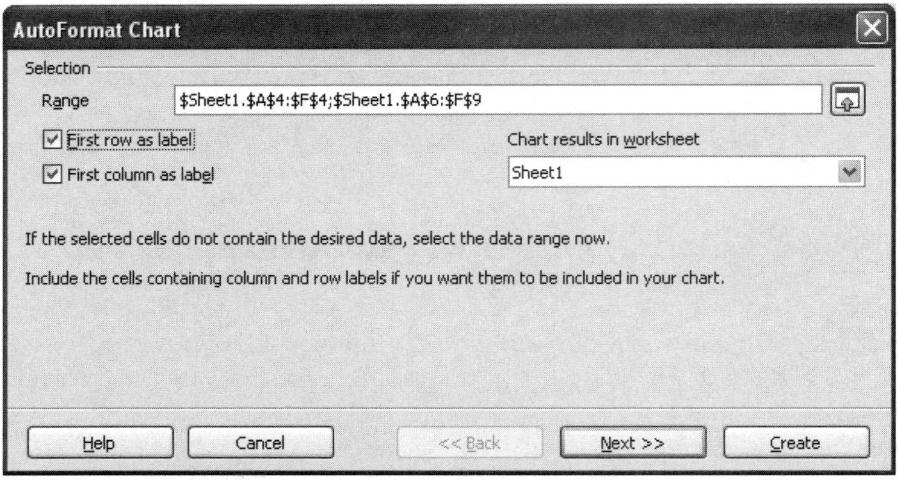

AutoFormat Chart

Selection

Range   `$Sheet1.$A$4:$F$4;$Sheet1.$A$6:$F$9`

☑ First row as label

☑ First column as label

Chart results in worksheet

Sheet1

If the selected cells do not contain the desired data, select the data range now.

Include the cells containing column and row labels if you want them to be included in your chart.

| Help | Cancel | << Back | Next >> | Create |

Figure 7–7   The AutoFormat Chart dialog.

 Note There is also an Insert Chart icon on the Standard bar. If you click that icon (instead of clicking Insert and then Chart from the menu bar), the software automatically assumes that you want the chart in the worksheet. Furthermore, your cursor changes to a small chart icon. Click a location on the document where you want the chart to appear, and the AutoFormat Chart dialog appears.

The next window lets you choose from chart types (bar, pie, etc.) and provides a preview window to the left (see Figure 7-8). That way, you can try the various chart options to see what best shows off your data. If you want to see the labels in your preview window, click the check box for Show Text Elements in Preview.

You can continue to click Next for some additional fine-tuning on formatting (the last screen lets you change the title), but this is all the data you actually need to create your chart. When you are done, click the Create button, and your chart appears on your page (see Figure 7-9).

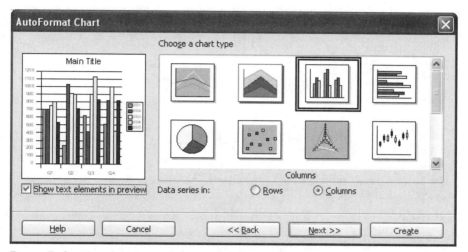

Figure 7–8   You can choose from lots of chart types.

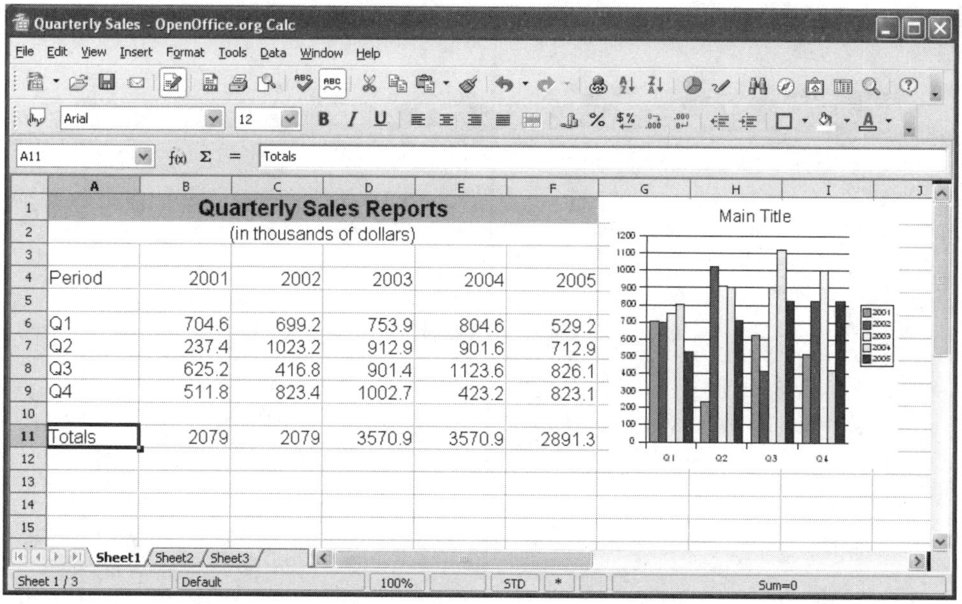

Figure 7–9   Just like that, your chart appears alongside your table.

To lock the chart in place, click anywhere else on the worksheet. You may want to change the chart's title, as well: double-click the chart, and then click the title to make your changes. I'm going to call mine Sales Over 5 Years. If the chart is in the wrong place, click it, then drag it to where you want it to be. If it is too big, grab one of the corners and resize it.

This chart is dynamically linked to the data on the page—cool! Change the data in a cell, press <Enter>, and the chart automatically updates!

Final Touches

If you select (highlight) the title text in cell A1 and click the centered icon, the text position doesn't change. That's because A1 is already filled to capacity, and the text is essentially already centered. To get the effect you want, click on cell A1, hold the mouse button down, and drag to select all the cells up to F1. Now click Format on the menu bar and select Merge Cells. All six cells merge into one, after which you can select the text and center it.

For more extensive formatting of cells, including borders, color, and so on, right-click the cell, and select Format. (Try this with your title cell.) A Format Cells window appears, from which you can add a variety of formatting effects (see Figure 7-10).

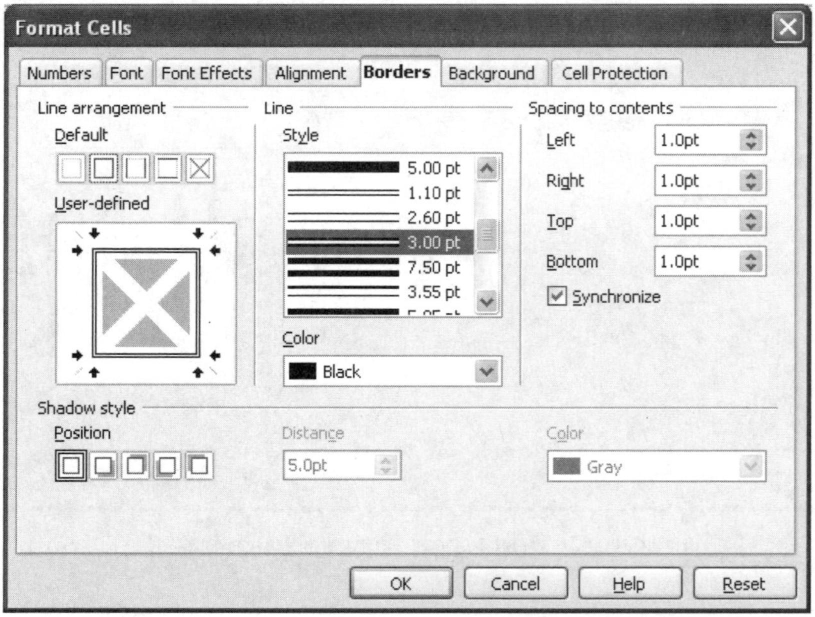

Figure 7–10   Adding borders and fill to cell.

A Beautiful Thing!

When you are finished with your worksheet, it is time to print. Click File on the menu bar and select Print. Select your printer, click OK, and you have a product to impress even the most jaded bean counter. While you are busy impressing people, keep in mind that you can also export this spreadsheet to PDF with a single click, just as you did with Writer in the last chapter.

Resources

OpenOffice.org Calc

http://www.openoffice.org/product/calc.html

Presentations with OpenOffice.org Impress (When You Need to Impress Someone)

Once upon a time, even a simple business presentation could be quite a costly affair. The person putting together a presentation would create his presentation using a word processor (or pen and ink), then transfer all this to a business graphics presentation tool. Alternatively, a special design service might be hired to take that next step, but eventually, the whole project would be sent to yet another service that would create 35-mm slides from the finished paper presentation.

On the day of the big meeting, the old carousel slide projector would come out, and the slides would be painstakingly loaded onto the circular slide holder. Then the lights would dim, and the show would begin. With any luck, the slides would all be in the right order, and the projector would not jam.

These days, we use tools that streamline this process, allowing us to create presentations, insert and manipulate graphical elements, and play the whole thing directly from our notebook computers. The projectors we use simply plug into the video port of our computers. There are other free software packages to do the job, but the most popular (and the one I will cover here) is part of the OpenOffice.org suite. It is called Impress. For those of you coming from the Microsoft world, Impress is very much like PowerPoint. In fact, Impress can easily import and export PowerPoint files.

Getting Ready to Impress

After having worked with OpenOffice.org's Writer and Calc, you should feel right at home when it comes to using Impress. Working with menus, inserting text, spell checking, and customizing your environment all work in exactly the same way. The editing screen is probably more like Calc than Writer in some ways. The Impress work area has tabbed pages so you can easily jump from one part of the presentation to the other. Each page is referred to as a *slide*. Given the history of business presentations—specifically, the making of 35-mm slides—it's probably no wonder that we still use the same terms when creating presentations with software like Impress.

To start Impress, click Start, Programs, and start OpenOffice.org Impress from the OpenOffice.org submenu. You can also start a new presentation from any other OpenOffice.org application, such as Writer or Calc. Just click File on the menu bar, select New, and choose Presentation from the submenu.

When you start up Impress for the first time, the Presentation Wizard appears and you are presented with a number of choices. You can start with an empty presentation (see Figure 8-1), work from a template, or open an existing presentation. Incidentally, some earlier versions of OpenOffice.org started with a blank page. You have the opportunity to select this behavior by clicking the Do Not Show This Wizard Again check box.

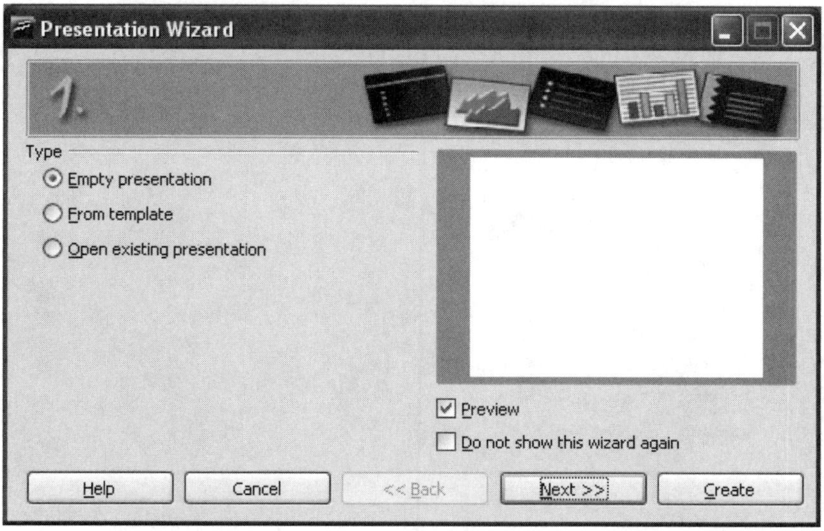

Figure 8–1 Starting a new presentation with the Presentation Wizard.

Quick Tip At the time of this writing, OpenOffice.org ships with only a couple of Impress templates. As I've mentioned before, one of the differences between OpenOffice.org and StarOffice (its commercial sibling) is that StarOffice comes with a number of templates. That said, you can still download some free templates from `ooextras.sourceforge.net`.

The Presentation Wizard allows you to select from existing presentations, as well as templates. For the moment, I'm going to stick with the very basics. Leave Empty Presentation selected, and click Next. Essentially, this starts you off with a blank slide. Step 2 gives you the opportunity to select a slide design (see Figure 8-2). You may find a few options for slide design here (these are your templates). Choose <Original>. Before you click Next, pause and have a look at the options for output medium. By default, Impress creates presentations designed for the screen (or a projector connected to your PC).

Figure 8–2   Impress defaults to creating presentations designed for the screen.

Step 3 lets you define the default means for slide transition (see Figure 8-3). You've all seen these transitions; as someone shows a presentation, slides dissolve to show the next one or fly in from the left or drop like a trap door closing. At this stage of the game, pick one of these effects from the Effect drop-down box, then choose the Speed of that transition. On the right side, there is a preview window that shows you what the effect looks like when you select it.

Directly below the Slide Transition section, you select the presentation type. Your choices are Default and Automatic. By default, transition from slide to slide is done by pressing a key, <Enter> or the spacebar (you can define this). Presentations can also run without any intervention from the person giving the presentation. By selecting Automatic, you can define the amount of time between slides or even between presentations. Accept the default setting here and click Create to start building your presentation.

We now have everything we need to start working on our presentation. Impress opens to a blank page that is divided into three main panes or frames (see Figure 8-4). On the left, small previews of all your slides are displayed (just a single blank one at this moment). As you work, you can quickly move to any slide you want by scrolling down the lists and clicking the slide. Below each preview is the slide's title. By default, the title is Slide, followed by the slide's number in sequence. If you don't like this naming convention, you can easily override it by right-clicking the title and selecting Rename slide.

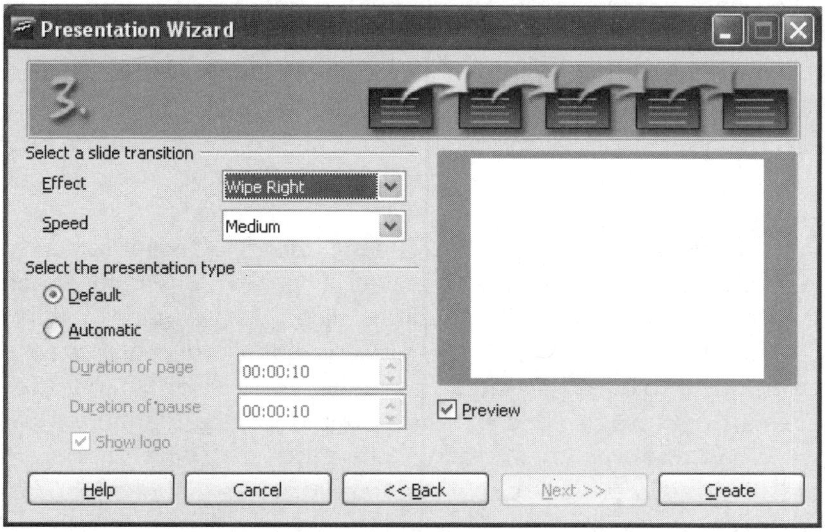

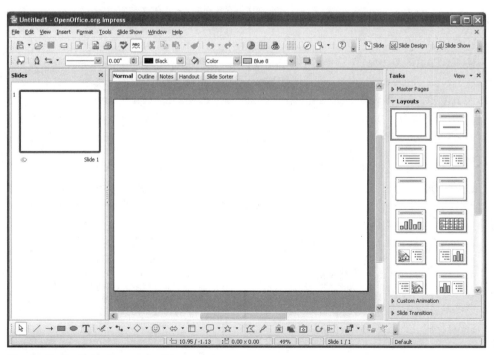

Figure 8–3   Selecting slide transition effects.

Figure 8–4   Selecting your slide layout.

To the right, another pane is visible with a number of potential slide layouts having small preview images. This is the Tasks pane and it is further divided into four sections: Master Pages, Layouts, Custom Animation, and Slide Transition. By default, the Layouts section is open. From here, you can decide on the appearance of the slide, the number of columns, title locations, and so on. If you pause over one of the images with your mouse cursor, a tooltip appears, telling you a little about the layout format.

Finally, there's a rather large central pane with five tabs labeled Normal, Outline, Notes, Handout, and Slide Sorter. The Normal view is where you do most of your work, creating and editing slides. The Outline view is a kind of bird's eye overview of the whole presentation. You can reorder slides, change titles, and so on. The Notes view does pretty much what you expect; it provides an easy way to add notes to the slides. The Handouts view is, I think, very handy. Sometimes, when you are doing a presentation, you are expected to provide printouts of the slides for those in attendance. With Handouts, you can define how those printouts look and how many slides fit on a single page. Finally, we have the Slide Sorter, which is just a larger version of the Slides preview pane on the left. With a larger area, sorting slides is made just that much easier. For now, we will be working with the Normal view.

Finally, you'll notice that the various toolbars and menus have some resemblance to those of both Writer and Calc (discussed in the last two chapters). The menu bar sits just below the title bar, and the Standard bar is directly below. You'll notice that the Formatting bar has a number of different options unique to working in the Impress environment. Along the bottom is the Drawing bar, which provides quick access to objects, drawing functions, 3D effects, and so on.

Let's jump right in and create a presentation. From the Tasks pane, select the Layouts section if it isn't already open. Choose the Title, Clipart, Text layout by clicking it, and it instantly appears in the main work area in the center (see Figure 8-5).

At any point, you can start the slide show by clicking Slide Show on the menu bar and selecting Slide Show. Pressing <F5> has the same effect. There won't be much to see at this point, but you can do this from time to time to see how your presentation is coming along.

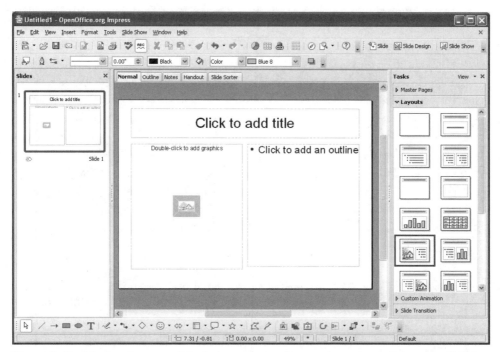

Figure 8–5 Having chosen a slide design, you are now ready to start editing that slide in the central work area.

To start editing your slide, click (or double-click for images) the section you want to change. Make your changes by typing into that area. For the title, you might enter **Why Use Free Software?** When you are happy with your changes, just click outside of the frame area. Over on the right, in the frame that says, "Click to add an outline," insert these bulleted points.

As high quality as any commercial software.

It is free. Gratis!

It does what you need.

You could use the extra money!

Bill Gates is already rich enough. Really.

As you might have noticed, this outline serves as talking points that mirror the first chapter of this book. Now, over on the left side, double-click the frame (as instructed on the default slide) and insert a graphic. The Insert

Picture dialog appears, allowing you to navigate your folders and look for the perfect image (see Figure 8-6).

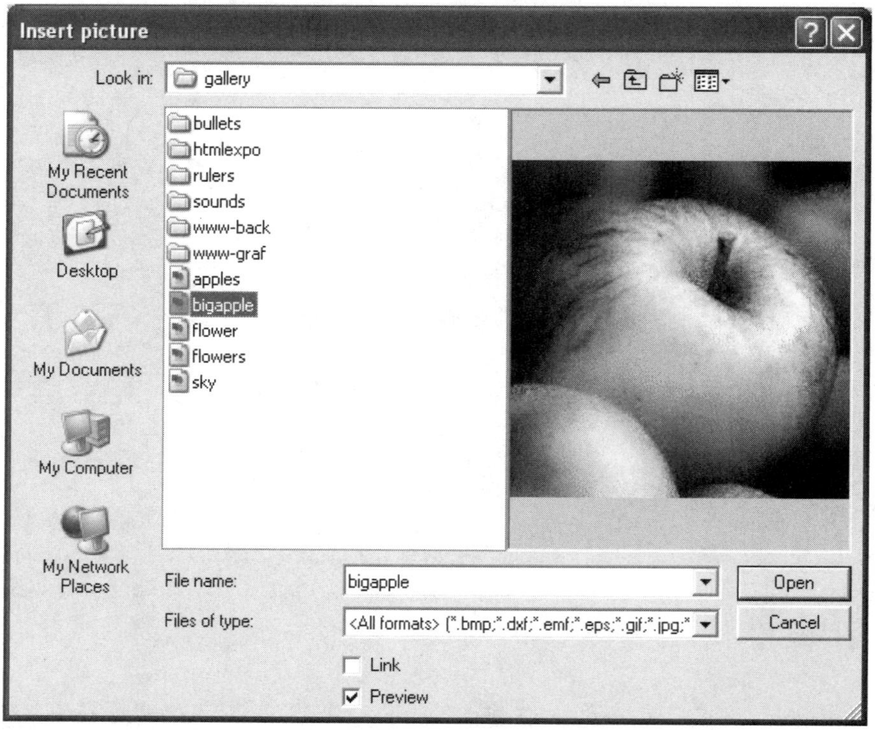

Figure 8–6   Inserting a picture into the presentation.

By default, the Insert Picture window opens in the OpenOffice.org gallery folder, but you can use any image you like here. For my image, I used the GIMP (covered in Chapter 15) to create a cartoon-like image from a photograph, and called it Empty Pockets. You may choose another image if you prefer. When you have your image selected, click Open, and it replaces the default text in the left frame.

Quick Tip   Another option is to single-click the default image and press <Delete>. Then, you can click Tools on the menu bar, select Gallery, and drag one of the included images onto your slide.

That's it. Your first slide is done. You might want to pause here and save your work before you move on. (Masterpieces must be protected.) Click File on the menu bar, select Save As, and then enter a file name for your presentation. I used Why Free Software as my title. Now, click Save, and we'll continue building this presentation.

Tip For thousands of free, high-quality, clipart images with no strings attached, visit the Open Clip Art project at www.open-clipart.org. The site provides access to thousands of user-contributed clipart images that are either in the public domain or licensed under the Creative Commons. You can search for what you need, download individual images, or download the entire library in one large bundle.

Inserting Slides

At the right end of the Standard bar, there's a Slide button. Clicking this button inserts a new slide after whatever slide you happen to be working on. You can also click Insert on the menu bar and select Slide. Once again, you are presented with a blank slide, ready for your creative vision (refer to Figure 8-4). In the left frame, a new blank slide appears below the preview of the completed first slide.

For this second slide, let's select a new slide design. Go back to the Layouts section of your Tasks frame and select the slide design called Title, Text (see Figure 8-7).

Because we had five points (after our introductory slide), let's do a quick add of the next four slides by just clicking the Slide button on the Standard bar. You should now have tabs labeled Slide 1 through Slide 6.

Okay, click the tab for Slide 2, then click the top frame where it says Click to Add Title. Enter the first bullet point from Slide 1. Then repeat the process for the next four slides, inserting the appropriate bullet point as the title.

Quick Tip You can give those slide labels more useful names by right-clicking them and selecting Rename Slide.

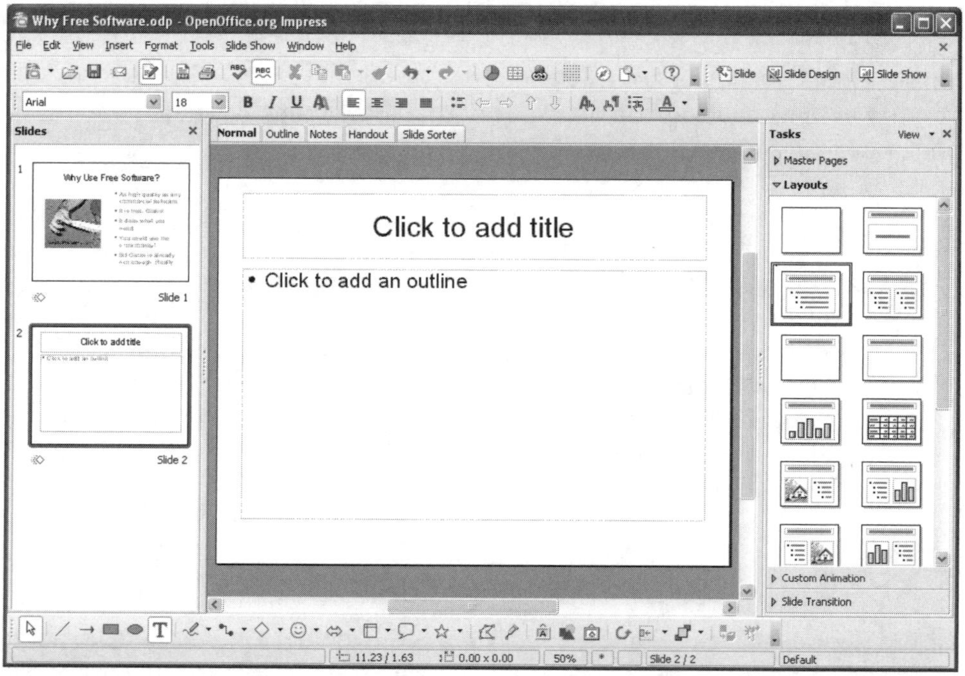

Figure 8–7   With the addition of a second slide, our presentation is starting to take shape.

Regarding what to enter in the text area of each slide: I leave that to either your imagination or your memory of Chapter 1. When you have finished entering all the information you want, save your work. I'm going to show you how to dress up those plain white slides.

Adding Color

Right-click your slide (not on the text), and select Slide from the pop-up menu. Now click Page Setup (see Figure 8-8).

You will see a two-tabbed window (the Page tab and the Background tab). Click the Background tab. You'll notice that it's a pretty boring page with nothing but a Fill drop-down list with None selected. Each item in the drop-down list provides an option for background selection, whether it be plain white, colors, gradients, hatching, or bitmaps. Select each to see the choices that they offer. The example in Figure 8-9 shows the Bitmap selection screen.

Figure 8–8 Modifying the page (slide) setup in preparation for color.

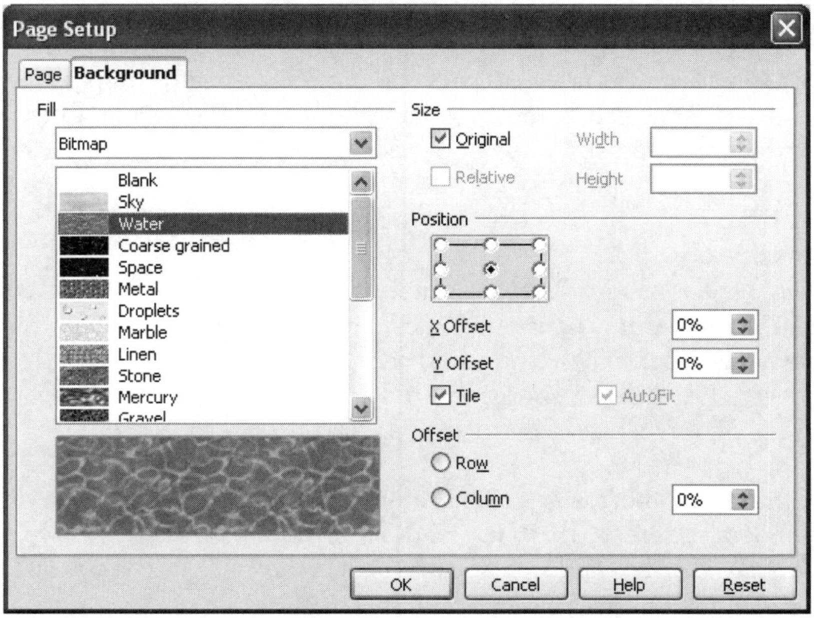

Figure 8–9 Selecting background decorations from the Impress Page Setup.

For example, you might choose the Linear blue/white gradient (a very business-looking background) or perhaps the Water bitmap. The choice is yours. When you click OK, you are asked whether you want this background setting to be for all slides. For now, click Yes.

All right. You've done a lot of work, so save your presentation. Click File on the menu bar and select Save (or Save As) from the menu. If you choose Save As, you have the opportunity to select the presentation format, whether native OpenOffice.org OpenDocument or Microsoft PowerPoint format.

Now, it's time to see the fruits of your labors. Click Slide Show on the menu bar and select Slide Show. You can also use the <F5> keyboard short-cut. The slides transition with a touch of the spacebar or a mouse click. You can exit the presentation at any time by pressing the <Esc> key.

Printing Your Presentation

As with the other OpenOffice.org applications, click File on the menu bar and select Print; you can also click the small printer icon on the Standard bar. The standard OpenOffice.org Print dialog appears, from which you can select your printer of choice.

Instant Web Presentations

Here's something you are going to find incredibly useful. Impress lets you export your existing presentation to HTML format. The beauty of this is that you can take your presentation and make it available to anyone with a Web browser. Best of all, the export functionality takes care of all the details associated with creating a Web site, including the handling of links and forward and back buttons.

To create an instant Web presentation in OpenOffice, here is what you do. Make sure that your current Impress presentation is open and that your work is saved. Click File on the menu bar and select Export. The Export dialog appears. Because all the generated pages appear in the directory you choose, it might make sense to create an empty directory into which to save your files before entering a file name. That file name, by the way, is the HTML title page, normally called `index.html`. If you would like a different name, choose it here, minus the `.html` extension (e.g., Free_Software), and click Export. A new window appears. This is the HTML Export dialog (see Figure 8-10).

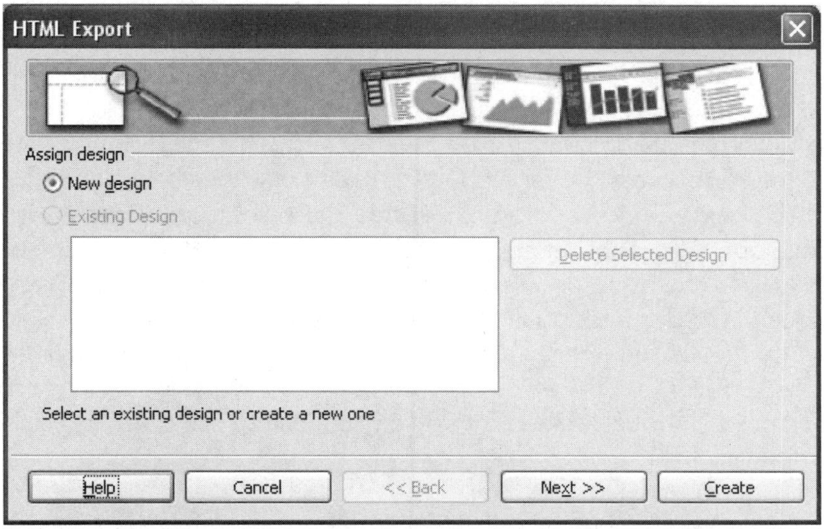

Figure 8–10   The HTML Export dialog on first run.

If this is your first HTML export, you only have one option on the first screen: to create a new design. Click Next and you are presented with a few additional choices (see Figure 8-11).

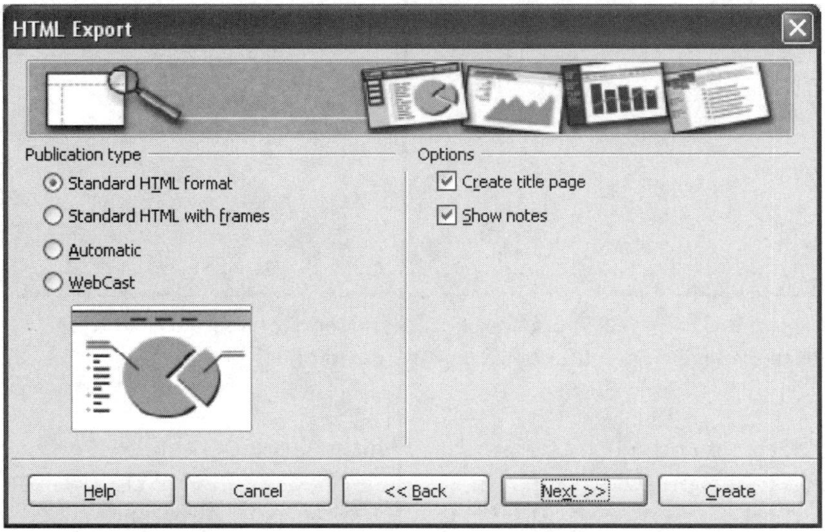

Figure 8–11   It is time to choose the format of your HTML presentation.

You are given the choice of several publication types. The default choice (and probably a very good one) is Standard HTML Format. You can also decide to create an HTML publication with frames, if you prefer. If you want to be totally in control of what your audience sees, you can also elect to create an automatic slideshow (using HTML refresh times of whatever you choose) or a WebCast. When you have made your choice, click Next.

On the next window, you must decide the resolution of the images created for your Web publication (see Figure 8-12). The default is to use JPG images at 75 percent compression. You can elect to set this all the way up to 100 percent for the best quality possible, but be aware that the higher the quality, the larger the images and the slower the download time. If this presentation is meant to be viewed on your personal office network, it probably doesn't matter. Notice as well that you can choose to use the GIF graphic format instead of JPG.

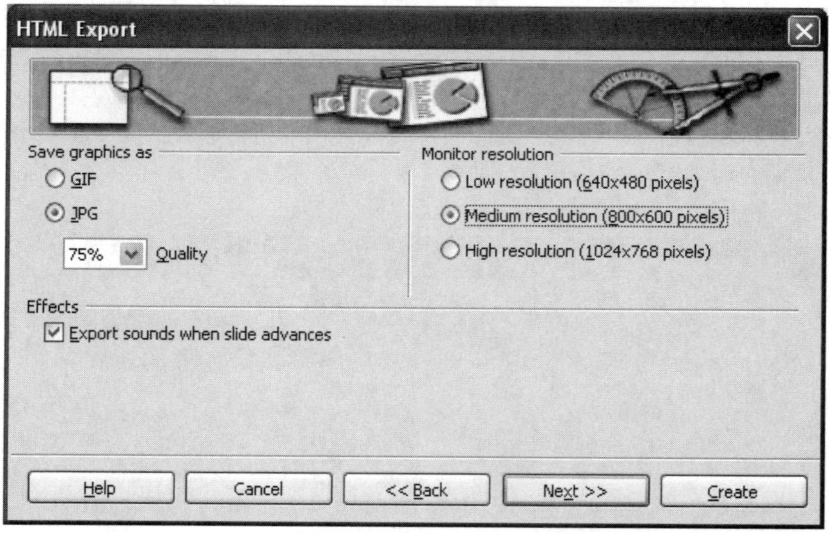

Figure 8–12   Select your image quality and monitor resolution. In this example, I've chosen to use JPG images instead of GIF.

You are also asked to choose the monitor resolution. This is an excellent question that is probably worth more than a few seconds of configuration. At some point in your history of surfing, you must have come across a Web site where the Web page was larger than your browser window. To view the page, you needed to move your horizontal slide bar back and forth just to read the text. Although we are used to scrolling up and down to read text, left to right scrolling is somewhat more annoying. If you want to be as inclusive as possible for your audience, use 640×480. That may be going overboard though. Most personal computer monitors these days will handle 800×600 without any problem and many people run 1024×768 displays. Is there a right answer? Probably not. Consider your target audience, make your decision based on those considerations, and then click Next.

One last thing before we move on. Notice the check box under the Effects section. I'm not a big fan of Web pages that play sounds when I do things. You can choose to export sounds whenever slides advance. The best way to decide what you like is to try both. It's all for fun, anyhow.

On the next window that appears, fill in title page information for the Web presentation. This is the author's name (you), your email address, and a link back to your own Web site, if you want. Click Next, and you then have the opportunity to decide on the graphics you want to use for the forward and back buttons. If you don't want to use graphical buttons, you don't have to. In fact, the default is to use Text Only, so to use a particular button style, make sure you uncheck the check box (see Figure 8-13), select your button style, and click Next.

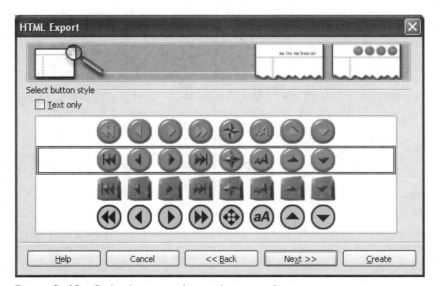

Figure 8–13   Pick a button style, any button style.

We are almost there. The penultimate window lets you decide on the color scheme for the presentation. The default is simply to use the colors from the original Impress publication, but you can override this, as well as the color for hyperlinks and the Web page background. Make your choices and click Create. One last window appears, asking you to name the HTML design. This is a free-form text field. Enter a brief description, and click Save.

The process of exporting your presentation may take a few seconds or a few minutes, depending on the speed of your machine and the complexity of your presentation. To view the presentation, open your browser and point to the title page. That is all there is to it.

How About a Little Flash? Shocking!

Before we wrap up, let's revisit that Export dialog one more time. Click File from the menu and select Export. When the Export dialog appears, have another look at the File Format selection box, just below the File Name field. The default is to export to an HTML document, but there are other options here. For one, we have a PDF export; the one button export (beside the printer icon on the Standard bar) is common to Impress as well.

Notice also that you also have a Macromedia Flash export capability. Isn't that interesting? Enter a file name for your presentation (no need to add the .swf extension). With a single click of the Export button, your presentation is saved to Macromedia's Flash format. Now your presentation is viewable from any browser with a Macromedia Flash or Shockwave plugin. The advantage of this over the HTML export is that all your animated slide transitions are preserved. Visitors to your site can view the presentation as it was intended.

Extra! Extra!

Before we move away from the classic office applications, I would like to take another moment to address the issue of templates. Although StarOffice, the non-free commercial sibling of OpenOffice.org, comes with a number of templates for word processing, spreadsheets, and presentation graphics, OpenOffice.org is still quite *light* in this area. As I mentioned earlier, the Impress package has no templates included at all.

To that end, I'm going to remind you of the Web sites I mentioned at the end of Chapter 6. They are Travis Bauer's OOExtras site and Scott Carr's

OpenOffice.org Documentation Project. Both are excellent starting points for adding to your collection of templates. Look for the links to both in the "Resources" section.

Perhaps in time, you too will contribute to this growing body of work.

Resources

OOExtras
http://ooextras.sourceforge.net

OpenOffice.org
http://www.openoffice.org/product/impress.html

OpenOffice.org Documentation Project
http://documentation.openoffice.org

Personal Databases: OpenOffice.org Base

Computers have thousands of uses, but in the end, the most important things they do come down to two major and equally important functions. The first is mathematics. More specifically, the computer makes it possible to do complex (or simple) mathematics quickly. The key word here is quickly. Whether it is figuring out ballistic tables to better ensure the trajectory of a missile and cracking complex codes (as was the impetus for the computer's development in the second world war), or processing a company's financial information, math is central to every computing operation.

The second most useful function a computer has is storing, sorting, and retrieving data quickly. (Again that word *quickly.*) Search engines like Google or Yahoo! are a testament to the computer's power of sifting through large amounts of information. In doing so, businesses can locate a customer's address in seconds, even though there may be millions of other customer records in the system. A hospital with thousands of patient records can pull up your medical history in a flash and update it with today's visit. The online bookstore maintains your personal information so you can buy a book with a click or two. A year's worth of financial information, arranged into a clear, concise report, appears on the printer seconds after the company accountant requests it.

As my wife, Sally, is fond of saying, "It's all about the data."

Storing data, or *information*, if you prefer, is what a database is all about. That's why the addition of a database into the OpenOffice.org suite is so exciting. OpenOffice.org Base makes it possible to create your own databases, retrieve and modify information, perform queries, create reports, and so on. Base can attach to an existing database engine such as Oracle, Microsoft Access, MySQL, and many others using ODBC or JDBC. If all you need is for your database to do simple operations, such as creating and maintaining a mailing list, OpenOffice.org Base comes with the built-in HSQL database engine.

The Beginning: Creating a New Database

Because I mentioned mailing lists, let's use that as the basis for our exploration of OpenOffice.org Base. When we are finished creating the database, I'll show you how to use it in another OpenOffice.org program, the Writer word processor. We'll take the information from our mailing list and create mailing labels.

When you start OpenOffice.org Base, you are presented with the Database Wizard (see Figure 9-1). This is a simple wizard with only two screens, the first of which is to select or identify a database. Your options are to Create a New Database, Open an Existing Database File, or Connect to an Existing Database. Let's just go ahead and create a new database by making sure that radio button is selected. Click Next.

On to the second step, where you must decide how to proceed after saving your database. There are only a few options on the second and final screen, but they are important and worth explaining (see Figure 9-2).

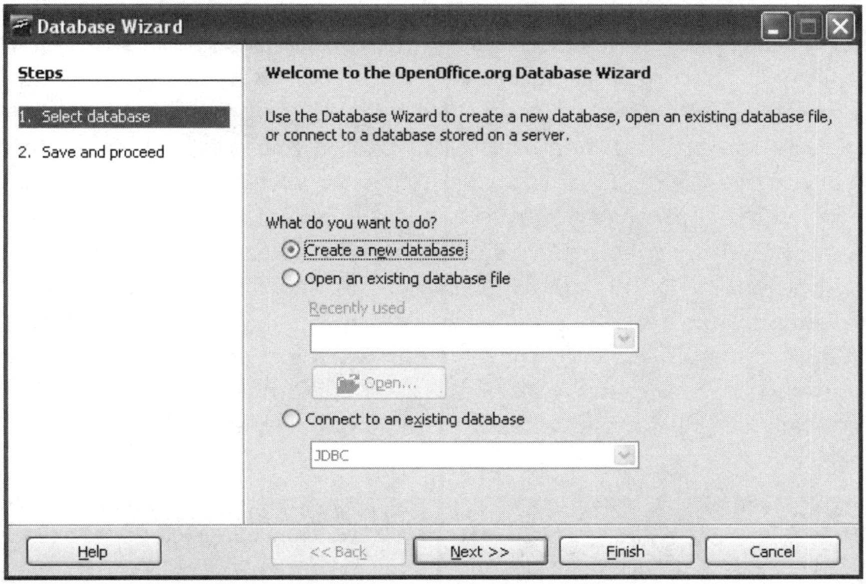

Figure 9–1 The OpenOffice.org Base Database Wizard.

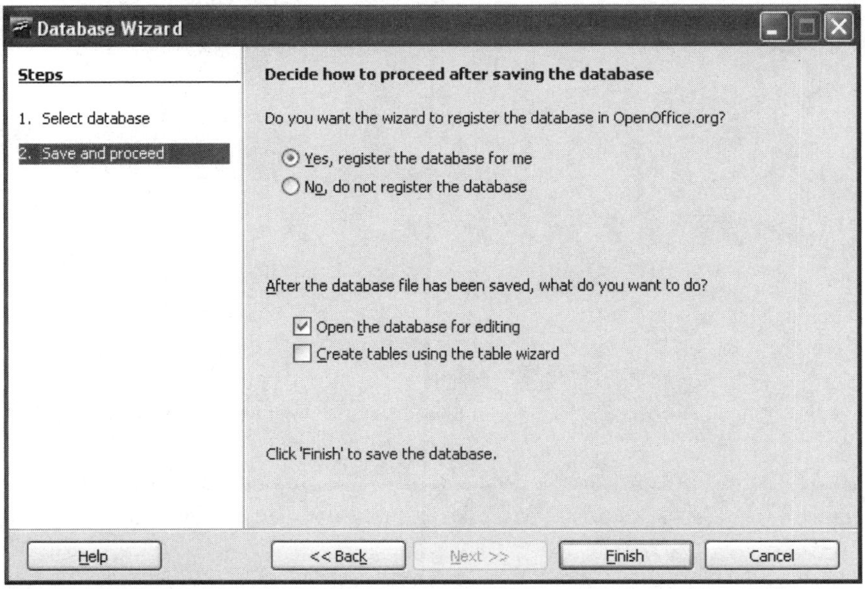

Figure 9–2 The final step in the wizard registers the database so that it is easily accessible by other OpenOffice.org applications.

The first has to do with registering a database. To quickly answer this question, ask yourself whether you want to use this database from inside other OpenOffice.org applications. If the answer is yes, click the Yes, Register the Database for Me radio button . Nothing stops you from creating a non-registered database and then registering it later, but in this example at least, we want to use the database in OpenOffice.org Writer.

The next section gives you two options. The first, Open the Database for Editing, should be checked (you can create a database and get back to it later). You could, at this point, jump right in and Create Tables Using the Table Wizard, but leave that unchecked for now.

When the Save As dialog makes its appearance, select a name and location for the database (see Figure 9-3). For this example, I'm going to create a simple mailing list database, which I'm going to call (wait for it) Mailing List.

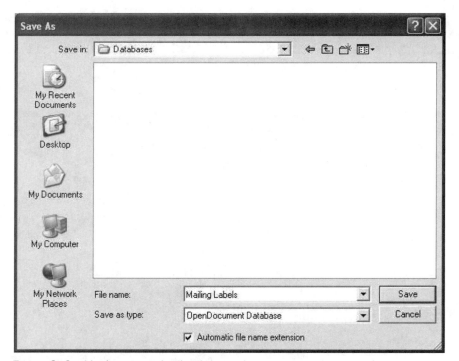

Figure 9–3   You've created a database and now you need a name for it.

That's really all you need to do to create the database. Click Save and OpenOffice.org Base's main window appears (see Figure 9-4). By default, the Forms view is selected but that's only useful if you haven't set up your tables yet. Nevertheless, let's take a look at the interface itself.

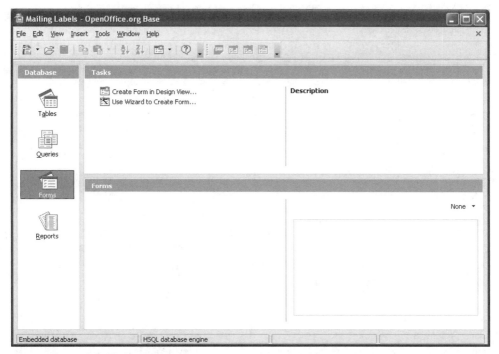

Figure 9–4 The OpenOffice.org Base window immediately upon creating a new database.

Along the top, directly below the menu bar is the standard bar, looking less standard in OpenOffice.org Base than in any of the other components you have worked with. Running down the left side is an icon bar providing quick access to needed database functions, including tables, queries, forms, and reports. The area to the right is divided horizontally into main areas. In the top part, we have tasks. These tasks are all in some way related to the four database functions in the left sidebar. The bottom part of the window is for forms.

Tip Pause your mouse cursor over any of the tasks and a description appears to right of it.

Before we get too deep into all of this, we need to prepare the database to accept data. We do that by creating tables. Simply stated, tables define what our data looks like. You can even define multiple tables that further define bits of data in a master table. For instance, you can have a table that is basically an address list with first and last names, addresses, and so on. A second table might tie in to the person's name, but the information may have to do with the number of hours the person worked. The person's name, in this case, might be the key you use to access both tables. A third table, using the same key, might be a list of movie rentals in the last year.

Let's go ahead and create a table.

Setting the Table

Yes, you could even have a table with recipes. Although that sounds like a tasty idea, I started out by saying my database was going to be a mailing list, so we will build an appropriate table.

The easiest way to get started is by using the Table Wizard. To do this, click the Table icon in the left sidebar. Now look at the top in the Tasks section. You'll see two entries there. The first, Create Table in Design View, is the more advanced approach, when you know what your data looks like. The second option is Use Wizard to Create Table. When you click this item, OpenOffice.org Base's Table Wizard starts (see Figure 9-5).

Tip When selecting the Table Wizard (or any of the Base wizards), you may get a message telling you that you need to turn on the Java runtime. First, you need to make sure you have a Java runtime installed. Luckily, OpenOffice.org automatically discovers its location. Click Tools on the menu bar, then select Options. On the Options window, click Java from the sidebar, then check the Use a Java Runtime Environment box.

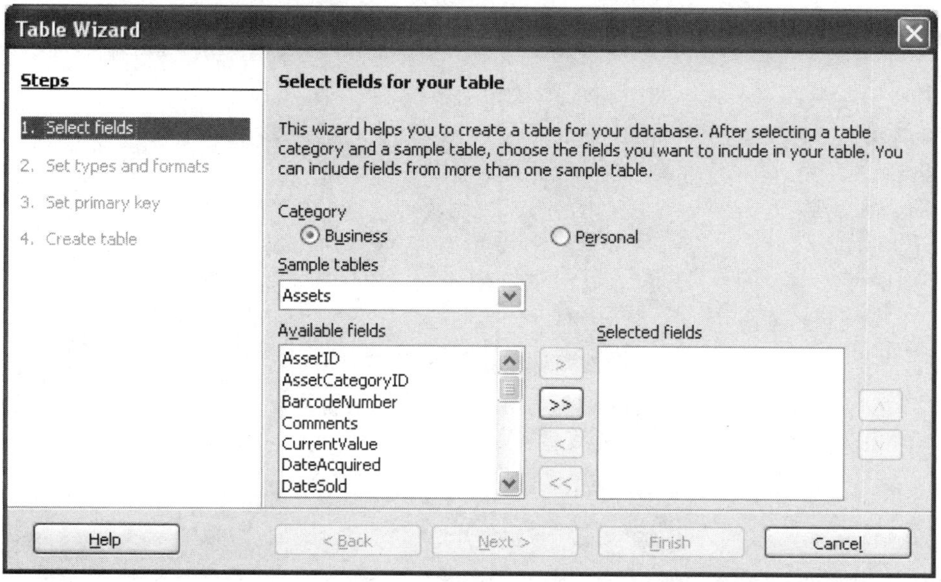

Figure 9–5 The Table Wizard comes with a number of predefined tables for business and personal use.

The Table Wizard comes with a number of predefined tables for common tasks. All of these table definitions are divided up into two categories, Business and Personal. Click the radio button for one or the other, and then click the Sample Tables drop-down box to browse the table types. Under Business, you find things like Assets, Customers, Employees, Expenses, Projects, Suppliers, and many more. The Personal list has items such as Accounts, CD-Collection, Diet Log, and Household Inventory, to name just a few. For now, click the Personal radio button and select Addresses from the Sample Tables list. A list of fields appears below (see Figure 9-6).

If you scroll down that list of available fields, you see a lot more information than you may need. You can click the double arrow in the middle (the right pointing one) and all the fields are selected. You can also select them one by one as I have done in Figure 9-6. In the case of a simple mailing list, you may not need anything more than name, address, city, state, phone number, and email address. After you have finished selecting these fields, you can click Finish or Next to edit the format of each individual field. Let's pretend that the definition and format of these fields are okay. Click Next to move to the primary key selection screen (see Figure 9-7).

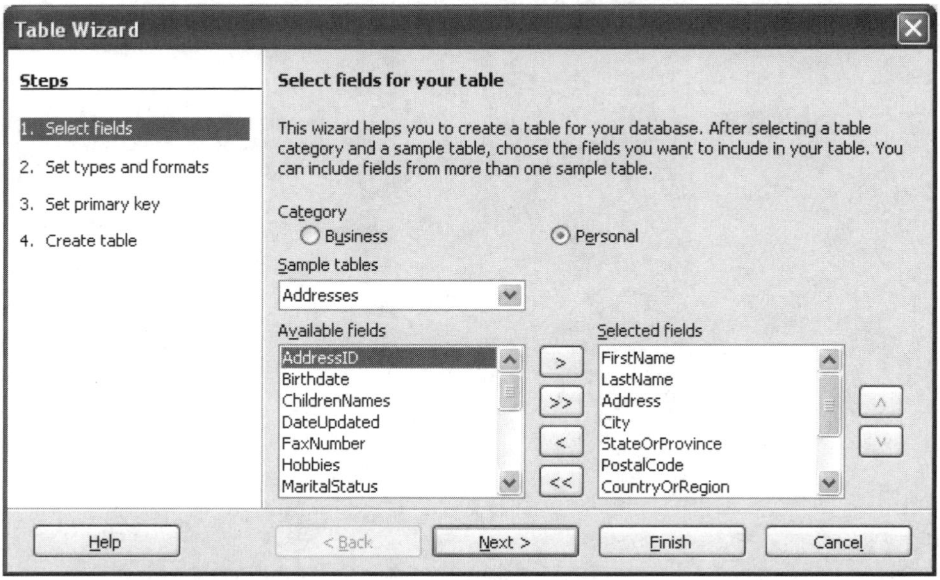

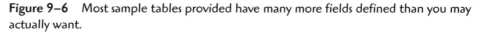

Figure 9–6   Most sample tables provided have many more fields defined than you may actually want.

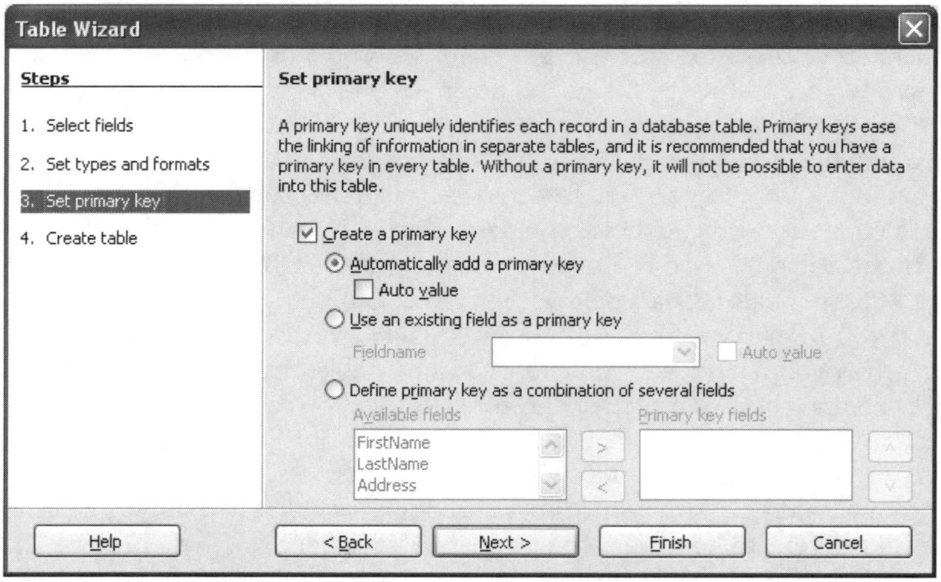

Figure 9–7   Each record in a database requires a unique, primary key. You can choose to base that key on your selected fields or let Base create one for you.

The primary key selection screen is important because a key is how you access and store information in a table. Although you can search on any field, a key needs to be a unique piece of information under which the record is stored. A classic example is the Social Security Number (or Social Insurance Number), which is unique to the individual. You can let Base generate a primary key for you, and that is the default. By checking the Auto Value box, Base automatically generates a key with each record you create.

Your other options are to use an existing field (like that SSN/SIN) or, if you prefer, to define a combination of your fields to create that uniqueness.

Let's go with the default for now. Check the Auto Value box as well. Click Next and the final part of the wizard, the Create Table page, appears (see Figure 9-8). If you are using the wizard, Base suggests a name for the table, but you can call it anything you like. I'm going to accept the default of Addresses because that suits me just fine. Keep in mind that although our database is called Mailing List, there can be a lot more associated with a mailing list, the Addresses table being just a small part of it.

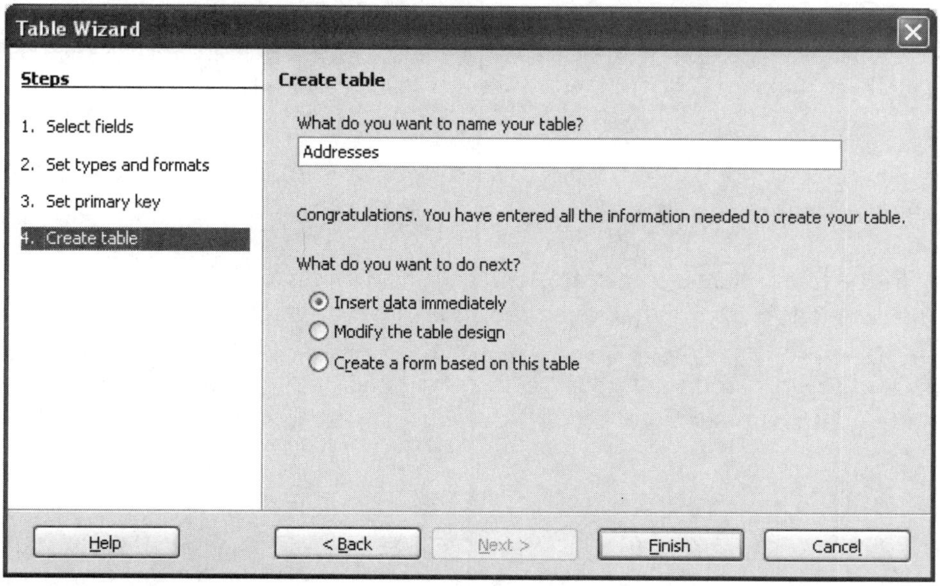

Figure 9–8 You're almost done. All you need now is a name for your table.

We are done with the wizard, but before you click Finish, you have one last choice to make, and three options to choose from. The first is to start adding data (I'll show you that in a moment). The second is to go back and make other changes to the table design. The final choice is to create a form based on this table. I'll show you what happens in both cases, but let's start with the default option, Insert Data Immediately. When you do that, a spreadsheet-like window appears with rows of data and columns representing the fields in your table (see Figure 9-9).

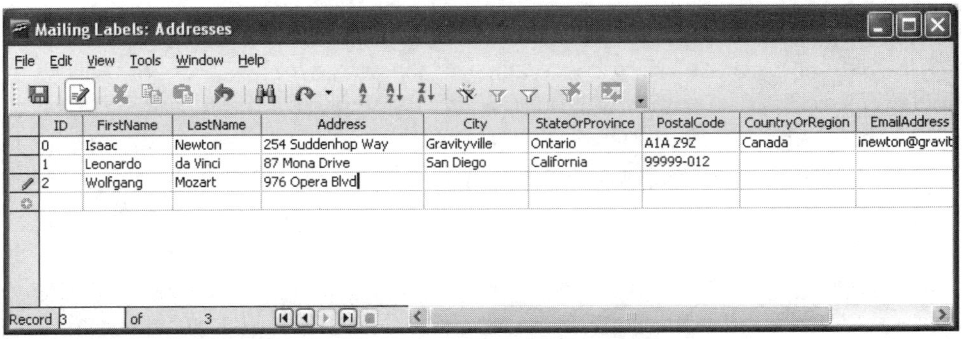

Figure 9–9   Inserting data is as easy as working with a spreadsheet.

There is one other item I'd like you to look at in the OpenOffice.org Base Tables view. It's not a big deal, but it's kind of cool so I'm going to tell you about it.

In the lower part of the main screen (the section labeled Tables), click the table labeled Addresses (at this time, there is only one). Now, look over on the right and you see a drop-down list with None selected. Click the list button and select Document. You get a pretty cool little preview of your table and the data in it (see Figure 9-10).

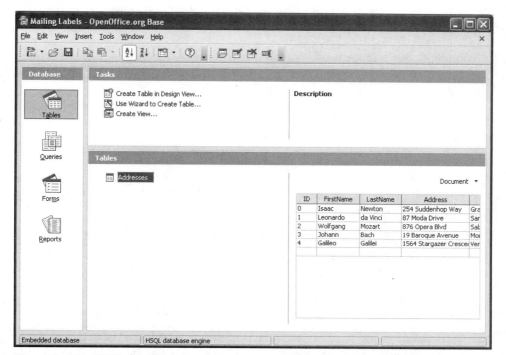

Figure 9–10 The lower part of the Mailing Labels left pane lists your tables and provides a small preview of the data when you click on a table.

No Wizards for Me!

Before we move on to the next step, I want to touch on the subject of creating a table in design view. There's no question that using the wizard is by far the easiest way to do this, but using the design view isn't much more difficult. It does have the advantage of giving you greater control over the format of your tables, but you have to think about what fields you want, and what you want those fields to look like (see Figure 9-11). In that respect, I recommend it only if you already have some experience in database and table design.

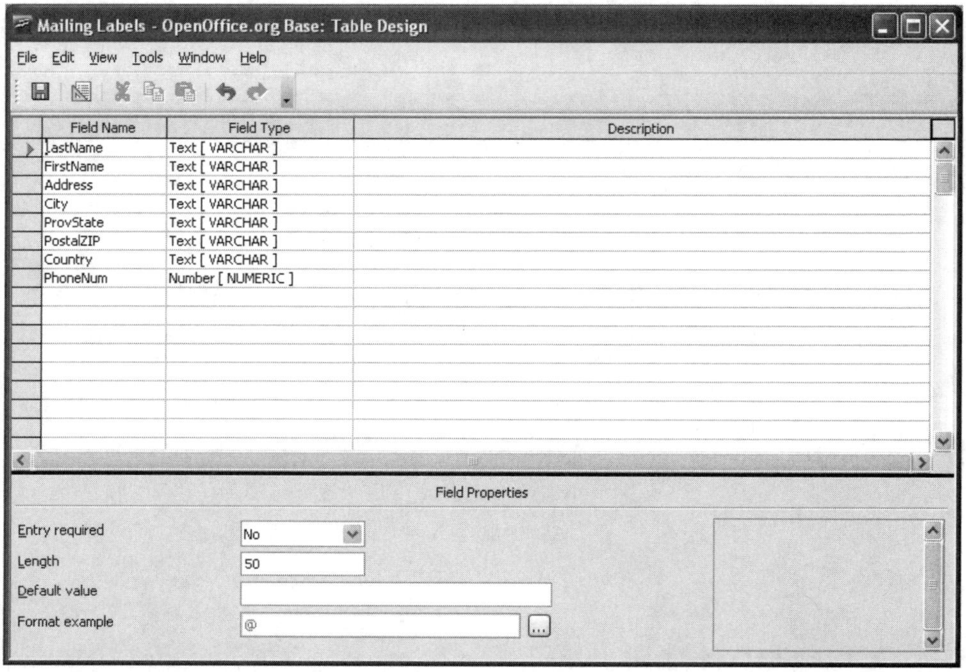

Figure 9–11   Creating tables using design view requires some knowledge of database and table design.

Creating Mailing Labels

Now that we have this great database of names, let's create a sheet of mailing labels. We do this with Writer, the word processor I covered in Chapter 6, but not with OpenOffice.org Base.

To begin, click File on the OpenOffice.org menu bar, and select Labels from the New submenu. You don't have to be running Writer to do this. Any OpenOffice.org application is a perfect starting point for creating labels. A few seconds after making your selection, the Labels dialog appears (see Figure 9-12).

Start by taking a look on the right, under the Database heading. This is where registering the database, that little step we did at the beginning, pays off. OpenOffice.org Writer already knows about the various databases and can pick my Mailing_List database from the drop-down list. Below that is another drop-down list labeled Table. Click here and select the table from which you will be pulling the information you need. At the bottom of the dialog, you can select the Brand (e.g., Avery Letter Size) and the Type (e.g., 5961 Address).

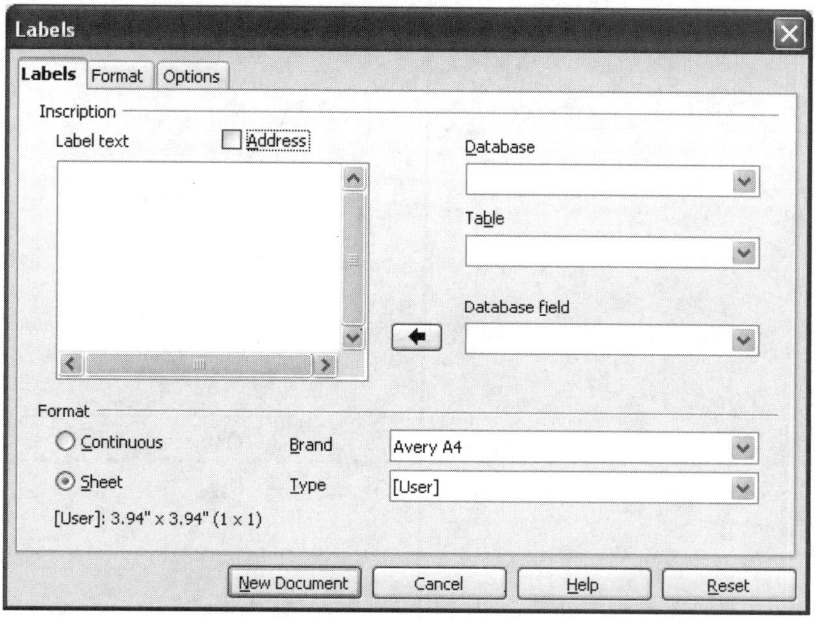

Figure 9–12 When creating a new sheet of labels, OpenOffice.org starts by asking you about the data source.

Now, look at the upper left, below Label Text. This is where we build the label we will be printing. At this moment, there are no fields visible there. Look again to the Database Field drop-down list. Click that list and you see all the fields that make up the records in your table. Select the database field you want, and then click the large arrow directly to the left. The field you selected appears in the Label Text field. Put a space after the filed name, select the last name, and click the arrow again. Press <Enter> to go to the next line in the Label Text field. Next is the address, city, and so on. You may want to put a comma between the city and province (or state). Line by line, transfer the fields that you want to have appearing in your finished label (see Figure 9-13).

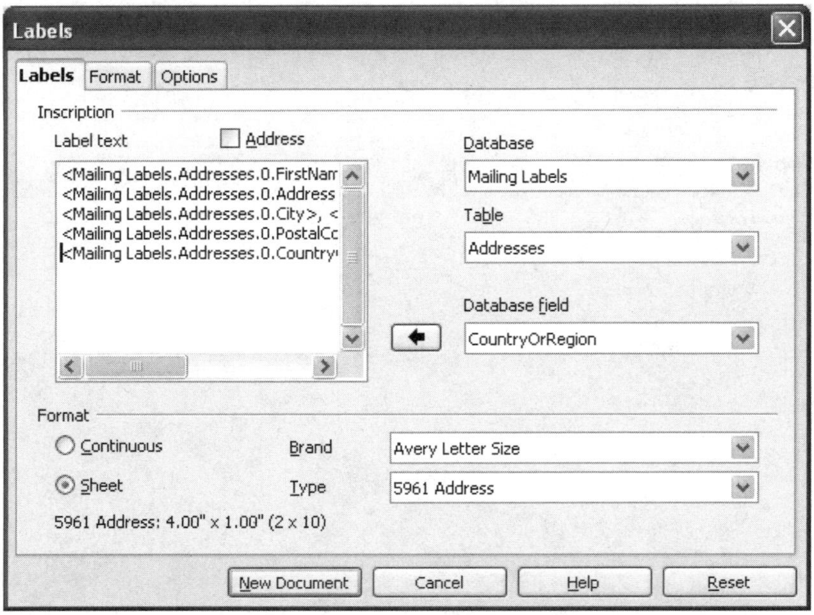

Figure 9–13   As you select fields, they appear in the Label Text window to the left.

Before we move on, let's quickly have a look at the other two tabs, Format and Options. The Format tab allows you to fine-tune your label dimensions. This includes margins, columns, rows, and pitch. If you selected one of the commercial labels from the list, this information is filled in for you, and you shouldn't have to worry about changing anything. Use the Options tab to select whether you are printing a full page of labels or a single label. The most interesting item here is a Synchronize Contents check box. Check this box and you can edit a single label and synchronize the contents of all other labels with a click.

Go back to the Labels tab and click the New Document button to create your label document. Each label is precreated with the field labels you selected in the proper place. At this stage of the game, there are no names or addresses in any of the labels, just the data fields. To populate these labels from your Mailing_List database, you need to tell the new document where to get its information. To do that, click View on the menu bar and select Data Sources (you can also just press <F4>). The top part of your label document now shows the databases and tables available. Make sure you select the Addresses table from the database list. When you do, the records in that table appear in the right side of the data sources pane (see Figure 9-14).

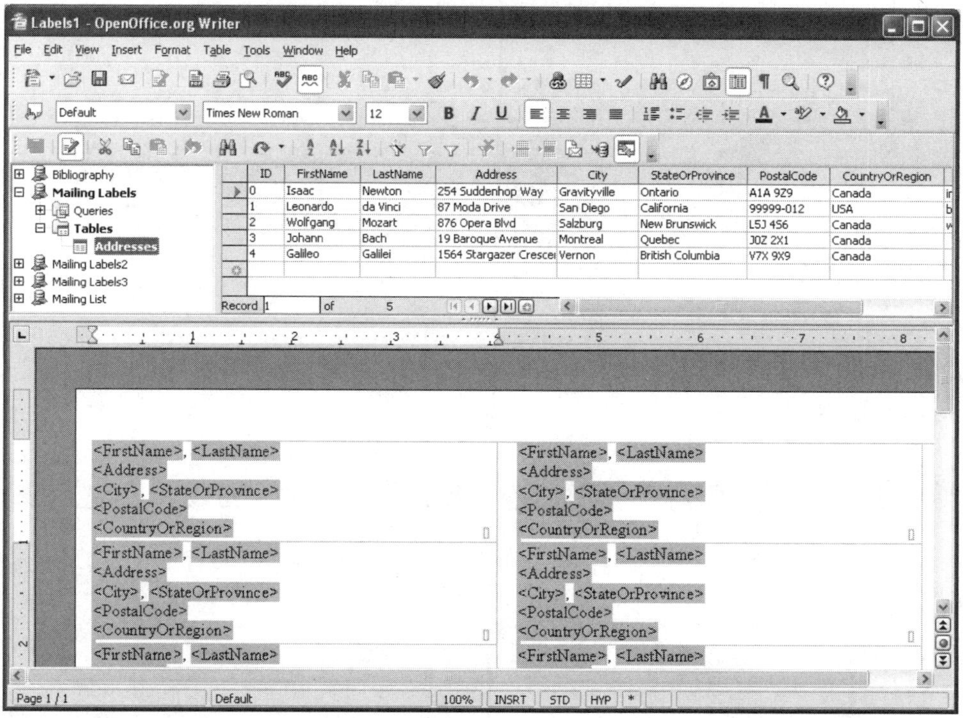

Figure 9–14   The data source for the labels appears directly above the actual label document, in the upper-right pane.

To populate your label document, you should now select which records you want included from the table view at top right. The easiest way to select them all is to click the button to the right of the top record, press the <Shift> key, and then click the last record. You can also select individual records by holding down the <Ctrl> key and clicking the records you want. When you have made your selections, look at the secondary icon bar, directly above the data sources. There's a button, fourth from the right, that displays a Data to Fields tooltip if you pause your mouse over it (see Figure 9-15).

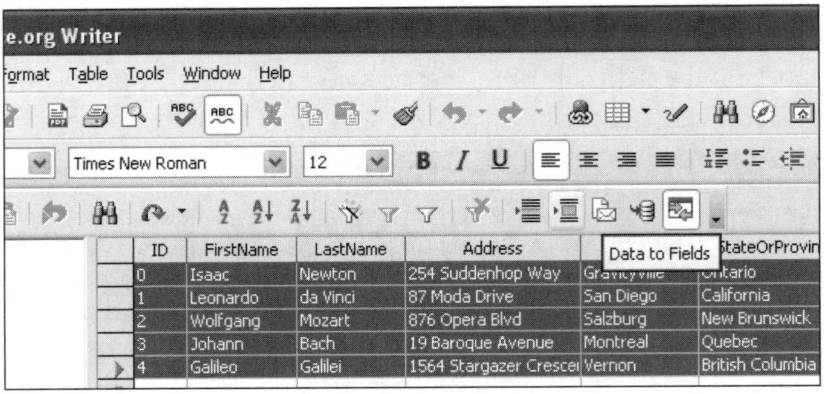

Figure 9–15   Close-up of the Data to Fields button.

Click the Data to Fields button and your document is instantly populated with all of the selected records (see Figure 9-16). You can then save this document for later use or you can print the page using your chosen label stock.

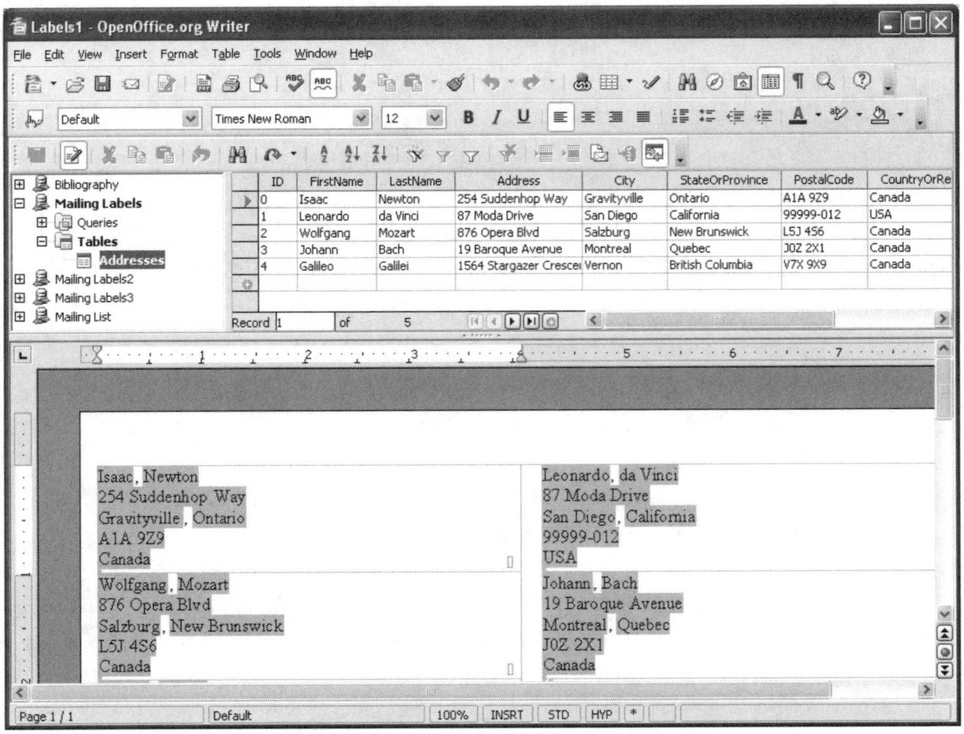

Figure 9–16   With a click, all of the selected record data is transferred to the label form.

Further Exploring

In this chapter, I introduced you to the basics of using OpenOffice.org Base and showed you how to use the database tables in a word processing document. Obviously, this is just the beginning.

Using Base, you can create custom forms for data entry. Wizards make this easy, but there is a manual forms creator as well. Simple or complex custom reports are also easily generated using the Report Wizard. Perform queries, connect to external databases, build indexes, and more. OpenOffice.org Base provides useful database access tools for users at every level.

Resources

BASE Homepage

http://www.openoffice.org/product/base.html

10

CDex: An All-Purpose CD Ripper and Audio Converter

Over the years, we have all purchased a lot of music CDs, or as some of us still call them, albums. Many of those albums, unfortunately, had only two or three songs we really liked, so playing the whole album wasn't what we wanted. As a result, we created collections of our favorite songs on tape and played the tapes, instead.

These days, we can create our own collections from those albums we have purchased and create CD collections of those songs we want to hear. Furthermore, if you have lots of disk space and you spend a lot of time at your computer, nothing beats a collection of songs ready to play without having to change CDs all the time. Pulling songs from a CD and saving them to your system as digital images is what is commonly referred to as ripping.

Intermezzo: Digital Audio Formats

Before I get into the mechanics of ripping and burning songs, I'd like to spend a small amount of time discussing music formats. When you purchase a CD, the songs on that CD are in a format not generally used by your system. In fact, when you copy songs to disk from a CD, you always encode them into another, usually more compact format. The format you transfer to is identified by a three-letter extension on the file name. The most common formats are .wav, .mp3, and (more recently) .ogg.

The *WAV* format was originally created by Microsoft. It is extremely common but not the most efficient in terms of compression. On the other hand, the *MP3* format (from the Motion Pictures Experts Group, aka MPEG) owes its popularity to the high compression ratio it uses—about 12:1. The newcomer on the block is the *OGG* (or Ogg Vorbis) format. Like MP3, it boasts a high compression rate, but unlike MP3, it is completely unencumbered by patents.

To give you an idea of the compression values, I ripped a 3-minute, 46-second song to WAV format. It came in at 39,866,444 bytes, whereas the same song in OGG format required only 3,438,407 bytes. If you do the math, that is a ratio of 11.6:1. Pretty impressive reasons for not using WAV format files.

Introducing CDex

CDex is a great little program primarily used for ripping songs so that you can convert your CD collection into compressed audio files to listen to on your PC (or take with your portable media player). I used the term *primarily* because CDex is also a tool for converting audio files from one format to another. Appropriately, CDex supports many different audio formats. The CDex package also comes with a simple audio player as well.

Start your CDex program and you see a screen similar to that in Figure 10-1.

Before you run off and start ripping your songs to disk, there are a few configuration items you should pay attention to. None of these is particularly complicated, but you should take a few moments and make the following changes.

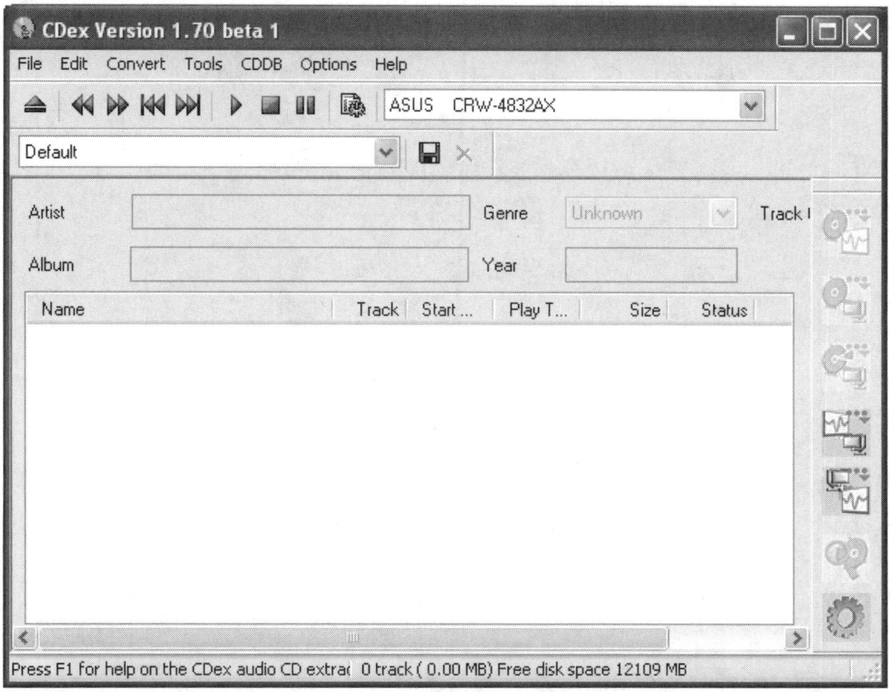

Figure 10–1 Without a CD loaded, CDex's interface is pretty easy to understand.

Configuring CDex

Bring up CDex's configuration dialog by clicking Options on the menu bar and selecting Settings (pressing <F4> also works). There's also a button at the bottom of the right sidebar that does the same.

After you pop your CD into the tray, you may find that all you see is a list of tracks with no title or artist associated.

The quality of the ripped files is defined somewhat by the bitrate you choose. By default, this is 128 kbps, but many people, myself included, like it a little higher than that. To change this, click the configure icon at the bottom of the right sidebar. When the configuration dialog appears, click the Encoder tab, and then select your bitrate from the drop-down list provided (see Figure 10-2).

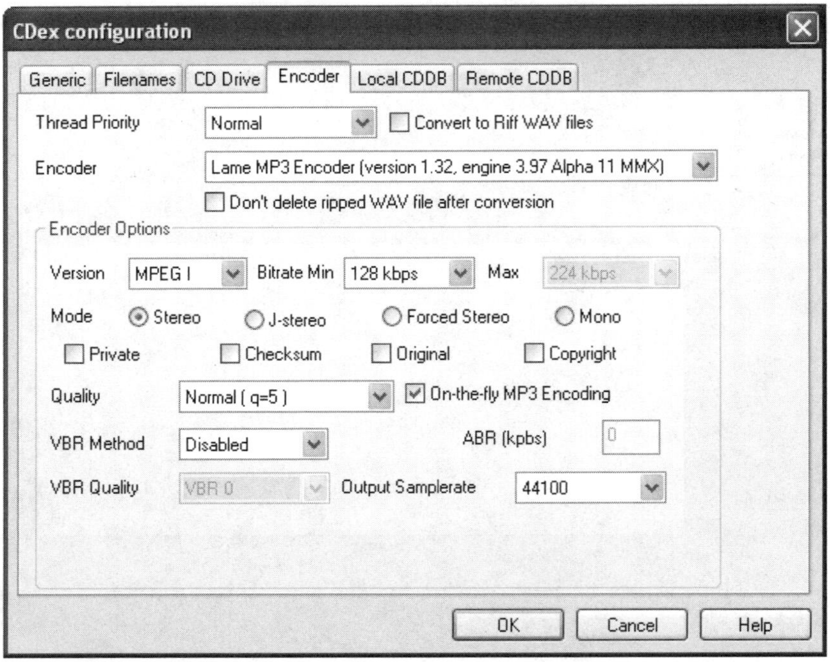

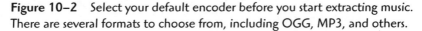

Figure 10–2   Select your default encoder before you start extracting music. There are several formats to choose from, including OGG, MP3, and others.

You want to remember that although a higher bit rate provides a better sound quality, it also generates larger files.

Another item you may want to attend to immediately has to do with access to the remote freedb.org CDDB (CD database). This is a free online database that you can use to look up CD information. When you put a CD into a program like CDex, the information on the disk is read to identify artist, title, and so on. To verify the content of the CD, a query to the CDDB may take place. If the information isn't there and you fill it in, your information updates the database so that future users can find what you provided. To use the freedb CDDB, click the Remote CDDB tab (see Figure 10-3).

You can leave pretty much everything as is, but you do need to enter your email address.

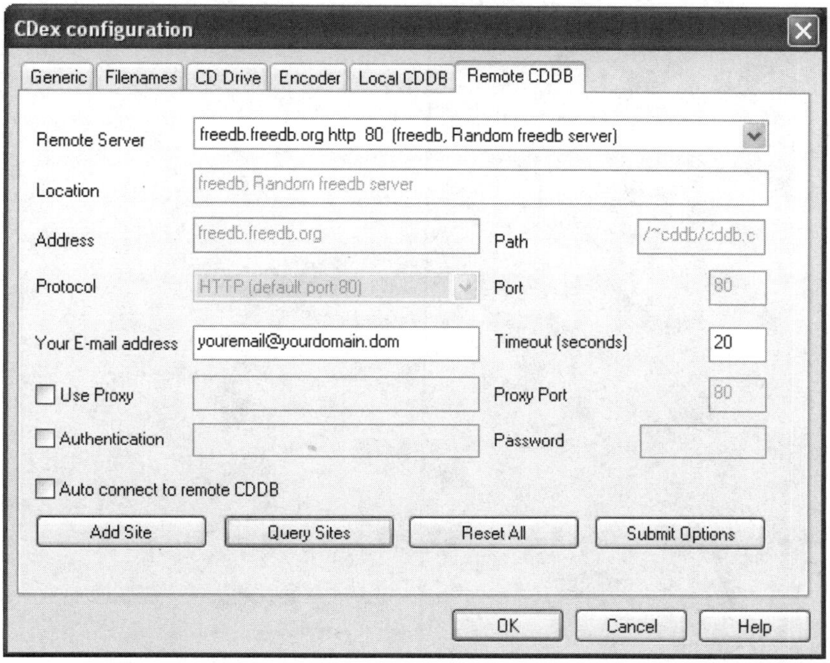

Figure 10–3   If you want to be able to look up album information online using the CDDB, you must supply an email address.

Ripping Music to Your PC

When you first insert a CD into your PC's drive, CDex reads the disk and tries to extract as much information as possible (see Figure 10-4). This includes the name of each song, the artist's name, the length and size of the various tracks, and so on.

Look on the right at the button bar that runs vertically. Click the Get Album Information from Remote CDDB button. The online CDDB contains an extensive collection of information (see Figure 10-5).

Select the track or tracks that you want to rip. This is the normal Windows select mode where you hold the <Ctrl> key to select individual songs or the <Shift> key to select a contiguous group of tracks. To select all tracks, press <Ctrl+A> or click Edit on the menu bar and choose Select All.

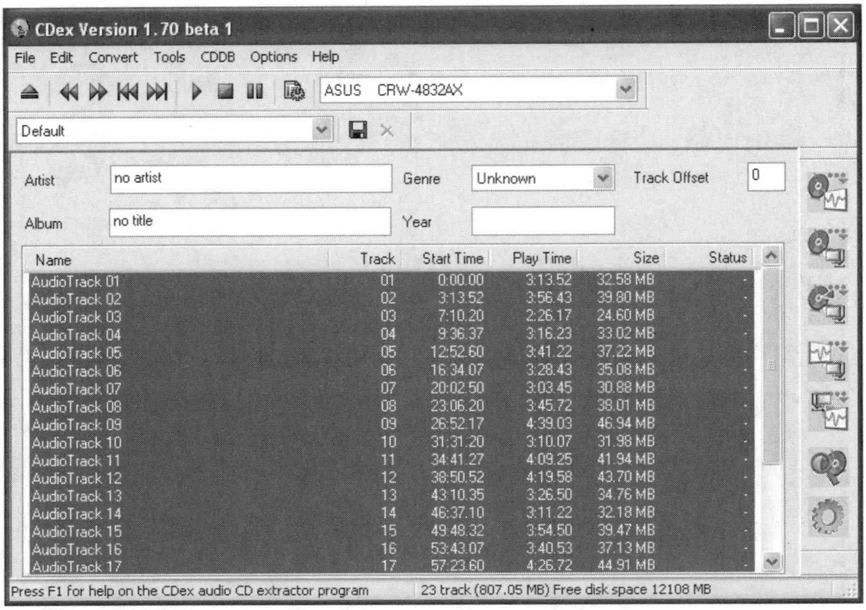

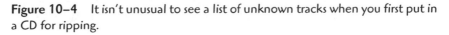

Figure 10–4   It isn't unusual to see a list of unknown tracks when you first put in a CD for ripping.

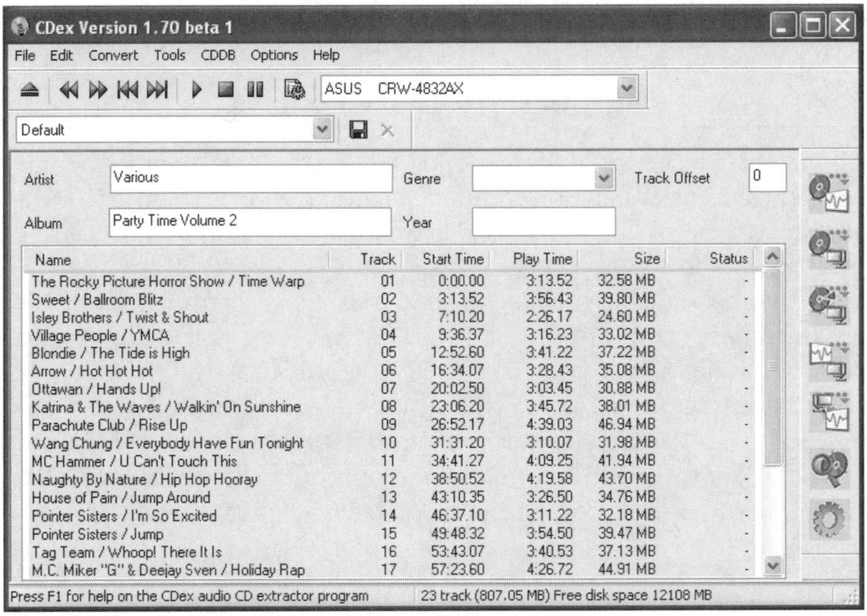

Figure 10–5   After the CDDB lookup takes place, a full list of songs on the CD appears.

When it comes time to rip your music files to disk, you have a couple of choices. The first is to extract them to WAV format files. To start this process, click the topmost icon on the right icon bar (pause your mouse cursor over this icon and it pops up an Extract CD Track(s) to WAV File(s) tooltip).

However, most people will probably want to extract and compress the files so that they can carry them on their portable music players. The most popular compressed audio format is probably MP3, and this is what CDex does very nicely. To do that, click the second button from the top, the Extract CD Track(s) to Compressed Audio File(s) tooltip.

After you start the process, a window informs you of the status of your extraction (see Figure 10-6).

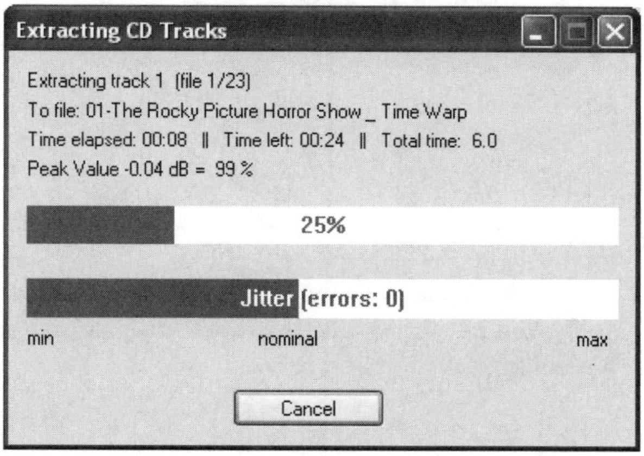

Figure 10–6 As songs are extracted and compressed to your disk, a progress dialog like this one gives you an idea of where you are in the process.

Ripping Just a Little

Generally speaking, you will probably want to pop in a CD, select the tracks (as shown in the last section), then sit back and wait for CDex to create your MP3 files. You can, however, also choose to extract only a section from the CD. That section could run anywhere from a second to the entire disk. This is how you do it.

Start by selecting a single song, multiple tracks, or the entire CD. For example, let's say you want to take a sample from one track. Select that track, then click the third button from the top along the right. The tooltip identifies the button with "Extract a section of the CD to WAV or Compressed Audio file(s)." Click the button and the Record Partial Tracks dialog appears (see Figure 10-7).

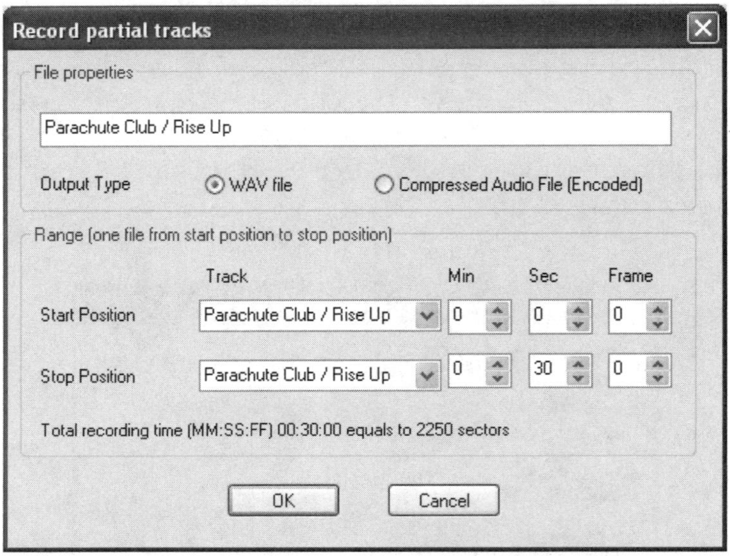

Figure 10–7 You can also choose to extract only a portion of a song, or any audio track for that matter.

The artist and title information are shown above and this becomes the file name (minus the extension). Change it here if you want. Next, select the output type from WAV or compressed audio (e.g., MP3, OGG, etc.). To identify the size of your sample, enter the start and end position in the Range section.

When you click OK, a progress dialog appears (refer to Figure 10-6). That's it. There is really no difference between this sample file and any other music file you might rip, other than its length.

Simple Music Player

The CDex package includes a simple music player. It is quite handy and you can bring it up from the CDex menu bar. Just click Tools and select Media File Player. Figure 10-8 shows the media player in action.

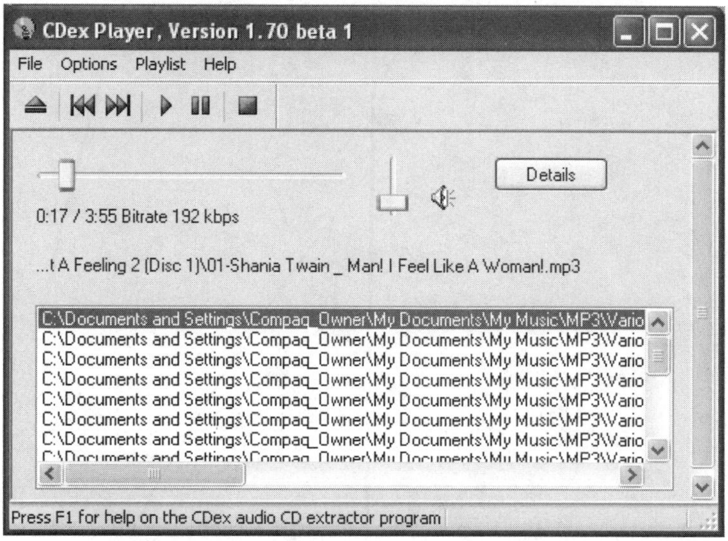

Figure 10–8 The included music player is only so exciting, but it does the job.

When the player starts, there are no files in the list. A file dialog appears, from which you can select individual files or a folder of songs. To select all the tracks in a folder, click the Select All button, then click the Select Files button, just below the File entry on the menu bar.

When the songs are loaded, you can choose to play tracks sequentially or in random order. Just click Options on the player's menu bar and select Play Random.

The player is only so exciting, but CDex's strength doesn't come from the included media player, but from its stellar capability to rip and encode music.

Resources

CDex

http://cdexos.sourceforge.net/index.html

Chapter

11

Audio Magic with Audacity

Unless you are in the audio editing business, Audacity is one of those programs that you aren't sure you really need until you've used it once. Then it becomes a program you can't live without. So, what is Audacity?

Audacity is a wonderful, easy-to-use, audio editing program. With it, you can record audio from a variety of sources, including a microphone—podcasts, anyone? You can use it to convert audio files into other audio formats. Take your old records or tapes, clean up the noise, and convert them to digital audio so you can burn them to CD. Edit, cut, copy, mix, add special effects, and splice sound sources to create new sounds. Audacity is a multitrack real-time audio editing system that can handle 16-, 24-, and 32-bit samples. Audacity is also just plain fun.

In this chapter, I'm going to give you a brief introduction to Audacity and some of its audio editing features. Then, I'll show you how to take that creation of yours and export it so you can produce your own podcast.

Installation Notes

Installation is pretty simple; in theory, you only need to download the Audacity package from the site. Installation is pretty simple and really doesn't require anything I haven't covered in the introductory chapter. However, most people also want to pick up one optional package from the site (sort of). It's called LAME, and it is an MP3 encoder. Without it, you can't encode your audio captures into MP3 format.

Yes, I did say *sort of* in the preceding paragraph. You see, there is a catch. Due to software patents, the encoder that lets you create MP3 files isn't available from the Audacity site. Neither is it included on the DVD that comes with this book. This isn't a big problem, but it does take an extra step. Your first step is to visit the Audacity Web site. In the download section of the Audacity Web site, there is a link for you to download the LAME MP3 encoder.

This part is going to sound a bit strange, but bear with me. You are downloading a zip file that, when extracted, leaves you with a Windows DLL file called `lame_enc.dll`. You can store this file anywhere you want on the system. The first time you export a file to MP3, Audacity asks you for the location of the DLL—but we are getting ahead of ourselves, so just keep that one in the back of your mind for now.

Touring Audacity's Interface

Audacity starts with a blank slate by default (see Figure 11-1). Along the top of Audacity's main window, you find a pretty standard menu bar with access to various categories of tools in Audacity's toolbox. Directly below the menu bar and toward the center, a number of buttons reflect Audacity's audio editing nature. These buttons are Pause, Play, Stop, Skip to Start, Skip to End, and Record. I mention these first because they are so familiar.

To the left of those buttons are six small icons representing some common tools used in Audacity. The vertical bar icon, which looks like a capital I, is the Selection tool, and it is selected by default.

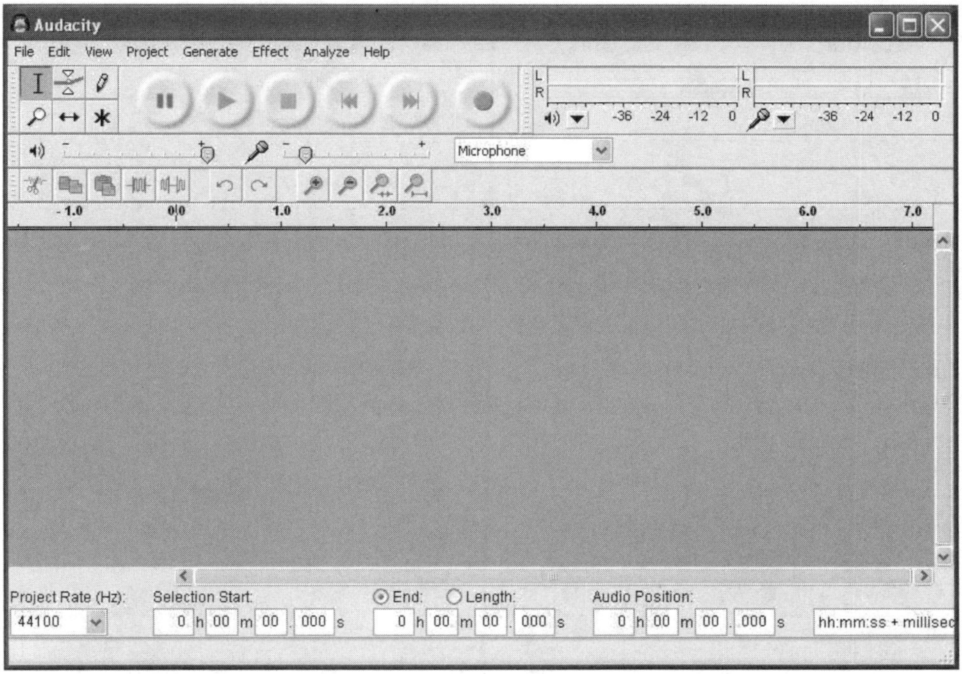

Figure 11–1   Audacity's interface at start time.

Let's Record Something

Make sure your microphone is plugged in, and then click the Record button to start. Be creative. Sing a short tune, recite a line or two of poetry, or just speak whatever nonsense pops into your head.

As you record, keep your eye on the microphone icon near the top on the far right. If you pause your mouse cursor over it, the tooltip reads, "Input level monitor - click to monitor input." When using a stereo input source, you'll see both the left and right channel levels being displayed. In Figure 11-2, you only see the right channel because I am using a single channel microphone.

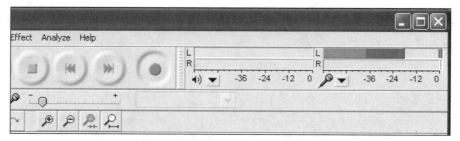

Figure 11-2   While you are recording, keep your eye on the input level meter on the top right.

As you record, you see the appearance of an audio track with details about the quality of the recording, whether it's a mono or stereo recording, and so on. When you are finished recording, click the Stop button. The full audio track remains with timing marks above (see Figure 11-3).

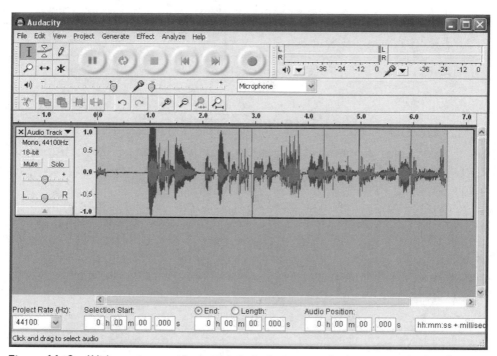

Figure 11-3   With a voice sample recorded, Audacity now displays one audio track.

As you can see from the preceding sample, I recorded just under seven seconds of speech. To listen to the recorded track, click the Play button (see Figure 11-4).

Figure 11–4   When playing back the sound clip, look at the meter directly to the right of the Record button.

At the bottom of the screen, there are additional details on the recorded track, the project audio rate (more on that shortly), as well as positional information.

Saving Your Project

Now that you have a sound clip to work with, this is a good time to save your work. At this stage, you don't have a finished product, but a work in progress. Audacity calls these projects. To save your project, click File on the menu bar and select Save Project As. A file navigation dialog appears where you can select the folder that will house your project. Give your project a name, and then click Save.

When you save a project, everything having to do with your project is saved, as it is at that moment. The only thing to remember is that Audacity project files (with an .aup extension) cannot be opened by other packages. The AUP file is accompanied by another folder of the same name, but with a _data extension.

Now that your project is safe and sound, let's edit that file.

Editing Audio

Basic audio editing consists of identifying a section of track, selecting that section, and performing some action on that section. Notice the beginning of my recorded sample in the close-up in Figure 11-3, where the first second or so is basically dead air. Yes, it's the dreaded dead air, the mini-*uhm* we tend to have sneak in at the beginning of these things. Click the beginning of the sample at the zero mark and drag the mouse pointer to select the first second or so (see Figure 11-5).

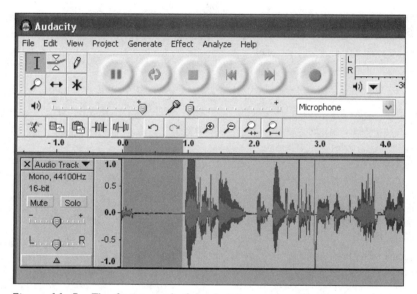

Figure 11–5   The first second of dead air in my recording is selected in preparation for trimming.

After you've selected the section of audio that contains the dead air, click the Play button to make sure that you haven't selected a portion of your speech. If necessary, adjust the selected area by positioning your mouse cursor over the beginning or end of the selected area and dragging to the left or right. The cursor changes to a hand with a pointing finger.

If you are satisfied with your selection, click Edit on the menu bar and select Cut. Now, click the Play button again to listen to your file without that little bit of dead air.

Fade to Special Effects

With Audacity, you can let your creativity run wild with tons of included effects. Let's say, for example, that you want to fade out the last few seconds of your recording. Select that section of the audio track, playing it first to confirm you have what you want, and then click Effect and select Fade Out.

Perhaps you need to emphasize a few words. Again, select the section of audio that you want, click Effects, and select Amplify. In the dialog that appears (see Figure 11-6), amplify your selection by using the slider for a decibel increase. For finer control, just type the number into the Amplification (dB) field. I should point out that despite the name, Amplify, you can enter a negative amplification to reduce the volume. Click the Preview button to sample the effect before you click OK.

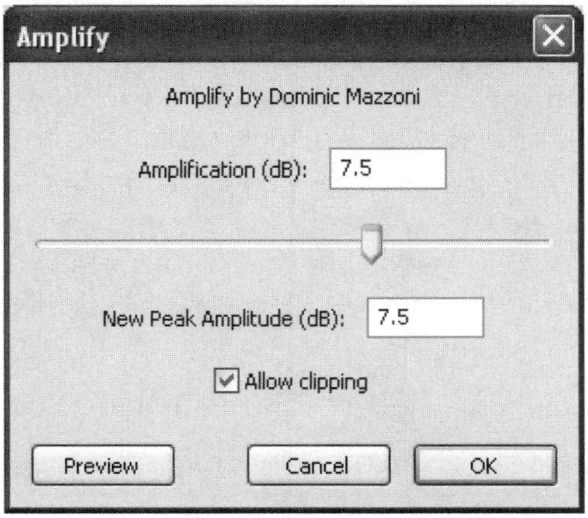

Amplify

Amplify by Dominic Mazzoni

Amplification (dB): 7.5

New Peak Amplitude (dB): 7.5

☑ Allow clipping

Preview Cancel OK

Figure 11–6 Despite the name, Amplify, this dialog can be used to decrease the volume as well.

Sometimes, repetition is the best way to get your point across. Make your selection, click Effects on the menu bar, and select Repeat. The default is to repeat the selected audio 10 times, but you can override that in the dialog (see Figure 11-7).

Figure 11–7 The Repeat effect identifies the length of the segment and then asks how many times you want that segment repeated.

This repeat can be a lot of fun if you select a very short segment (or a single word) and set it to repeat for several beats.

I highly recommend that you spend time playing with Effects. Aside from being a great way to waste some time, you'll be impressed with the arsenal of effects at your disposal. Change your pitch (without changing tempo), change the tempo, equalize soft and loud portions of your audio, add tremolo, remove noise, and more.

Okay, it's nostalgia time! One of my favorite effects is something those of us who can still remember vinyl albums will appreciate. On the occasional album, there were sections of a recording where you could play the sound backward to reveal a *secret* message. Granted, some of these so-called hidden messages were imagined and playing your album backward did nothing but add wear and tear to your needle, but others were really there. Well, you can create your own hidden message by using the Reverse effect.

Have fun!

Creating Podcasts with Audacity

One of the hottest topics of the last couple of years has been podcasting and the rise of the podcast. I enjoy several podcasts and download them to enjoy while I'm sitting at my computer working. I also copy them to my handheld and take them on the road. Podcasts are a great diversion on trains or while sitting in waiting rooms. Best of all, there are tons of great programs out there from pros and amateurs alike with topics covering pretty much anything you can think of.

> *Note* In the next chapter, I'm going to show you a great pod-
> cast receiver and aggregator for your system. Stay tuned for all the
> juice.

I've even recorded a few podcasts myself, very occasionally, and only
when the mood takes me. It can be a lot of fun, especially when you have the
right tools. Luckily, if you've ever felt the pull of the microphone, Audacity
was written for you. Record your podcast. Edit the file, adding here, cutting
there, and inserting special audio effects where you see fit. When you are finished with your masterpiece, you want to save that file in a format that your
listeners can use.

Exporting to MP3

When creating podcasts, people tend to publish them in MP3 format. You can
choose other formats, such as the open and patent-unencumbered OGG format, but most people tend to use MP3. The reason for this is primarily iner-
tia, but that doesn't change the fact that MP3 remains the most popular
format there is. With that knowledge in mind, you can select from a wide
variety of formats, but in all likelihood, you will want to choose MP3 as your
format. Let's do that.

After you have an audio segment that you are happy with, click File on
Audacity's menu bar, and then click Export as MP3 from the submenu.

This is where the information I gave you about the LAME encoder comes
into play, and a good time to remember where you stored the LAME DLL
(see Figure 11-8).

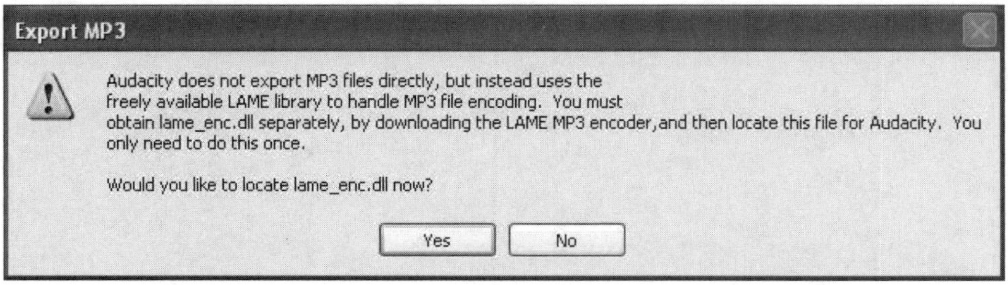

Export MP3

> Audacity does not export MP3 files directly, but instead uses the
> freely available LAME library to handle MP3 file encoding. You must
> obtain lame_enc.dll separately, by downloading the LAME MP3 encoder, and then locate this file for Audacity. You
> only need to do this once.
>
> Would you like to locate lame_enc.dll now?

Yes   No

Figure 11–8   Before you can export to MP3, Audacity needs to know the location of the
LAME MP3 encoder.

Click Yes and the Windows navigation dialog appears, allowing you to navigate to the folder into which you extracted the `lame_enc.dll` file.

Resources

Audacity

http://audacity.sourceforge.net

LAME Binaries for Windows

http://www-users.york.ac.uk/~raa110/audacity/lame.html

LAME (Official Site)

http://lame.sourceforge.net

Chapter

12

The Juice: A Podcast Aggregator

For those who may not be familiar, podcasts are audio programs, generally provided in a format that is convenient for handheld media players. The name is a play on Apple's popular iPod multimedia player, but podcasts work with any number of compatible devices. You can even play them on your home computer. Because they are portable, however, podcasts are great diversions on trains or while sitting in waiting rooms.

Podcasts can be music programs, news programs, or just some gal talking about whatever floats into her mind at the time. In terms of subject matter, you can probably find a podcast that covers just about any subject imaginable. There are slick, professional podcasts, and there are strictly amateur presentations. In the previous chapter on Audacity, I gave you some tips on joining the legion of podcasters by creating your own audio program.

What generally sets a podcast apart from any other audio program you can download on the Internet is that you can subscribe to podcasts using an RSS aggregator. I introduced you to Internet news feeds using RSS when I covered Firefox and Thunderbird. You could think of podcasts as audio news programs, although news may be the least of it when it comes to podcasts.

When you really start to get into podcasts, you need some way to effectively download and collect them. Chasing down podcasts, looking for new programs, and downloading them can take a frightful amount of time. That's why podcast aggregators are such a great idea. In this chapter, I'm going to cover one of the best podcast aggregators out there.

The Juice on the Juice

For starters, the perfect podcast aggregator would contain its own directory of podcasts categorized into an easy-to-search list of topics. Add to that an easy one-button system to add feeds, a new show scanning feature so you don't have to go looking for the latest shows, and a system of automatic scheduled downloads running in the background, and you've got the makings of a great program. As it turns out, the Juice does all those things.

When you start Juice for the first time, it creates a folder in your My Documents folder called My Received Podcasts. You can override this default by selecting Preferences from the File menu. I'll discuss preferences a little later, but let's start with a little tour first.

The Juice interface has the usual menu bar running along the top offering access to all the program's features. There are four main tabs: Downloads, Subscriptions, Podcast Directory, and Cleanup (see Figure 12-1). You most likely will find the Subscriptions tab selected by default. The larger portion of the interface under this tab is a two-paned view that shows a list of subscribed podcasts in the upper pane. If you click one of these shows, the bottom pane loads the latest episodes for those shows and lists them in the bottom pane.

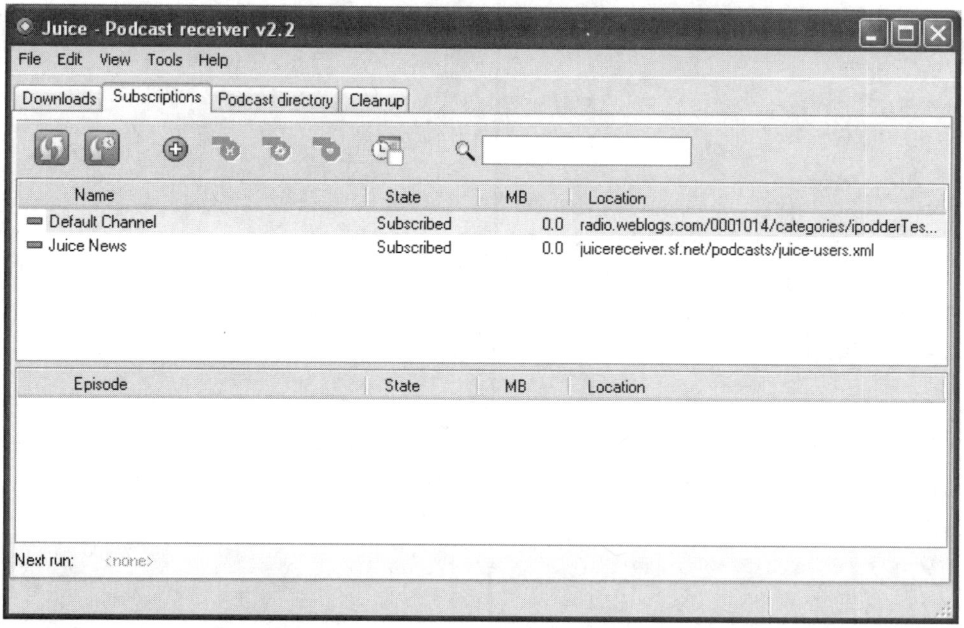

Figure 12–1 The Juice podcast receiver starts with a couple of default podcasts in its subscription list.

Note A fifth tab labeled Log may also be present. The presence of the Log tab can be turned on or off via Preferences. I'll cover Preferences a little later.

Let's move to the Podcast Directory tab now. You see a list of folders describing various directories and top podcast collections available. Click one of these collections and it downloads the most current list. At any point, you can force a refresh by clicking the Refresh icon on the far left of the icon bar. That's the best way to make sure you are working from a recent list. Click the plus sign beside any of these directories and the directory expands to show you all the programs listed there (see Figure 12-2).

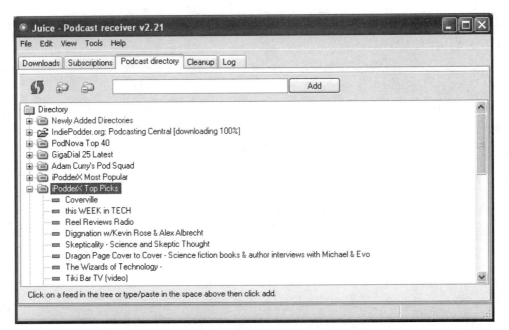

Figure 12-2   No need to go hunting through podcast directories. Juice provides its own, extensive list.

Note As soon as you start downloading content, a new tab, labeled Log, appears. As it sounds, this is a log of the work Juice is doing for you.

Now, let's get back to those podcast directories. Take some time to go through them. Notice that some are organized by popularity, others by the rating of a particular podcast directory service. Others still are listed according to the type of content. Perhaps the most interesting here is the one called Libsyn Podcasts, because it contains a massive list of podcasts.

Subscribing to a Podcast

To subscribe to a podcast, click the title and it appears in the top field to the left of the Add button. Next—you guessed it—click the Add button. If the podcast you want isn't listed here, you can add it manually by clicking Tools on the menu bar and selecting Add a Feed (see Figure 12-3).

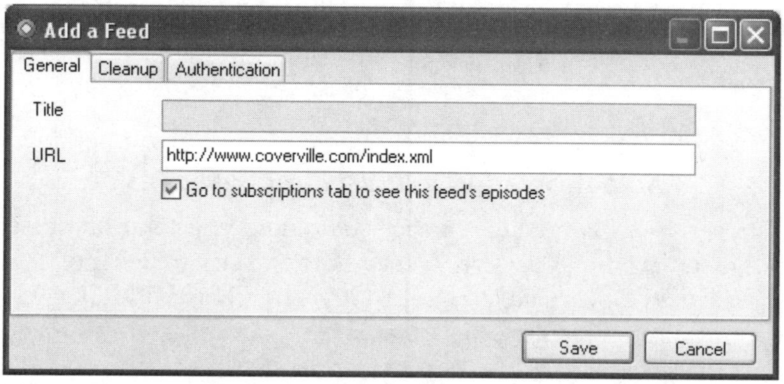

Figure 12–3 When you add a feed, a window appears, allowing you to modify some settings on that feed.

The dialog has three tabs: General, Cleanup, and Authentication. The feed's URL is automatically entered for you. The title is filled in for you automatically when the feed is added. Notice the Go to Subscriptions Tab to See This Feed's Episodes check box. If you are adding a lot of feed up front, you may want to uncheck this because it takes you from the directory to the Subscriptions tab.

The Cleanup tab is interesting because it provides a means of automatically cleaning up old episodes. Check the Automatically Delete Episodes More Than check box (see Figure 12-4). This activates a field where you can specify the age of the podcast before it is deleted. The default, upon activation, is 14 days. Think of it as a free maid service for your PC.

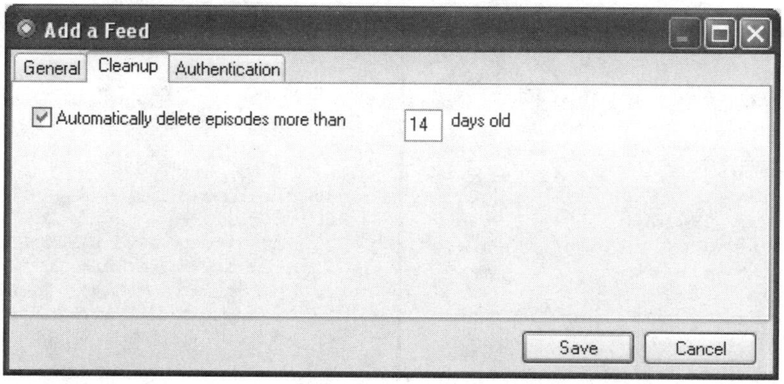

Figure 12–4 No need to worry about cleaning up after yourself. Select the Cleanup tab and tell Juice you want it done automatically.

The Authentication tab is rarely used, but if you subscribe to a podcast that requires you to enter a username and password, this is where you enter this information.

Selecting and Downloading Podcasts

As you subscribe to various podcasts, subfolders with the names of those podcasts are created in your My Received Podcasts folder. For instance, I have folders called Coverville, KFI Tech Guy, and Quirks and Quarks, among others. Each folder holds that particular show's podcasts, so it's a good thing to have lots of disk space. I'll discuss housecleaning shortly.

Let's go back to the Subscriptions tab (see Figure 12-5). A list of all the podcasts to which you have subscribed are in the top half of the main window. Click any of these shows and the bottom pane lists the various episodes, the size of the show, and its location on the Web. Look to the far left next to the episode title and you see a check box. Click this box to flag the episode for download. A little green arrow next to the episode title means it has already been downloaded to your system.

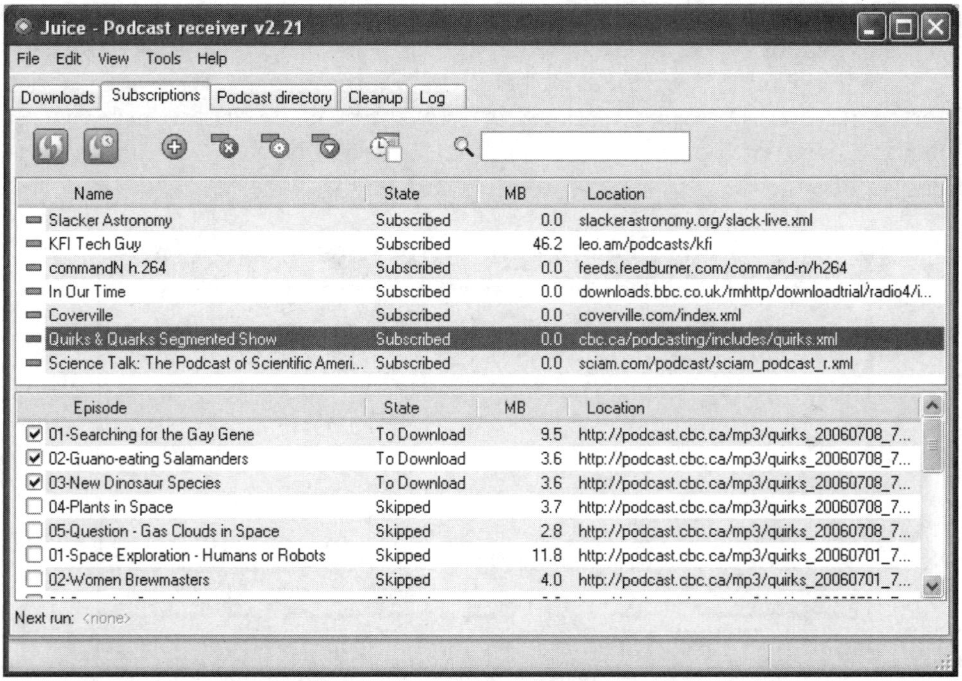

Figure 12-5 Subscription lists allow you to individually select episodes for download.

After you have selected the episodes you want, click the first button on the left of the icon bar, the one that says, "Check for New Podcasts," when you pause your mouse cursor over it. The button turns gray and the download of your podcasts begins. To see the progress of those downloads, click the Downloads tab. You see the current state of the download, as well as the speed and percentage completed of the transfer (see Figure 12-6).

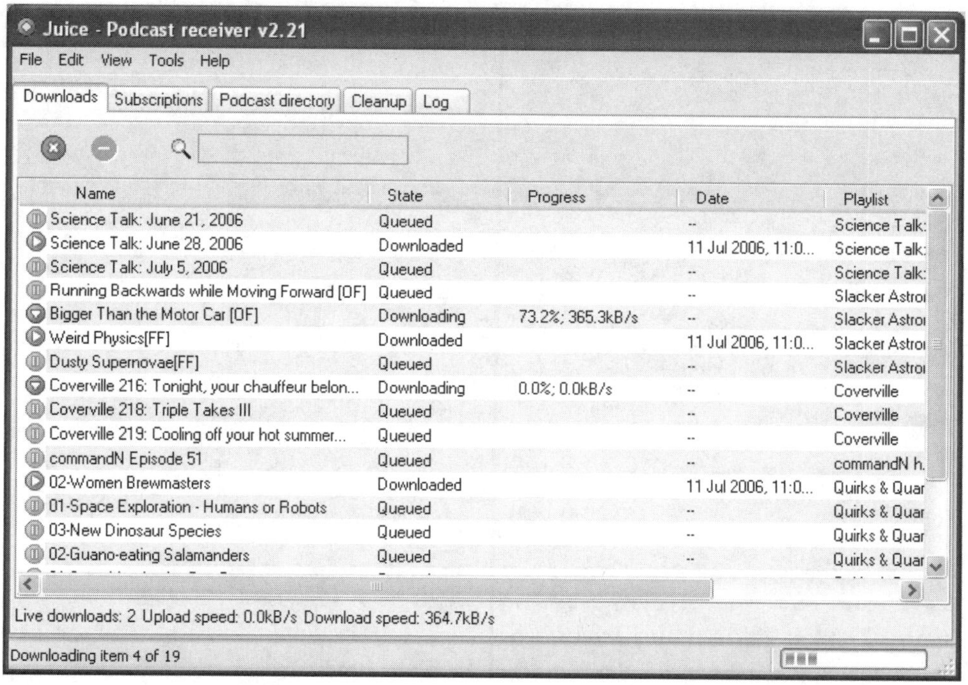

Figure 12-6   As the download progresses, status reports are provided via the Downloads tab.

Finally, we get to the whole point of finding and downloading all these shows, and that's listening to them. Take a look again at that little green arrow to the left of your downloaded episodes (this applies to both the Download and the Subscriptions tab). Either double-click the entry or right-click and select Play Episode in Media Player from the pop-up menu.

By default, Juice uses the iTunes music player, but this is not the only player it supports. The default Microsoft Media Player is supported as is Winamp. To change your player, click File on the menu bar and select Preferences. A multi-tabbed window appears. (I'll discuss the Preferences dialog a little more shortly.) Select the Player tab, and then click on the radio button to select your favorite player. Looking at Figure 12-7, you'll notice that I switched mine to use Winamp. There is one other choice: to use no player at all.

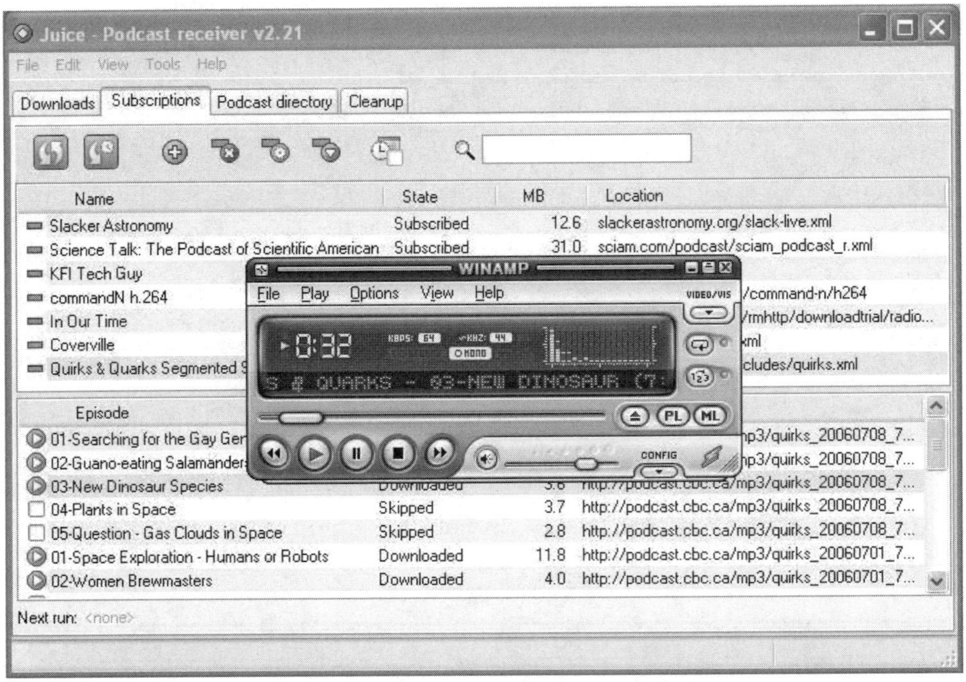

Figure 12–7   By default, the Juice launches iTunes to play your podcasts, but you can set the configuration to use other players such as WinAmp, as seen here.

Tweaking the Juice

Having just mentioned the Preferences dialog, I feel I should spend just a little more time on it. I had you change the player a moment ago, but there is a lot more to see here. Click File and select Preferences. If you did change the player to something else, the Player tab is selected. Click the General tab and you see a number of start and runtime options (see Figure 12-8).

For the Juice to fold nicely into the panel, you need to click the Continue Running in the Background When I Close the Main Window check box. To keep your new settings, you must click the Save button.

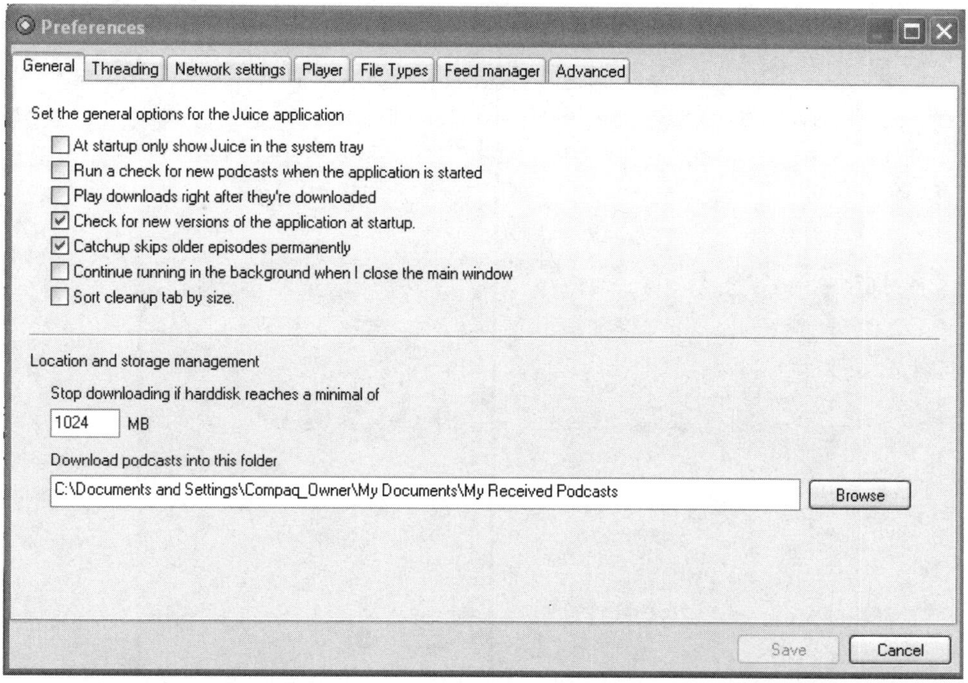

Figure 12–8 The Preferences dialog is worth close examination. There are several settings that will interest you.

There are other settings that are worth looking at as well as tweaking. Under the Threading tab, you may want to change the number of downloads per session, assuming, of course, that your machine or network connection can handle the load. Network Settings are important if you are running behind a proxy server of some kind. I've already covered the Player tab, but there are some iTunes and Winamp specific settings should you choose either of these. The last thing I'll mention here is the Feed Manager tab, where you can enter a URL to synchronize your subscriptions.

Running on Automatic

One of the great things about using Juice is that after you have it set up, it can handle all your podcast needs without you having to lift a finger. Juice swallows down into a nice, lemony applet in your system tray so that the program can keep running out of the way.

This is particularly handy when you consider Juice's scheduling functionality. From the Subscription tab, click the Scheduler button on the icon bar (or click Tools from the menu bar and select Scheduler) to automate your podcast downloads. The Scheduler window appears but the system is not yet running. To activate the Scheduler, click the Enable Scheduler check box (see Figure 12-9).

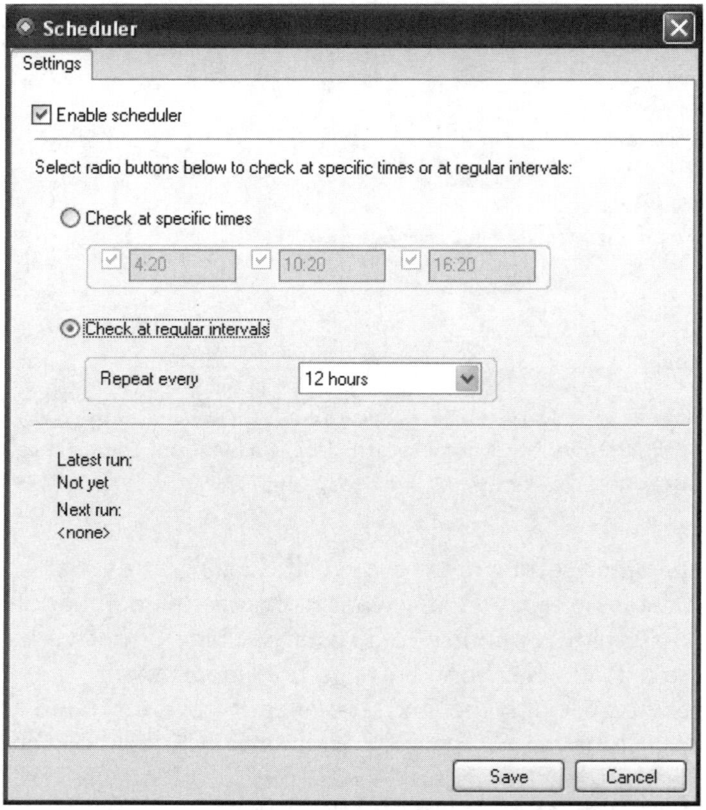

Figure 12–9   By activating the scheduler, Juice will automatically scan for updated podcasts and download them for you unattended.

Automatic updates and downloads to subscribed feeds can be set to run at a specific time of day or at regular intervals throughout the course of the day (e.g., every 12 hours). That way, you don't have to spend time checking up on new episodes. Just let Juice squeeze the fresh podcasts for you.

Cleaning Up

Although you may have set your podcasts for automatic cleanup when you added the feed, it is possible that the sheer number of podcasts on your system may begin taking up more space than you expected. It's time for a little cleanup.

Click the Cleanup tab, and then select one of your feeds from the dropdown list. A list of episodes associated with that feed appears in the lower pane (see Figure 12-10).

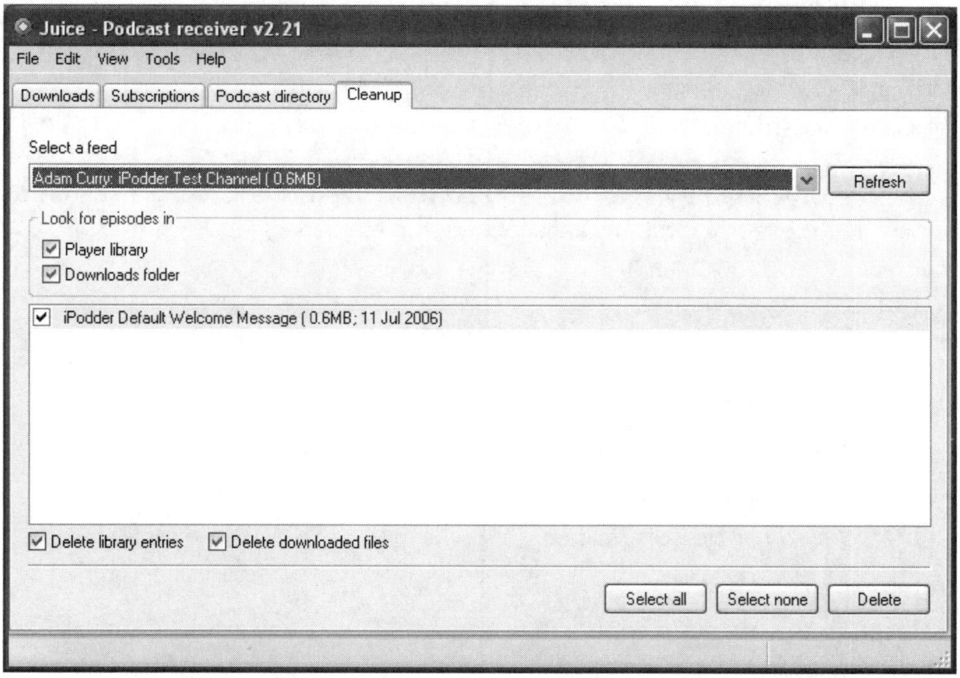

Figure 12–10 From the Cleanup tab, it's easy to select and clean up old podcasts. Select all or choose from individual episodes.

Select the episodes individually or click the Select All button to delete everything. When you are ready, click Delete.

Locating More Podcasts

The built-in directory of podcasts is a nice place to start, but you may find yourself asking for more as the podcast madness takes hold. As I suggested earlier, you can find links to podcasts on a number of sites, then enter them into your subscription list manually. Still, there is something very nice about a large directory, organized by category. On that note, take a look at the following list and you'll find tons of podcasts covering every imaginable subject.

Indiepodder.org	`http://www.ipodder.org/`
Podcast.net	`http://www.podcast.net/`
PodcastDirectory.com	`http://www.podcastdirectory.com/`
Podfeed.net	`http://podfeed.net/`
Yahoo! Podcast Directory	`http://podcasts.yahoo.com/`

All are organized by subject area and most feature a keyword search to help you find exactly what you are looking for. Enjoy!

Resources

Juice
http://juicereceiver.sourceforge.net

iTunes Music Player
http://www.apple.com/itunes/

Winamp
http://www.winamp.com

13

Nvu: A Graphical Web Site Design Tool

Web sites are everywhere and it seems that everyone, including newborns, has his or her own Web site. If you happen to be among the (seemingly) few who don't already have a Web presence, or if you would simply like to try out a little Web design but don't know where to start, take heart.

In this chapter, I'm going to take you through the creation of a simple, five-page Web site, complete with bulleted lists, links, and images. I'll even show you how to publish that Web site to your server. The tool I'm going to use to do all this is called Nvu (pronounced N-view).

Nvu is an easy-to-use, WYSIWYG editing and publishing program for the Web. Using this program, you can author a great-looking Web site without any prior knowledge of HTML or writing code for the Web.

Installation Notes

The Nvu installer is a pretty standard setup wizard. Click Next past the introductory screen and you have an opportunity to read the license agreement (Mozilla Public License). Click the I Accept the Agreement radio button, and then click Next to continue. For the most part, this is just a case of accepting defaults and clicking Next. When the installer completes, it offers to start Nvu for you. This is where you see something a little unusual.

The first time you start Nvu, an extra window labeled Please Let Us Know appears asking you to add yourself to a counter of Nvu users. The company would like to know that you have downloaded the software and, in addition, would like to know how many people are using the software. A privacy statement accompanies the window. If you want to add yourself (and this is optional), click OK.

Touring Nvu

When Nvu starts, an Nvu tip is displayed with a Did You Know That window floating above the main window (see Figure 13-1). You can turn this tip feature off by unchecking the Show Tips at Startup check box. Some people find these little tips at startup annoying. I happen to believe that they can be quite useful until you get comfortable with an application; besides, reading the tip takes a few seconds at best. Alternatively, if you want to read every tip up front, click Next Tip or Previous Tip to move forward or backward through the list.

Let's take a little tour of Nvu. Along the top, directly beneath the menu bar, is the Composition toolbar. This is where you find many commonly used functions such as opening a document, publishing it to your Web site, adding a link or image to your page, running spell check, and more. Each of these functions is represented with a large icon for one-click access.

Below that is the Formatting toolbar. I should probably call this the Formatting toolbar parts one and two, or upper and lower. That's because its functions are spread out over the next two rows (see Figure 13-2).

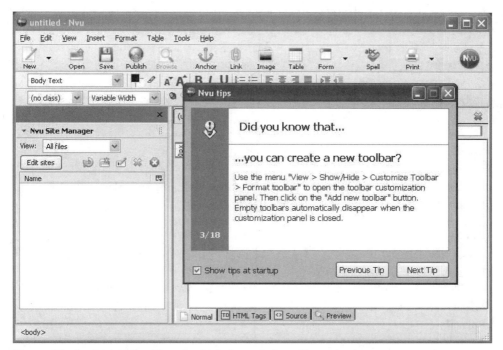

Figure 13–1   Launching Nvu also includes a tip box. If you don't want to see these, uncheck the *Show Tips at Startup* box.

Figure 13–2   If it has to do with how your text looks, it's on one of two formatting toolbars.

These toolbars are concerned with most anything having to do with text itself. That includes changing the paragraph format, heading level, font color and type, alignment, and so on. It is here where you italicize, bold, or underline words as well.

Below all these toolbars and to the right is Nvu's main editing window where you type the text from which your Web page is created. Over on the right is the Site Manager. To publish a Web site through Nvu's interface, you need to create at least one site in the site manager. I'll talk about how you do that when I discuss the steps required to publish a site a little later in this chapter. For now, let's concentrate on the editing window.

As with Firefox (way back in Chapter 2), Nvu uses tabbed views of the pages you are working on. That means you can have multiple Web pages open at any given time and switch from one to the other by clicking its tab. At the bottom of the editing window, there are four tabs: Normal, HTML Tags, Source, and Preview. Each of these provides a different view to the page you are working on. By default, the Normal view is selected and this is where you enter your text. The HTML Tags view shows your page and displays all HTML tags.

The main interface can be resized to suit by clicking an edge or corner and dragging. When you do this, the main editing window is affected as well. At the top of the window, below the tab (currently labeled Untitled), there's a white bar with a number in the center. This is the current view width of your window in pixels. This is useful for letting you know what your Web pages will look like on different monitor sizes.

Finally, over on the right is the Nvu Site Manager window. We'll take another look at it later in this chapter when I show you how to publish your Web site.

Editing a Web Page

It is always so difficult to start something new. There is nothing worse than staring at a blank page and trying to come up with a little brilliance to fill it. Let me help. Start by entering a simple first line that welcomes the visitor. Then, add a list of five things the surfer can find on your site (e.g., family pictures, links to friends, etc.). These five things will eventually be links to the other pages that make up your Web site.

Finally, enter a paragraph of text; anything will do here, so feel free to get as creative or silly as you want. You can use the following if you like.

> Three long hours ago, the great and mighty warrior god, Mangidor the Fierce, found himself trapped in rush hour traffic where he tried vainly to keep his road rage in check while he wondered about the curse that brought him here and how a warrior god could get himself into a mess like this, far from the bustling heavenly halls of Kintryal, the songs of great deeds echoing through its cavernous beauty, and the best damned eggs benedict in the universe.

Remember, I didn't claim that my example would be any good. If anything, it sounds more like something bound for the Bulwer-Lytton fiction contest, but it's just an example. Feel free to write something else. In the meantime, this is what your Nvu editing window should look like (see Figure 13-3).

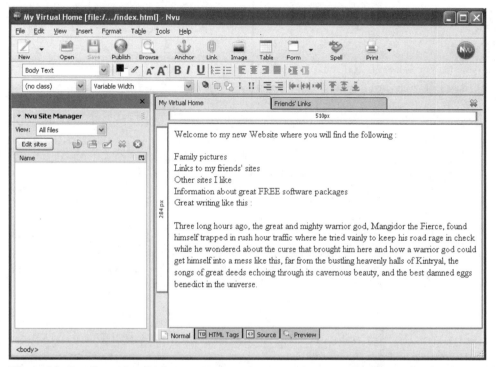

Figure 13–3   Creating a Web page is as simple as entering text into the main editing window.

Now that your first page is no longer blank, select the first line on the page. You can bold the line and increase the font size slightly. To do this, click the bold button on the formatting toolbar. Then, click the Larger Font Size button directly to the left of the bold button (see Figure 13-4).

Figure 13–4   Close-up view of the main editing buttons (font size, bold, italic, etc.).

Tip For some people, it can be faster to use keyboard shortcuts than to chase around with the mouse. Using the keyboard also gives the old mouse wrist a bit of a break. For instance, to bold selected text, press <Ctrl+B>. To italicize, press <Ctrl+I>. Pressing <Ctrl+U> underlines the selected text.

Another way to create a bold heading is to use the standard HTML heading tags. There are six of these, identifying different levels in your text. For a title, it's traditional to use the heading level 1 tag, or H1. Common text, or paragraph, formats are available at the upper-left side of the formatting toolbar. It defaults to Body Text, which is plain, nonbolded, nonitalicized, non*anything*, text. Select the paragraph you want to enclose (or the line, in the case of the heading), and then click the drop-down box directly below the New and Open buttons on the icon toolbar. Select your heading level (see Figure 13-5) and click to apply.

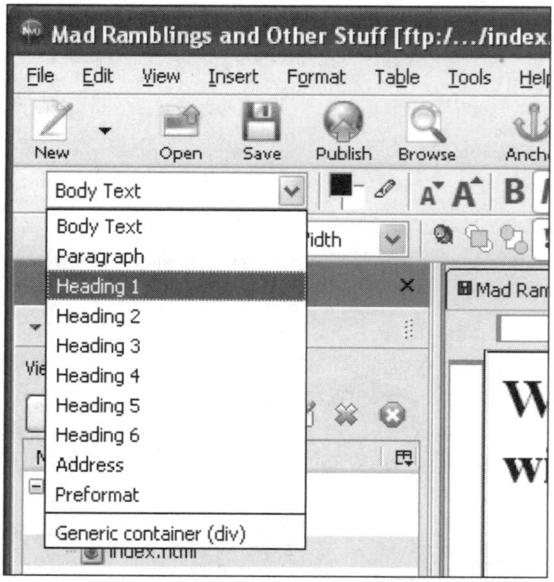

Figure 13–5 Paragraph formats can be easily applied from the drop-down list on the formatting toolbar.

Tip At any time in the course of your page creation, you can see what the actual HTML code looks like by clicking the Source tab at the bottom of the editing window. To go back to the WYSI-WYG editing screen, click the Normal tab.

Bulleted Lists

I had you come up with a list of five items that would become links to other pages. Let's take those lines and make a nice, bulleted list with them.

Select all five lines of text, and then click the Bulleted List button on the formatting toolbar. In the close-up in Figure 13-4, the bulleted list button is the last on the right. You can also click Format on the menu bar, navigate to the List submenu, and select Bulleted from the list. Instantly, your five lines indent on the screen with five bullets, one before each of the five lines.

Take a moment to look further at that List menu and you see that you can also specify a numbered list for your items. Instead of bullets, you get a nice sequential list from one to five.

Saving Your Work

Anyone who has ever lost a few minutes' or, worse, a few hours' worth of work because the computer crashed knows the importance of doing regular backups. If you've been working on that Web page for a few minutes now, it's time to save it. Click File on the menu bar and select Save (or Save As). A pretty standard Windows Save As dialog appears, from which you can navigate to a desired folder (see Figure 13-6).

Because a Web site is usually a collection of multiple pages, images, and other files, it makes sense to create a folder for that site and to store the pages there. When you create the next site, you can then make a new folder for that one.

The file name can be whatever you like, but the top page of a standard Web site is usually called `index.html`. That's because Web servers automatically serve up pages called `index.html` without you having to add it to the end of your Web site address. For instance, when you go to www.yoursite.dom, the Web site is actually giving you the first page for that site without you having to ask for it. If the page was `myfirstpage.html`, your visitors would have to enter www.yoursite.com/myfirstpage.html to get there.

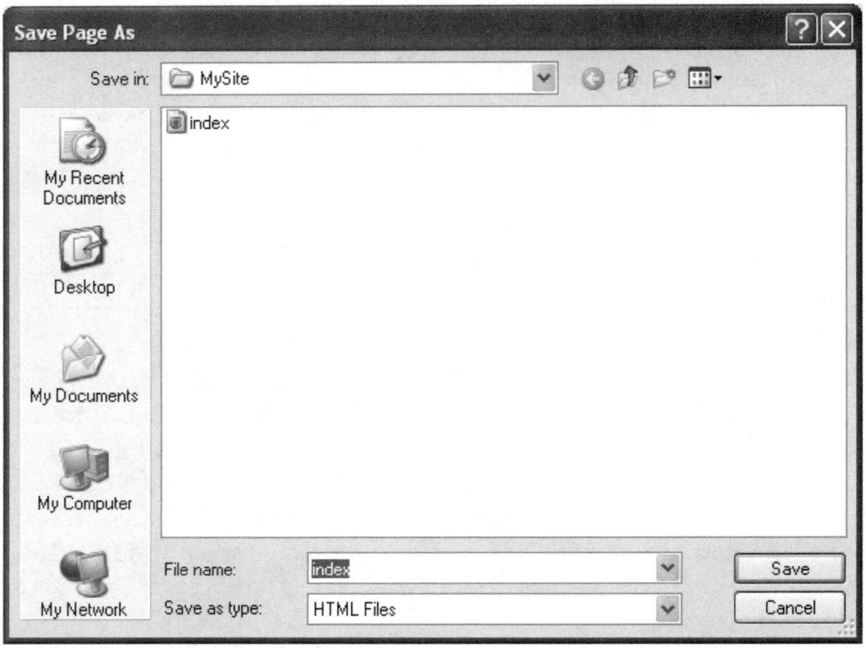

Save Page As   ? X

Save in: 📁 MySite   ▼   ○ ↱ ↰ ▦▾

📄 index

My Recent Documents

Desktop

My Documents

My Computer

My Network

File name: index   ▼   Save

Save as type: HTML Files   ▼   Cancel

Figure 13–6   It probably helps to save all your files in the same folder if they are part of the same site.

Tip So, is it `.htm` or `.html`? People who have been creating Web sites on UNIX or Linux systems for a long time always use `.html` for the file name extension. On the other hand, people working on Windows systems (and DOS systems before that) have been creating HTML files with an `.htm` extension. That's because in the old days of DOS and Windows, file names could only have a three-letter extension. That hasn't been the case for a long time and now, even though both formats work, it's probably more right to use the `.html` extension. Luckily, Nvu automatically adds the four-letter extension for you when you save.

Creating Subsequent Pages

Creating the second page is easy. Click File on the menu bar and select New. You can also just click the large New button on the top left.

The default behavior is to have the new page appear in a tab in the main work area to the left. This is similar to the tabs you saw in Firefox in Chapter 2. I'm rather fond of this behavior because tabs give me quick access to my pages without cluttering my desktop, but you can override this. If you desire, you can easily have the new page open in its own Nvu window. Next to the New button, there is a small, black, down arrow. Click and hold that button, and then select Page in New Window from the drop-down menu.

Just as you did with your index page, enter text relevant to this page. If it's the Family Pictures page, you might add a title. When you are happy with the text on this page, save it in the same folder you used for the index page.

Adding Images

Because I'm discussing the Family Pictures page, it seems like the right time to talk about how you get images into your Web site. Put your cursor where you want it on the page, and then click the Image icon on the top icon bar (or click Insert on the menu bar and select Image). The Image Properties dialog appears with four tabs: Location, Dimensions, Appearance, and Link. Under the Location tab, you must now enter the path to the image you want to add. You can find a Choose File button that brings up the Windows file navigator to assist you in finding the image you want.

After you've made your selection, the image appears in a small preview area at the bottom of the Image Properties window, along with the image dimensions. This brings us to the Dimensions tab (see Figure 13-7).

Of course, the ideal situation is to have an image sized appropriately, but if you don't, this is where you can take care of that. Just click the Custom Size radio button. If you change your mind and you really do want your image to be 800 by 600 pixels on the page, click the Actual Size button.

Perhaps the most important thing here is that Constrain check box. You can set whatever width and height you want for the image, but odds are that you want to maintain proportional dimensions so that you don't wind up with a distorted or squashed image. With the Constrain box checked, all you need to do is enter the desired width and the height is automatically calculated for you.

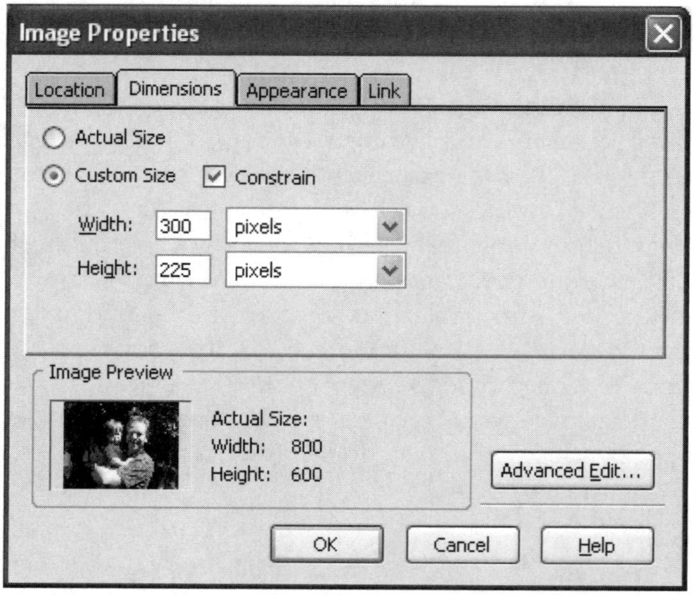

Image Properties

Location | Dimensions | Appearance | Link

○ Actual Size
◉ Custom Size   ☑ Constrain

Width: [300]   pixels ▾
Height: [225]   pixels ▾

Image Preview

Actual Size:
Width: 800
Height: 600

[Advanced Edit...]

[OK]   [Cancel]   [Help]

Figure 13-7   If your images are too large for the page, you can set it to display in a smaller format.

Tip Keep in mind, however, that even if you are displaying a larger image in a smaller format, it still takes up as much room on disk and in memory. To make your pages load as quickly as possible, you should shrink your images to the size you want them to appear before you upload them.

The Appearance tab allows you to select whether the object has a border around it, and how much space there is around the image. I find that even a five-pixel border makes text much easier to read because it isn't pressed right up against the image. The last important item on this tab is the alignment of the image. Does text wrap to the left or right, or is the image aligned vertically (top, center, or bottom) with the text? For the most part, wrapped text looks much better, but your design may require a different look.

Finally, we come to the Link tab. Is this a standalone image or does clicking the image take you to another page, another site, or a larger version of the image? When you want visitors to look at a large image, it often makes sense to use a thumbnail version of the image. Then, that thumbnail links to a larger version of itself. Alternatively, the link might be to an email address where the image is the person you want to send a message to. In the case of an email, make sure The Above Is an Email Address check box is checked (see Figure 13-8).

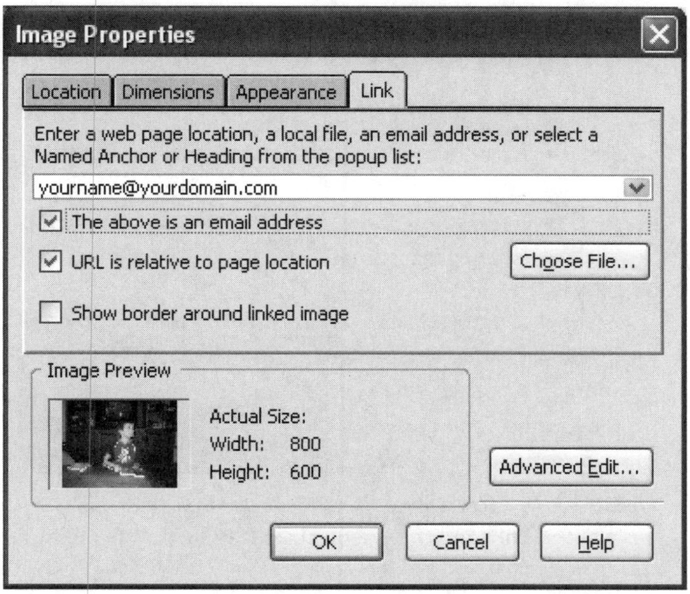

Figure 13–8 When specifying an email address as the link, you must remember to check the appropriate box.

After you've finished adding images and links to your Family Pictures page, make sure you save your work.

Hmm . . . all this talk of links provides a nice introduction for the next section in this chapter.

Linking to Your Other Pages

Now that you've created the second page, it's time to create a link to it from the main page. If you were following along with me, you now have a title page called `index.html` and a second page called `familypics.html` and four other pages, which I leave to you to create and name.

To create a link from the first item in your bulleted list, select the Family Pictures text. Then, right-click the text and a menu appears with several choices, including the usual cut, copy, and paste (see Figure 13-9).

Figure 13–9   To create a link, select the text that will
serve as the link, and then right-click to bring up the menu.

The items in the menu vary depending on the nature of the selected text. For instance, there is a List Properties menu entry here because the selected text is part of a bulleted list. Of course, another way to do this is to select the text, and then click the Link button in the icon bar at the top.

After you click Create Link (or click the button), the Link Properties dialog appears (see Figure 13-10).

In the Link Location field, you can enter an outside link to another Web site, an image, or a file. You can even enter an email address. As with the image example in Figure 13-8, this link could also be an email address. Just make sure you click the check box, The Above Is an Email Address. For this example, you want to enter the link of your Family Pictures page. Click OK and your selected text appears with the classic blue underline signifying a hyperlink.

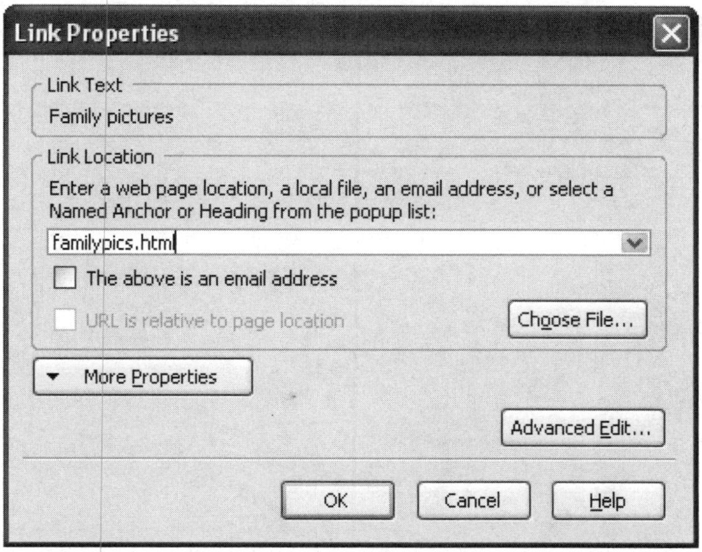

Link Properties ✕

Link Text

Family pictures

Link Location

Enter a web page location, a local file, an email address, or select a
Named Anchor or Heading from the popup list:

familypics.html   ⌄

☐ The above is an email address

☐ URL is relative to page location   Choose File...

▼   More Properties

Advanced Edit...

OK   Cancel   Help

Figure 13–10   To link to another page, just enter the name of
the Web page.

Publishing Your Web Site

One of the things that makes Nvu a really nice program to use is that you can
publish your Web site directly from the editor. It's really an easy-to-use process and after you set it up for a page, publishing your updates is a one-click
affair.

Let's go back to the main index page for this example. Make sure you've
saved your page, and then click the Publish button on the main icon tool bar
(you can also click File on the menu bar and select Publish). The Publish Page
dialog appears (see Figure 13-11). This is a two-tabbed dialog with one Publish
tab and the other Settings tab. Make sure the Settings tab is selected.

In the Web Site Information section, enter the address of your Web site.
The preceding example shows a folder with the username (my name, in this
case) directly below the Web site address. Many ISPs who offer free Web
space often use the format of a tilde character just before the username (e.g.,
www.myisp.dom/~myname) for the site address. Make sure you check with
your ISP so that you know what format you should use.

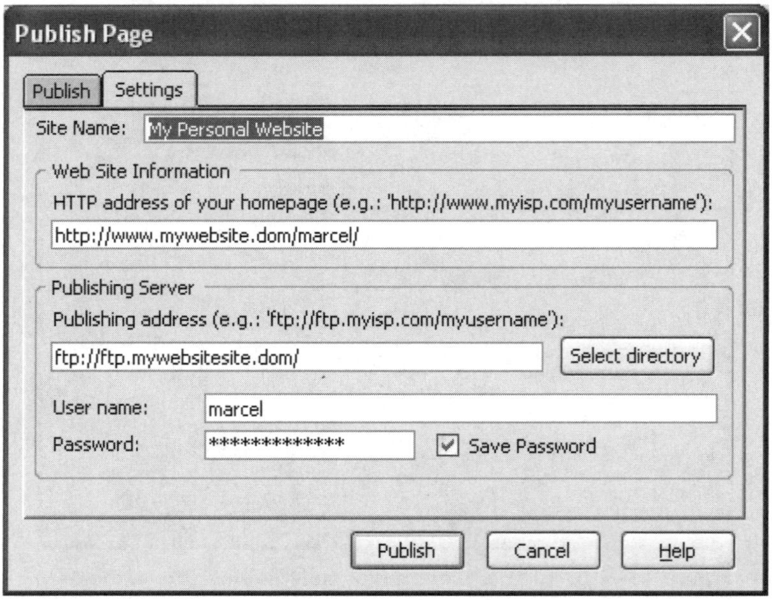

Figure 13–11   Settings for your site include the FTP login information and password so that pages can easily be uploaded.

In the Publishing Server section, you should enter the address information you were provided to publish via FTP. This address generally has the format of `ftp://ftp.myisp.dom`; but again, you should check. Below all this, enter your username and your password for access to the site. If you don't want to be asked for the password each time, click the Save Password check box.

Now, click the Publish tab and you have the opportunity to provide some information about this page (see Figure 13-12).

Enter a site name (assuming you don't already have one in the Site Manager) and a title for your page. This title appears at the top of your Web browser's title bar. The file name should be already filled in for you, but you could change the name here. If you've published the page before, change the name next time you publish; the result is that you wind up with two versions of the page, but with different names.

One last thing before you click the Publish button. Notice the section on images near the bottom. By default, all your images are stored in the same folder as your Web pages. If you want to use a subfolder, let's say one called Images, enter that here. Just make sure the folder already exists on your site first (you can use Site Manager to create it). When you are done, click the Publish button at the bottom.

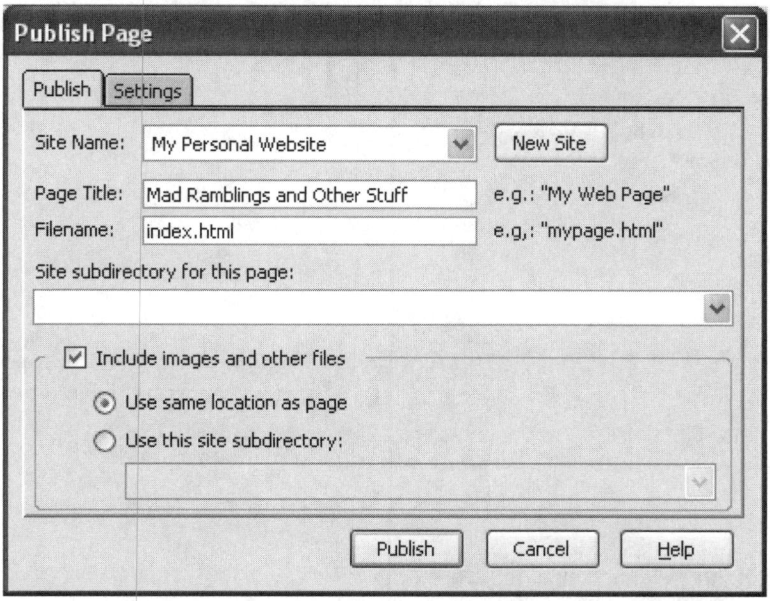

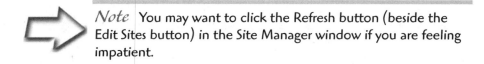

Figure 13–12 It's time to supply some information about the site and the page you are uploading.

With a simple page that consists of nothing but text, the whole process is likely over in a heartbeat. As you add more text, images, and other files, the process may take a little longer. As the page and its components are published, a small window informs you of the progress (see Figure 13-13).

If you have images associated with your page, they also are uploaded to the site when you publish. Meanwhile, the information in the Site Manager (on the right side of the Nvu window) reflects the files on your Web site (see Figure 13-14).

Note You may want to click the Refresh button (beside the Edit Sites button) in the Site Manager window if you are feeling impatient.

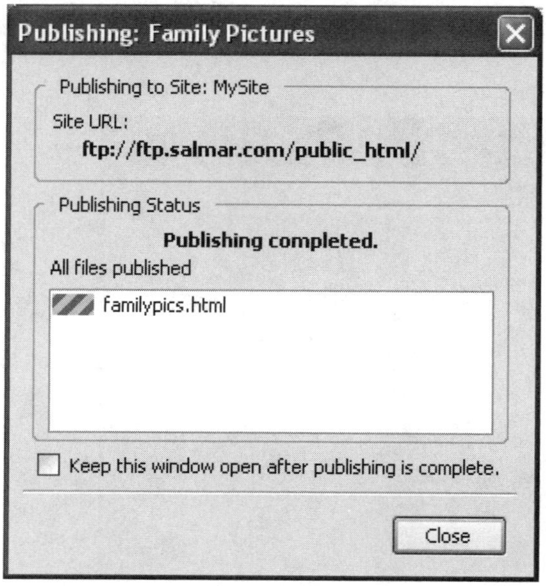

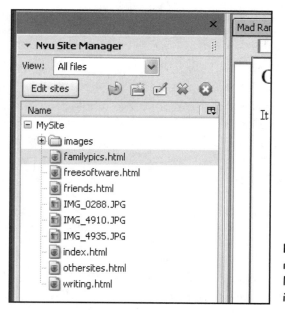

Figure 13–13 As the page and its components are published, a progress dialog keeps you up-to-date on what is happening.

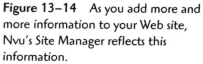

Figure 13–14 As you add more and more information to your Web site, Nvu's Site Manager reflects this information.

Site Manager is actually a mini, remote file manager. The buttons above the site listing make it possible to create new folders, rename folders and files, and even delete files.

It's a Beautiful Thing

Getting started with Nvu is easy, and publishing a basic site takes little effort. Nvu is also up to the job of far more complex sites. Nvu supports forms, tables, and Cascading Style Sheets (CSS). When you get a little more comfortable with HTML and Web design, you can even edit code manually using the Source tab in the editing window.

Take the time to get to know Nvu and your site will be a beautiful thing.

Resources

Nvu
http://www.nvu.com

Nvu User Guide Online
http://nvudev.com/guide/1.0PR/ugs01.htm

Chapter

14

Inkscape: A Vector Drawing Program

When you use Inkscape, it's hard to believe that something that is this much fun and so easy to use could help you create high-quality, professional artwork. Inkscape is a drawing program in the spirit of Corel Draw, Adobe Illustrator, or Macromedia Freehand. The drawings you create with Inkscape are scalable vector graphics (SVG), a W3C-standard graphic format. The SVG format is fully open and based on XML. As such, there are plenty of applications that can read and write SVG files.

You might ask, what is so special about vector art versus any other type of digital art? Good question. When you create digital art in nonvector programs, the image is bitmapped, with different colored dots turned on or off. The more dots you pack into a small area, the better the quality. If you then scale (or blow up) that drawing, you lose more and more quality as the image gets larger. Here's another way to look at it. Most of us have, at one time or another, blown up an image on a photocopy machine. The bigger the copy, the worse the quality gets. This is also true of photographs.

On the other hand, vector art describes what a drawing looks like using a system of points, curves, and lines. You don't just zoom in on a vector drawing. A larger image uses the same mathematical description to create the image, but it is scaled to whatever size of canvas you are working with. You aren't just making bigger, fuzzier, dots. As a result, Inkscape's artwork can be scaled up or down without loss of quality. Inkscape features freehand and geometrical drawing tools, shape tools, text tools, color tools, gradient tools, and a whole lot more. You can export your creation to PostScript, EPS, PNG, or PDF, among others.

Ready to get started? Let's start by taking a look around.

A Friendly Introduction

Let's start this overview of Inkscape by having a little fun. I'll give you a little bit of information, and then have you go ahead and do a little doodling, Inkscape style. I don't know about you, but when I was a young lad in school, I spent an amazing amount of time just doodling in my books. Doodling, I believe, is a great way to let your creative juices flow. And doodling is what we'll do. First, let me introduce you to Inkscape's interface and some basic tools.

Inkscape starts with a blank canvas in the center of a rather purposeful looking interface (see Figure 14-1). Along the top is the classic menu bar (e.g., File, Edit, View, etc.). Directly below the menu bar is the Commands bar, a row of icons representing some basic and useful commands. Some of these icons are pretty standard and you'll recognize the New document, Open, and Print icons, to name a few. I'll explain some of the others in more detail shortly.

Figure 14–1 The blank Inkscape canvas, ripe with possibilities.

Below the Commands bar is the Tool Controls bar. The icons represent controls for the drawing tools, and this whole bar changes as you select individual drawing and editing tools to work with. The drawing tools themselves are available through those icons you see running down the left sidebar. I'll tell you about those tools in detail a little later. Down at the bottom of the screen, there's a color palette that runs the length of the Inkscape window. Inkscape gives you fine control over colors using RGB or CMYK, but the palette provides quick access to a handful of colors for less demanding projects.

At the bottom, below the color palette, there is a status bar (see Figure 14-2). There can be a lot of information here, including tips on using the current tool, the zoom level (more on zooming in a moment), the current layer, style information such as the flat and stroke colors currently in use, and the pointer's position on the canvas.

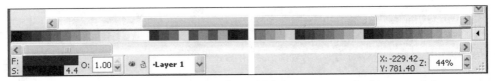

Figure 14–2 A close-up of the color palette and status area at the bottom of the Inkscape main window.

That plain rectangle in the center is your page, the white background around it is called the canvas. Around the canvas, along the top and left, there are rulers. Your creation can take place on or off the page. Nothing like a blank page to get the creative juices flowing, right?

Tip You can pull the vertical (or horizontal) ruler down into your canvas. The ruler itself doesn't move, but a line *guide* appears that you can use to more clearly align objects in your drawing. When you are done with the guide, just pull it back.

Moving and Zooming Around

Right now, that blank page is pretty small because it's scaled to fit the entire page on the screen. The first thing you probably want to do is zoom in a little bit. Using the + and – keys is an easy way to zoom in and out, but I find that there are other, more convenient ways, particularly if you are using the mouse. Click the magnifying glass icon in the left sidebar (it's called the Zoom tool), and then click the page to zoom in. To reverse the process and zoom out, hold the <Shift> key, and then click with the mouse.

Those of you with a wheel mouse have other options. In fact, using the wheel mouse, you can zoom in and out, move around, and more. Scroll up to move up the canvas, which has the effect of moving the page down away from you. Ah, relativity. Scroll down to move down. At the bottom of the canvas, there's a scroll bar. Position your mouse there, and scroll up to move right and down to move left. You can also hold the <Shift> key, and then scroll the wheel to move left or right.

Tip With so many ways to do things, it's easy to forget the basics, but you can always just use the scroll bars on the right and bottom to pan the canvas.

To zoom in, you don't need to use the Zoom tool. Instead, hold down the <Ctrl> key, and then move the scroll wheel up or down to zoom in or out.

You've already seen one of the drawing tools, the Zoom tool, so it's almost time to explore the rest of the drawing tools in detail; but first, I'm going let you to do a little doodling, just to get the feel of the program.

Doodle Away

Look along the left side of the Inkscape main screen and you see a column of icons. These represent commonly used tools and, before the end of this chapter, you'll be familiar with all of them. For now, I want you to take a look at the fourth (it has a square on it), the fifth (this one has a circle), the sixth (that's the star), and the seventh icon (that one has a spiral on it). Now, skip two icons and you'll see one that looks like a fountain pen doing a calligraphic stroke.

I've just told you about the Rectangle, Ellipse, Star, Spiral, and Calligraphy tools. Start by clicking the Rectangle tool. Then, click somewhere on your canvas and drag the mouse pointer to create a square or rectangle. Cool? Now, click the star and do the same thing. This time, a star appears on the screen. Drag the star to make it bigger or smaller. Try the ellipse tool and you can create circles or ellipses. Spirals are kind of fun, too. Do this for a few minutes and, even if you aren't, you'll feel like a kid again.

This is pretty simple stuff right now, but we can do a few simple things beyond this. If you don't think yellow is a good color for a star, click one of the colored squares at the bottom of the screen and the corresponding tool changes. When you are ready to wrap up, why not add a final flourish with the Calligraphy tool? To see my intro doodle, check out Figure 14-3.

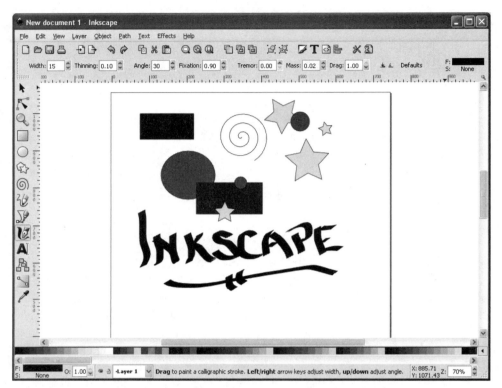

Figure 14–3   Using the stock shape tools, you can try a little doodling to get comfortable with the interface.

Drawing Tools

There are 14 tools running down the left side. You've already seen and played with a few of them, but now it's time to see what they all do.

Pause over each one and a tooltip appears with a short description of its function. To make it easier to keep track of where we are, I've broken the 14 tools into two sets of seven and provided close-ups of the icons. I've also detached the tool icons and aligned them horizontally as with the first set of seven in Figure 14-4.

Figure 14–4   The first seven of 14 drawing tools, arranged horizontally.

The Selector Tool

The first tool is the Selector tool. This is by far the most used and useful tool available to you. As the name implies, you use it to select objects. Select single objects by clicking them. You can also select multiple objects by clicking outside an object, and then dragging the selection area to encompass two or more objects.

The effect of selecting an object activates handles around the object (see Figure 14-5). Click once and the handles point toward and away from the center of the object. Click and drag any of these handles and you resize the object in any direction you choose. Do this now and you'll notice that the ratio of width to height is not maintained. To maintain a consistent (or proportional) set of dimensions relative to whatever changes you are making, press and hold the <Ctrl> key as you drag the handles. Now, click the object again and another set of handles appears. These are skew and rotate handles.

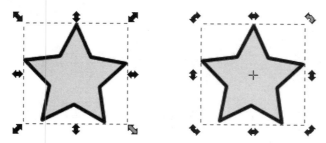

Figure 14–5   Click once with the Selector tool and resize handles appear. Click twice to activate the skew and rotate handles.

The skew handles are top and bottom, as well as left and right. The handles on the corner rotate the object. What's the difference? When you rotate, it's a simple circular motion, as though you were spinning the object clockwise or counter-clockwise. When you skew, you tilt the object obliquely.

Tip If you have multiple objects overlapping and you want to select them as a group, hold down the <Shift> key and click each individually. To treat those objects as a group so that any changes to one affect the others, press <Ctrl+G>. Pressing <Shift+Ctrl+G> ungroups selected objects.

Look along the top, at the Tools Control bar and you'll see that it has changed to reflect the tool you are currently using. Along the left side, icons allow you to easily rotate the selection.

Node Tool

Every object is a collection of paths running between mathematically defined points. Nodes, the points along the way, define the object's shape. The Node tool allows you to click, drag, and otherwise manipulate those points and, as a result, the paths themselves. To illustrate this, I've created a small freehand drawing using the pencil (or freehand) drawing tool (which I'll cover shortly). After the drawing was created, I clicked the node tool to select it, and then clicked the drawing I created. The resulting points (nodes) appear as squares along the path (see Figure 14-6).

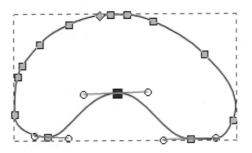

Figure 14–6   Nodes appear as squares with circular handles that let you modify the curve.

When you move your mouse over a node, it turns red. Select it by clicking it, and it turns blue. When a node is selected, it sports handles, round points at the end of a bar that extends from the node itself. You can click and drag a node to a different position to change the shape of your drawing (or curve), but you can also use the handles to refine the curve, or vector, along that point. Handles can be turned or dragged and extended to modify the amount of curve along that point.

> *Tip* You can also click the line between two nodes and drag it to create a new curve or alter an existing one.

Along the top, on the Tools Control bar, a new set of icons has also appeared that lets you do things with nodes. For instance, select a segment between two nodes, click the first icon, and new nodes are inserted between your selected path. Using the second icon, the reverse takes place. Just select a node, click the icon, and away it goes. You can break the path between two nodes, join two nodes with a path, and make segment curves or lines. Pause your mouse over each icon for a tooltip to help you along the way.

Playing with nodes is a surprising amount of fun. The bonus here is that the more you play, the better your control over the points, lines, curves, and vectors that make up your drawings.

You'll see the Node tool in action again when we get to some of the shapes, starting with the Rectangle tool.

Zoom!

We've already covered the Zoom tool to some degree so I won't spend a lot of time on it here, but I do want you look at the tools control bar when you click the tool. Pause your mouse cursor over the icons and you find some interesting things you can do there. With a single click, zoom to automatically fit the page, the page width, or even the current selection in the window. Other icons offer a one-click 2:1 or 1:2 zoom.

The Rectangle Tool

This tool can be used to draw both rectangles and squares, squares being just another type of rectangle. After selecting the tool, click and drag to create your rectangle. After it's created, you'll notice three active nodes on the square (see Figure 14-7). Two of them, at opposite corners, are square in shape. The third node (or handle, if you prefer) is a circle.

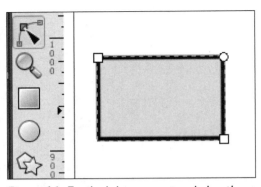

Figure 14–7   An Inkscape rectangle has three nodes, one of which has a circular handle.

Dragging either of the square nodes is another way to resize the rectangle. Clicking and dragging the round node vertically down, however, does something very different. The corners become rounded, in a perfectly circular arc (see Figure 14-8).

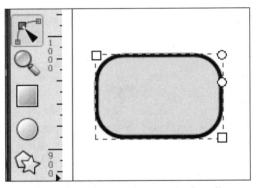

Figure 14–8   Moving the circular handle rounds the corners, but also uncovers another circular handle to modify the horizontal aspects of the curve.

Having dragged the circular handle down, you might notice that you now have a second circular handle in the corner. This one can be dragged horizontally and produces somewhat more elliptical corners.

Ellipse Tool

In the fifth position (and remember, my image is horizontal, but the tools are actually aligned vertically) is the Ellipse tool. Ellipses also cover the creation of circles, and arcs as well. Select the tool, and then click the canvas and drag. Creating an ellipse is easy, but trying to create a perfect circle just by dragging can be tough. To make this simple, hold down the <Ctrl> key as you drag your ellipse, and it is a perfect circle every time.

As with the Rectangle tool, the ellipses you draw have special nodes already assigned. The top and left squares allow you to shape the ellipse vertically and horizontally, stretching or shrinking as you desire. The circle node is particularly interesting and is called the arc handle. Drag the arc handle in any direction and you'll see that there are now two handles.

If your pointer happens to be inside the dashed lines that make up the border of your ellipse, the arc opens up as in Figure 14-9.

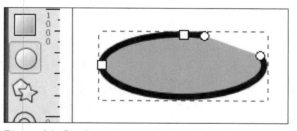

Figure 14–9   Drag the circular handles outside and the arc is open.

However, if your pointer is on the outside of the dashed lines, the arc is closed, with an anchor point at the center of the ellipse, as though somebody has taken a slice out of your pie (see Figure 14-10).

To undo an arc, you need to direct your attention to the Tools Control bar. Notice the Make Whole button. Click here and your ellipse returns to its original closed state. I should also point out the Open Arc check box. Earlier, I had you move the arc handles inside or outside of the selection to open or close the arc. You can also do that by checking (or unchecking) that check box.

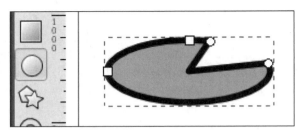

Figure 14–10   Keep the pointer inside the dashed lines and your arc is closed to the center of the ellipse.

Star Tool

In position number six, we have the Star tool, although it's also a Polygon tool, something that becomes important shortly. Select this tool, click the canvas, and drag. Presto! Perfect five-pointed stars just like that! Now, look at the tools control bar (see Figure 14-11). There's a Polygon check box.

Figure 14–11   The Star and Polygon tool has a number of useful tweaks in the tool controls bar.

Check this box and your five-pointed star turns into a pentagon. Uncheck it and the star returns. Now, look directly to the left in the Corners box. It's set for five, as in five points. Increase that and suddenly your five-pointed star is a six-, seven-, eight-, or more pointed star.

Now, let's look at the nodes (or handles) on the star. There are two of them. One is on a tip and the other is inside—on the inside tip, if you prefer. The outside handle controls the star's size. Click and drag the inside handle and you can alter the star's shape and that of its points (see Figure 14-12). If you just want to pull the points in with out changing the distance between two points, hold down the <Ctrl> key as you drag the inside handle.

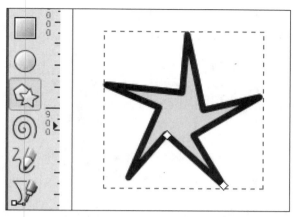

Figure 14–12 Pulling on the inside handle distorts the star's shape.

Here's a neat trick. Click and drag the inside handle past the center of the star and off to one side. You wind up with a star inside a star overlapping other stars (see Figure 14-13).

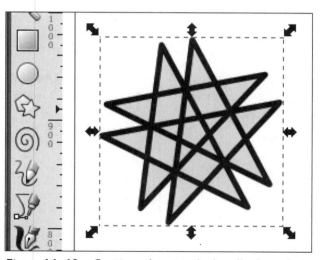

Figure 14–13 Continue dragging the handle through the center of the star and beyond to create a fascinating echo of the original.

Spiral Tool

I'm going to wrap up this first set of seven with the Spiral tool.

When you draw a spiral, there are two handles. One is inside at the inner end of the spiral, and the other is outside, at the outer end. Each handle can be dragged away from the center or toward it. Pulling the outside one extends (or decreases) the number of turns that make up the spiral—the default is five turns (see Figure 14-14). The inside handle lets you adjust the inner radius.

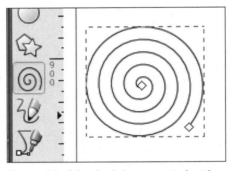

Figure 14–14   An Inkscape spiral with inside and outside control nodes, or handles.

At first, it may not seem as though you can change much with spirals, but try pulling the inside handle while holding down the <Alt> key. Now, drag the outside handle while holding down the <Shift> key.

Fill and Stroke Genius

Before I move on to that second set of drawing tools, I want to cover a special dialog that is especially relevant to some of the tools I've already covered, specifically the shape tools.

One of the most important tools you are going to work with is the Fill and Stroke dialog. Each time you create an object using the Square, Ellipse, or Polygon tool, there is the shape itself but it is bordered by a black line. The inside color is your fill. The bordering line that gives the object definition on the page is the stroke. Both fill and stroke can be modified using the Fill and Stroke dialog. To activate the dialog, select an object using the selector tool.

Now, click Object on the menu bar and select Fill and Stroke from the drop-down menu (keyboard jockeys can just press <Shift+Ctrl+F>). There's also a handy icon on the top icon bar, about six icons from the end.

When the dialog appears, you see a three-tabbed window (see Figure 14-15). The first tab is labeled Fill, followed by Stroke Paint, and Stroke Style. Click the Fill tab to start.

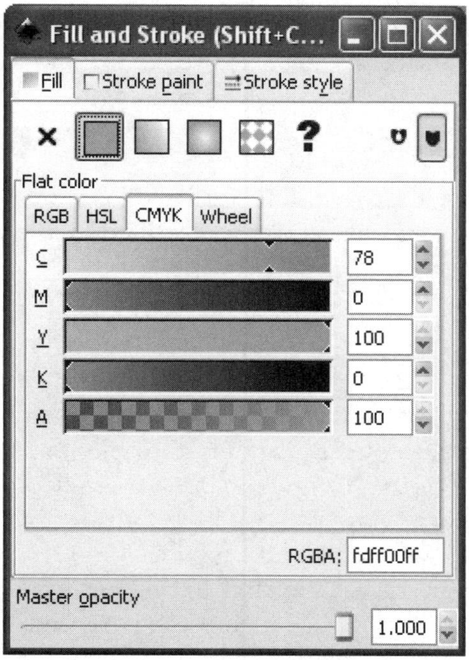

Figure 14–15   Using the Fill and Stroke dialog to define a color using the CMYK palette.

Directly underneath the tab, icons allow you to select the type of fill you want. The first icon, with an X on it, turns fill off. The result is an object that consists of the lines around it with nothing inside, much like the pictures in your coloring books before you add your special touch.

The second icon is for color selection. Given the nature of this program, there are many ways to select color. Simple *RGB* (Red, Green, Blue) is based on, well, the three primary colors indicated. Next, we have *HSL*, which stands for Hue, Saturation, and Lightness (think of a rainbow, then increase or decrease the light and saturation). The next tab is for *CMYK*, also known as Cyan, Magenta, Yellow, and Black, a system of specifying color that graphic artists and those in the paper printing business are quite familiar with. Finally, there's the wheel, a popular means of choosing color in many computer programs. It's effectively another take on the HSL rainbow, wrapped around a wheel this time.

 Note When you change colors, using whatever format you choose, look at the status area over on the lower-left of the main window. You'll see the fill and stroke colors change there.

The other icons that follow the fill icon are for gradient fills. Choose from horizontal gradients as well as circular gradients. Once again, you'll find yourself selecting a color and gradient type.

Stroke! Stroke!

Okay, I couldn't resist that. Strokes combine two sets of decisions. The first has to do with the stroke color. By default, the color used by the tools is black, but you aren't limited to that by any means. Color selection is much the same as it is with fill, so there's nothing new here. Stroke style, however, is worth spending a little time investigating (see Figure 14-16).

The first item at the top of the stroke style window deals with the width of the stroke in pixels (you can change the measurement if you want). Join style deals primarily with corners, turns, and so on. Do you want a square edge? Rounded, perhaps? Similarly, for simple lines you can also specify the style for the end cap.

Directly below these line styles there's a Dashes drop-down box. Dash style can vary dramatically, from various dash widths to dotted lines to nothing at all. What I find interesting about this is that the default dash style is an unbroken line—not really a dash at all.

The last three drop-down boxes on this part of the window are for start, mid, and end markers. Imagine you have drawn a curved line of some sort using the pencil tool or a straight line using the pen tool (both of which I'll cover shortly). Classic start and end markers are an arrow head and tail (see Figure 14-17).

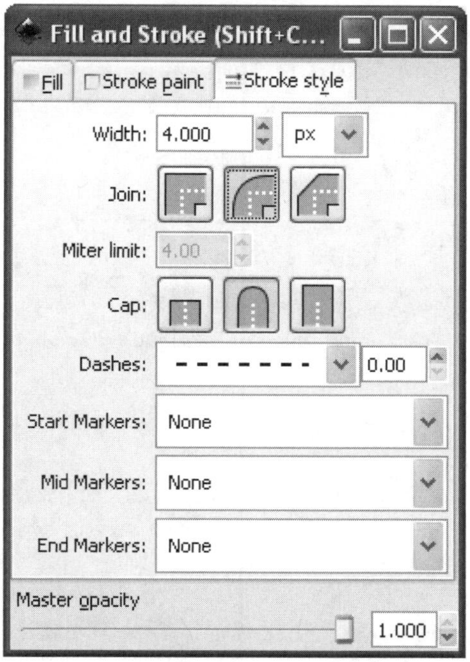

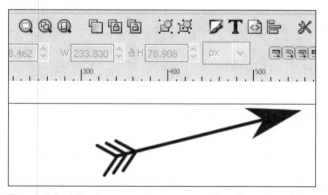

Figure 14–16   The stroke is the outside line that defines a shape. You can change its side, look, cornering, and more.

Figure 14–17   An arrow using start and end markers from the Fill and Stroke dialog. Directly above the arrow (to the left of the big T is the icon for the Fill and Stroke dialog.

A mid marker might be a smaller arrow head inviting the eye to follow the path in a particular direction. Arrows are certainly the most popular markers, but you do have other alternatives such as dots, squares, and so on.

Drawing Tools, Part Deux

On to the next batch of seven tools (see Figure 14-18)! Once again, I've assembled them horizontally starting with the pencil and making our way to the eye dropper at the end of the list.

Figure 14–18   The second seven of Inkscape's drawing tools, arranged horizontally.

Let's look at these tools one by one.

Given that this is a drawing program, the first tool in our list (directly below the spiral tool) is the pencil, also known as the Freehand tool.

The Freehand Tool (The Pencil)

Select the Pencil tool, click the canvas, and draw as you would with a pencil. When you are finished, release the mouse button. The shape of the object you've just drawn may not be 100 percent accurate, but don't worry about that. You can adjust the shape by clicking the node tool (the second in our first set) and then clicking your shape.

Several nodes, or handles, appear at various points along the length of your freehand work. Depending on how steady your hand or how complicated your object, you may find it looking very rough with a great number of nodes along the way. Now, you can drag the nodes (or the curves between two nodes) to smooth out and adjust the drawing, but you could also let Inkscape take a shot at it for you. Click Path on the menu bar, and then select Simplify (or press <Ctrl+L>). This is something you can do multiple times until you are happy with the result.

In Figure 14-19, I've drawn the outline for a cartoon face (forehead, ears, and chin). The first incarnation of it has multiple points (visible on the left), too many in fact to easily manipulate. After pressing <Ctrl+L> eight or nine times, I ended up with the figure on the right.

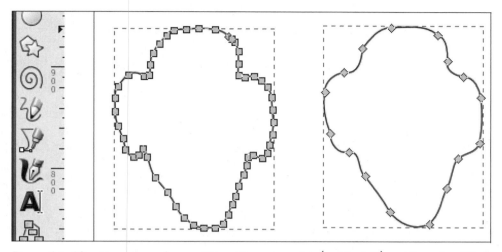

Figure 14–19 My cartoon face outline with many points (on the left) and then simplified multiple times on the right.

Bezier Curves and the Pen Tool

The Freehand tool is great for simple hand drawings, but it isn't your best bet for straight lines. For this, use the Bezier tool, or pen. Although it may seem strange to suggest something that is obviously meant for curves to create straight lines, it might help to remember that a straight line is just a flat curve.

To create a straight line, select the Bezier tool and then click a part of the canvas and release. Now, extend your line in any direction as far as you like, then double-click and you have a perfectly straight line. To draw shapes consisting of multiple lines (such as zig zag), click to a location, move, then click, then move, and so on until you are finished. At the final point, double-click to lock in your shape. Using this technique, you can draw any kind of nonsymmetrical polygon as well.

A curve is a bit different, and this is one of those times where the description doesn't help nearly as much as actually doing it. Click a point on your canvas, and then drag the line to a second point. Release the click, but don't double-click. A round node point appears at the end of this line. Now, move your mouse away from this point and a curve follows your cursor. When you are happy with the curve, or the look of the curve, double-click to lock it into place.

Tip Remember that you can fine-tune your curve using the Node tool.

The Calligraphy Tool

Calligraphy essentially means beautiful writing. Calligraphy tends to be hand-crafted text created with special brushes, quills, or pens. It is an art form that goes back centuries, often seen in early texts, Asian writing, and modern wedding invitations.

The Calligraphy tool included with Inkscape by no means compares to a master with a brush, but it does make it possible to create brush strokes evocative of the calligrapher.

You'll notice I haven't mentioned the Tools Control bar when discussing the last two tools. That's because there weren't any tool options to discuss. With the Calligraphy tool, the tool controls reappear. Play with these and you find that you can change the angle of the brush (or pen, if you prefer), add a trembling effect to the stroke, see how much the velocity of the stroke affects the thickness (or thinness) of the stroke, and so on.

Text Me!

Okay, it's not that kind of text. But for normal text, using a specify font, you want to use the Text tool. This tool is pretty much second nature to anyone who has ever used a word processor. Select the Text tool, click the canvas, and start typing. At the top of the screen, in your tool controls, you'll see that you can select the font, the point size, whether text is in bold, normal, or italics, the style of justification, and so on.

Another way to do this is to use the Text and Font dialog. This is the large T icon on the icon bar. Alternatively, click Text on the menu bar and select your dialog from there. When the window opens, you can modify the text, including the font, line spacing, and more (see Figure 14-20).

As you type, a dashed text box grows around your text. To go to a second line, press <Return>. By clicking and dragging with the Text tool, it's also possible to pre-create a text box into which text flows and automatically wraps. The catch here is that you are limited by the size of the box, and if you go beyond its dimensions, your text simply vanishes. It isn't really gone, however. Notice that the text box has a little handle in the lower-right corner—either change the size of the text to fit or drag the box to increase its size on the page.

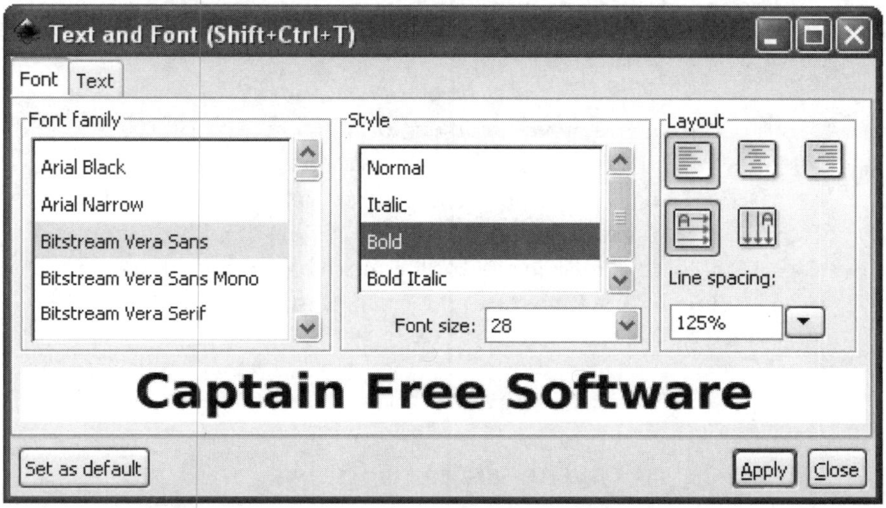

Figure 14–20   Using the Text and Font dialog to fine-tune your text.

Tip When created, text is just another object. Use the Selector tool to select it, and you can flip your text to create a mirror image, rotate it, stretch it, flip it, and whatever else you like. Then, use the Fill and Stroke dialog to change its color or introduce a gradient.

Creating Connectors

All of us have seen connectors in action, or at least their function. Just think of any company organization chart where boxes with names and titles link to other boxes with names and titles of somewhat lesser importance (or at least, pay scale) below. The lines that link those boxes are created with the connector tool. What is particularly cool about the connector tool is that the connectors you create follow the boxes if you move them around.

To use connectors, go ahead and create your text boxes, or any object for that matter, and arrange them on the canvas as you see fit. Now, select the connector tool and hover over the first box. A square appears in the center of that box. Click that square. Now move your mouse to the next object and another square appears in the center. Click that second square and the boxes are joined.

Tip When you move an object, or join any two objects, the lines may go through other objects (or boxes in the case of an org chart). To have the connectors go around an object, select the object that is currently in the way by clicking it with the connector tool. Now, look in the tools control bar and you'll see a couple of icons. Click the first and it makes the connector avoid the selected object.

The Gradient Tool

I've already told you a little bit about gradients when I introduced the Fill and Stroke dialog. The Gradient tool makes it possible to fine-tune a gradient in place, with the changes occurring dynamically on the screen. Select the Gradient tool, and then click the object you want to edit. Select a color, and then click and drag across the object where you want to apply the gradient. A line with two square handles appears on the canvas. You can click and drag those handles in any direction and pull to stretch or shrink the gradient as you see fit.

If you are doing this for the first time, you will be working with a linear gradient by default. Look at the Tool Options bar and you see that you can switch from linear gradients to circular gradients (see Figure 14-21) by clicking the appropriate icon. When you choose to work with a circular gradient, a different set of handles appears. There's a central node and two outside handles to adjust the gradient.

Tip We tend to think of gradients as something you do with the fill. When discussing text, however, I suggest that you play with color gradients there as well. You can also add gradients to the stroke.

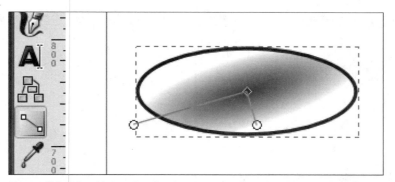

Figure 14–21   Using the Gradient tool to fine-tune a circular gradient.

The Eye Dropper

The eye dropper is a simple tool to use. Its purpose is to let you select a color, anywhere on the canvas, to use elsewhere. If there's a particularly cool shade of blue in your current artwork and you don't want to guess at it by playing with the color wheel or the CMYK numbers, just click it with the Eye Dropper tool, and that becomes your current color for both fill and stroke.

The Full Meal Deal

Inkscape provides you with a collection of powerful tools. Using these tools in conjunction with your artistic flair, you can create high-quality vector art. Even a novice can create something useful and maybe even beautiful with a little time and experimentation. In time, you'll go from just having fun (as with my vampire in Figure 14-22) to professional quality artwork.

Unfortunately, it's quite impossible for me to cover everything. There are plenty of features I haven't even touched on. For instance, you can import a bitmap image, such as a digital photograph or a picture from a Web site, and convert it to a vector drawing. Then, using the tools at your disposal, you can transform it into something entirely new.

Shapes can be stacked on top of other shapes, raised and lowered in the stack of images. The *ears* on my vampire are two ellipses that I lowered below the face contour. The Frankensteinian hairline is a separate item, sitting below the face. Similarly, the rectangle on my Captain Free Software logo sits beneath a circle with a see-through gradient.

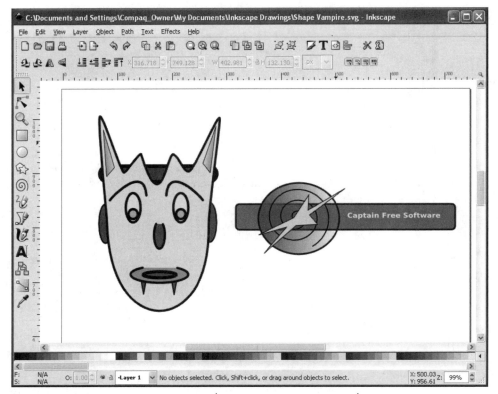

Figure 14–22   My Inkscape vampire (aka Captain Free Software) won't win any prizes, but it was fun to create nevertheless.

Inkscape lets you combine shapes or create entirely new shapes by excluding parts of others. Select two objects using the node tool, and then click Path on the menu bar and see what effect Union, Difference, Exclusion, and other selections have. There are several special effects tools included to let you render complicated structures easily. Just click Effects on the menu bar and try each one out.

Saving Your Work

As you go along, creating your artwork, making changes, tweaking here and there, it's a good idea to save your work. Don't wait for the finished product to safeguard all the work you've done. To save your work, click File on the menu bar and select Save or Save As. You'll immediately notice that the Save dialog is a little different than the standard Windows dialog (see Figure 14-23).

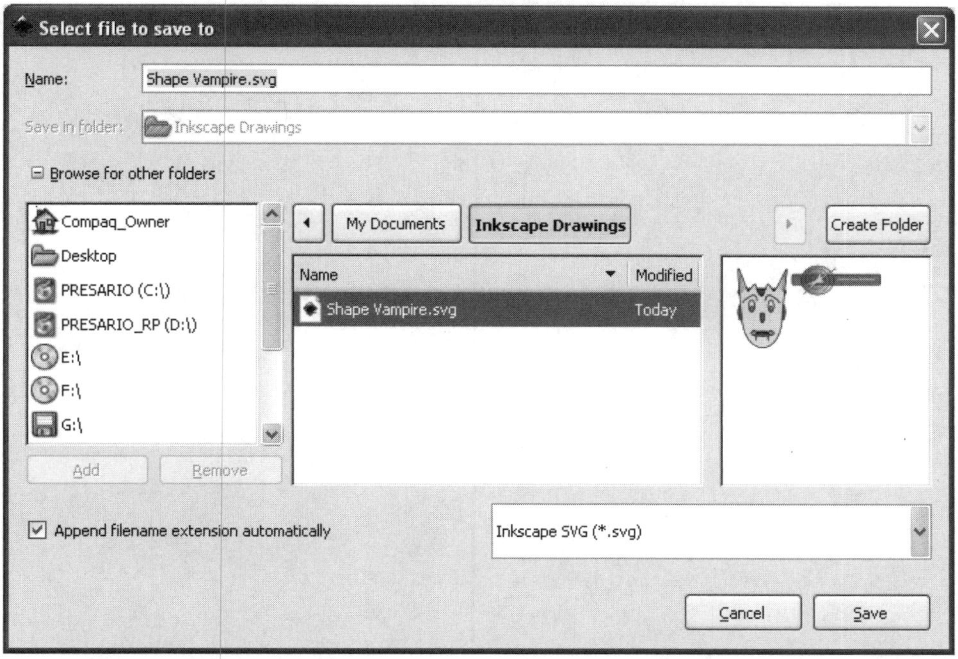

Figure 14–23 The Save As dialog defaults to Inkscape SVG, but other formats are also available.

If there is already an image by the same name, the Save dialog shows you a preview so you can decide whether you want to overwrite it. Just above the Save button, notice that Inkscape SVG format is the default. If you want to reedit your drawings and continue working on them, make sure you stick with the high-quality SVG format. Other choices available to you here include Postscript (and Encapsulated Postscript), PDF, ODG (used by Open-Office Draw) LaTex, and others.

Resources

Inkscape

http://www.inkscape.org

Chapter

15

Digital Art with the GIMP

When it comes to great graphical software, you can get one of the most powerful and flexible image manipulation packages there is for free. It's called the GIMP, which stands for GNU Image Manipulation Package.

The GIMP is an amazingly powerful piece of software, yet its basic functions are easy to use as well. With a little bit of work, a lot of fun, and a hint of experimentation, anyone can use the GIMP to turn out a fantastic piece of professional-quality art. You doubt my words? Then follow along with me, and in just a few minutes you'll have created a slick-looking logo for your Web page or your desktop. With time and practice, you may learn to wield the GIMP with the power of a Hollywood special effects master.

Play. Experiment. And don't be afraid.

Note I'm going to devote this chapter to showing you how to use this amazing program, but I want to mention an interesting side program. The GIMP is a free alternative to the commercial Adobe Photoshop package. Almost anything you can do in Photoshop, the GIMP can do as well. Still, the GIMP does have a very different interface than what you may be used to if you are familiar with Photoshop.

Ladies and Gentlemen, Start Your GIMP

The installation program creates an icon for the GIMP on your desktop. To start the program, just double-click that icon. Alternatively, you can click the Start button, look for the GIMP submenu, and click the GIMP 2 menu item.

Tip When you start the GIMP for the first time, a wizard runs through a few setup steps, part of which creates a work environment in your home folder. This is a simple process that only takes a few seconds. Read the information on the screens, click Continue a few times, and you are ready to start.

You probably get a number of panels aside from the GIMP's main screen. You also likely get the GIMP Tip of the Day. As with all such tips, you can elect not to have them appear each time the program starts—just uncheck the Show Tip Next Time GIMP Starts button before you click Close, and you aren't bothered with them again. What you are likely to see (minus that tip of the day) should look a bit like Figure 15-1.

The long window on the right is split into two main areas. At the top is the Layers, Channels, and Paths dialog. The dialog below has three tabs, one for brushes, another for patterns, and another for gradients. If you choose to close this window, there is no harm done, but you'll end up calling up dialogs as you need them. We'll visit this again when I cover brushes later on.

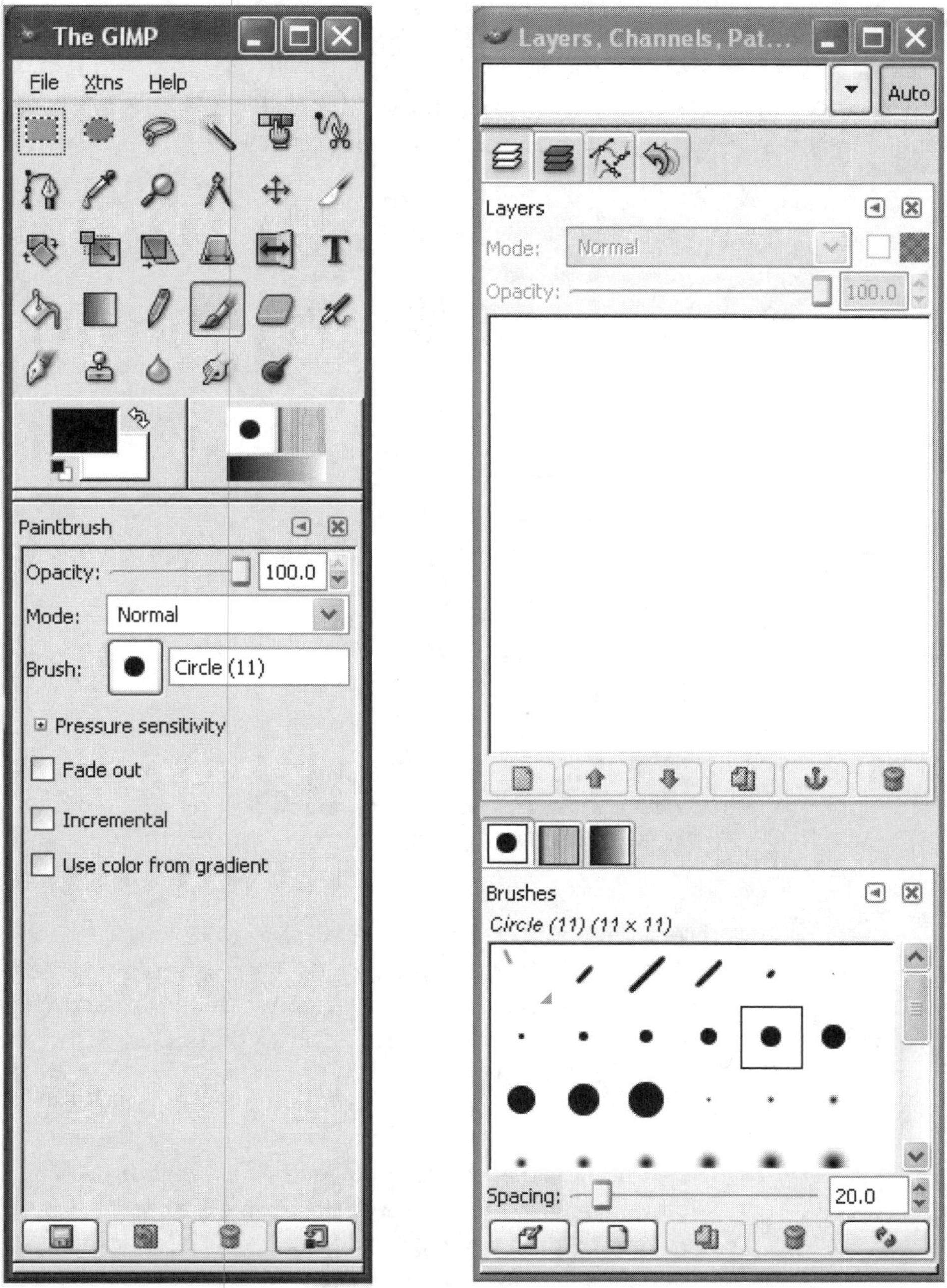

Figure 15–1 The first time through, the GIMP starts with the Layers, Channels, and Paths dialog (right) open.

The most important of those windows is the GIMP toolbox—that's the window to the left in Figure 15-1. The toolbox itself is the top half (see the close-up in Figure 15-2). The bottom half of the dialog represents the options available to the currently selected tool. If you are using the Text tool, you have a choice of fonts, styles, and sizes at your disposal.

Figure 15–2   The GIMP toolbox.

Along the top, directly below the title bar, is a familiar-looking menu bar labeled, quite simply, File, Xtns, and Help. Clicking these shows you additional submenus. Below the menu bar is a grid of icons, each with an image representing one of the GIMP's tools. I will cover all of these things shortly, but first let's take the GIMP out for a spin.

Note The GIMP help files are not installed by default, but you can download them from the same Web site from which you downloaded your GIMP program. You don't actually need to install the help files, however, because the GIMP lets you search the help files online using Firefox.

Easy Logos with the GIMP

The nitty-gritty can wait. I think we should do something fun with the GIMP right now. I'm going to show you how to create a very cool-looking corporate or personal logo with just a few keystrokes. If you don't have the GIMP open yet, start the program now. From the main toolbox menu bar, select Xtns, scroll down to Script-Fu, and another menu cascades from it.

> *Quick Tip* Notice that the menus have a *dashed line* at the top. These are menu tear-offs. By clicking the dashed line, you can *detach the menu* and put it somewhere on your desktop for convenient access to functions you use all the time. In fact, all the menus, including submenus, can be detached.

From the Script-Fu menu, move your mouse to Logos. You should see a whole list of logo types, from 3D Outline to Cool Metal to Starscape and more. For this exercise, choose Cool Metal.

Every logo has different settings, so the one you see in Figure 15-3 is specific to Cool Metal. Particle Trace has a completely different set of parameters. To create your Cool Metal logo, start by changing the Text field to something other than the logo style's name. I'll change mine to read Free Software Rocks! The font size is set to 100 pixels, and you can leave it at that for now.

In many of these, a default font has been selected for you. You can override the current choice (written on the button itself) and pick something else by clicking the font button. The Font Selection window shows you the various fonts available on your system and lets you try different font types, styles, and sizes. A preview window gives you an idea of what the font looks like (see Figure 15-4).

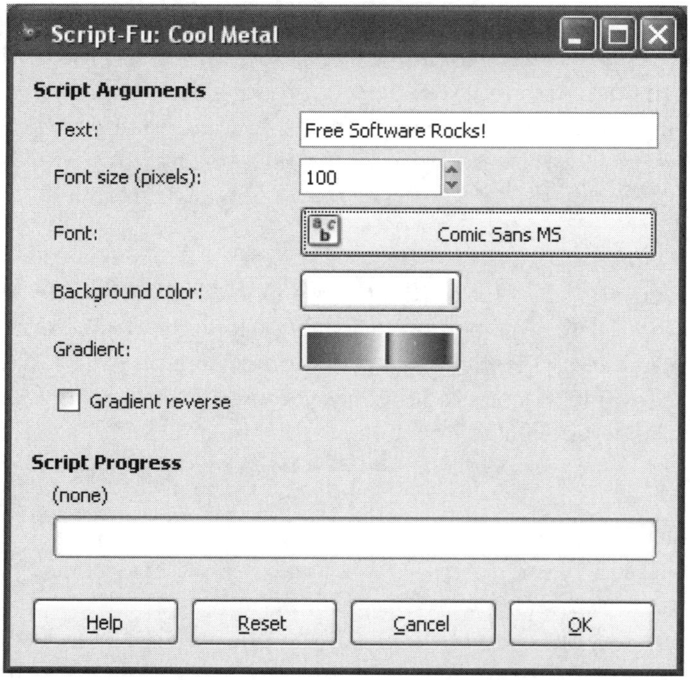

Script-Fu: Cool Metal

Script Arguments

Text: Free Software Rocks!

Font size (pixels):   100

Font: Comic Sans MS

Background color:

Gradient:

☐ Gradient reverse

Script Progress

(none)

Help   Reset   Cancel   OK

Figure 15–3   Script-Fu logo settings for Cool Metal.

Script-Fu Font Selection

Aa Gautami

Aa Georgia

Aa Georgia Bold

Aa Georgia Bold Italic

Aa Georgia Italic

Aa Impact Condensed

Help   Close

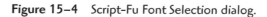

Figure 15–4   Script-Fu Font Selection dialog.

To create my logo, I'm going to choose a font on my system called Georgia Bold (not sure why, but suddenly I'm hearing Ray Charles music in my head). You may choose whatever you like. When you have decided on a font, click OK. Then click OK again, this time in the Script-Fu:Logos/Cool Metal window. The result should be something similar to my own logo in Figure 15-5.

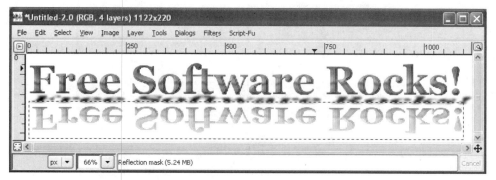

Figure 15–5 Just like that! A professional-looking logo.

If you don't like the results, close the image by clicking the Close button in the corner (usually an X unless you have changed your desktop theme or style). A warning box pops up, telling you that changes have been made and that perhaps you might want to save your work (more on that in a moment). Your options are Save, Don't Save, and Cancel. Click Don't Save and it goes away. Then start over with another logo. You might try changing the background color or the gradient this time. You might even want to try a different type of logo altogether.

Saving and Opening Your Work

It is time to preserve your masterpiece. It's also a good time to have another look at the image window, in this case, your logo. Every image created in the GIMP has a menu bar across the top labeled File, Edit, Select, View, and so on. These menus can also be called up by right-clicking anywhere on the image. To save your work, click the File menu, and then select Save As. The Save Image dialog appears (see Figure 15-6).

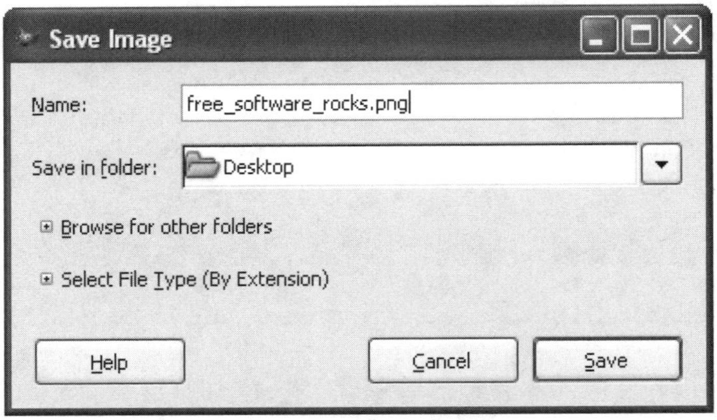

Figure 15–6   It's time to save your creation.

Notice the plus sign beside the words Select File Type (by Extension). If you already know that you want to save your image as a JPG or a TIF file (or any number of formats), you can simply add it to the file name. The GIMP can figure it out for you. If you prefer to see a list of available formats, click the plus sign and the Save Image dialog changes to display the various formats supported by the GIMP. There's also a plus sign beside the label Browse for Other Folders. By default, the GIMP uses the current folder to save your work. To choose another directory, click the plus sign and a more comprehensive navigation dialog appears (see Figure 15-7).

When you have entered your file name and selected a file type, click OK, and you are done. Opening a file is similar. From the GIMP toolbox menu bar, select Open (or use the <Ctrl+O> shortcut) to bring up the Load Image dialog. The difference between this and the Save Image dialog is that when you click a file name, you can also click Generate Preview to display a small thumbnail preview in the Open Image dialog.

Printing Your Masterpiece

You've created a masterpiece. You are infinitely proud of it, and you want to share it with your friends, who, alas, are not connected to the Internet. It's time to print your image and send it to them the old-fashioned, snail-mail way.

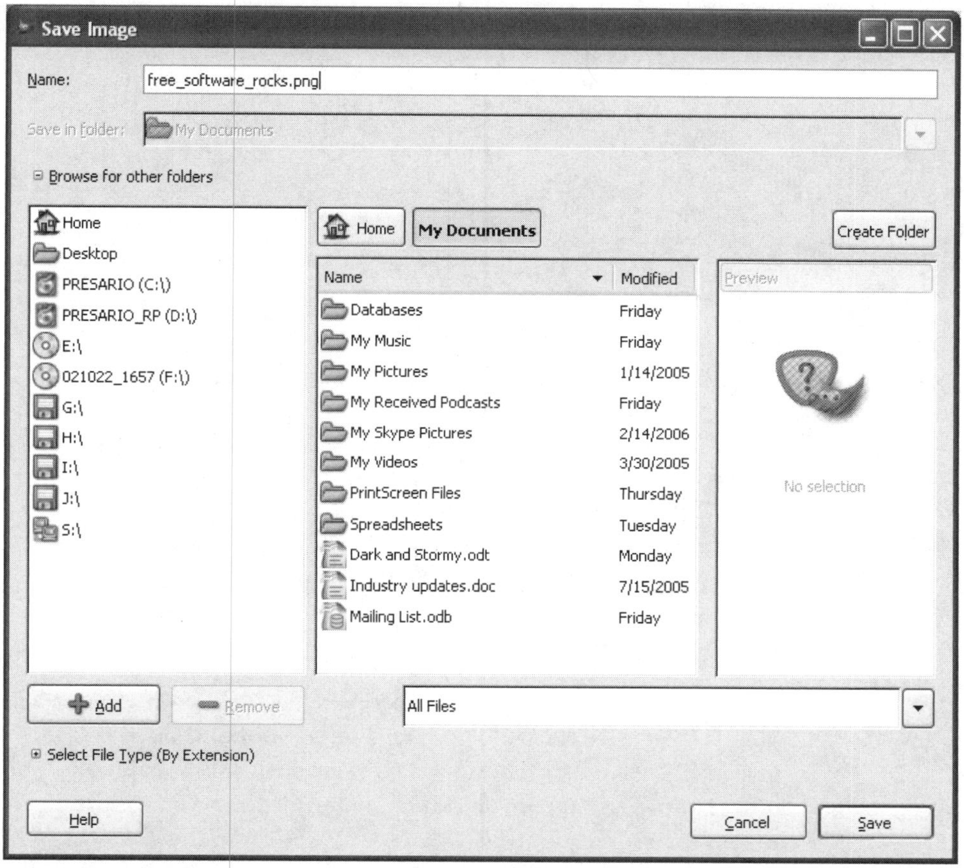

Figure 15–7 A more comprehensive folder navigation dialog to save your work.

Okay, perhaps you aren't feeling quite that sharing, but there are times when you want to print the results of your work. Simply click File on the image menu bar, and select Print (you can right-click your image, if you prefer). A Print dialog appears (see Figure 15-8), from which you can specify a number of print options, including, of course, which printer you would like to use.

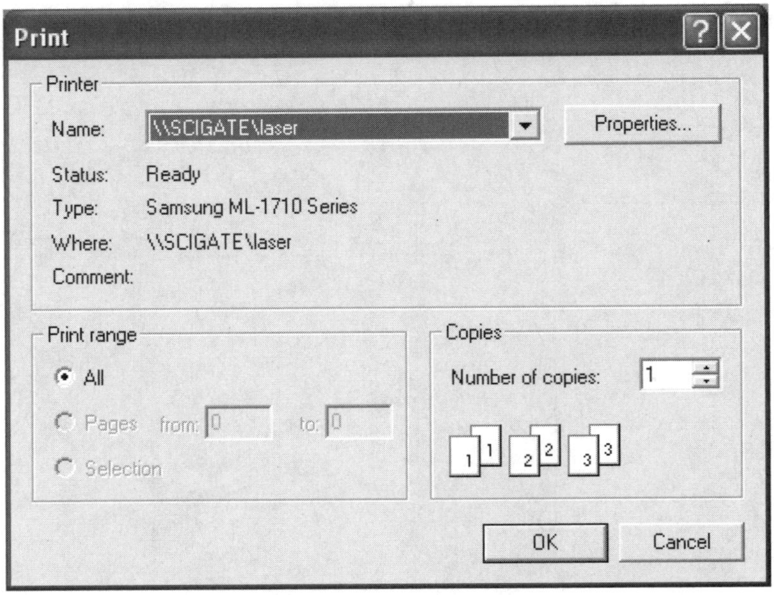

Print   [?] [X]

Printer

Name: \\SCIGATE\laser   ▼   Properties...

Status: Ready
Type: Samsung ML-1710 Series
Where: \\SCIGATE\laser
Comment:

Print range

⦿ All

○ Pages from: 0   to: 0

○ Selection

Copies

Number of copies: 1 ⬍

[OK]   [Cancel]

Figure 15–8   Time to print your masterpiece.

Quick GIMP Trick Want to take a screenshot and open it up to edit in the GIMP? It's easy. Click File on the GIMP toolbox menu bar, move to Acquire, and click Screen Shot. The image size is the same as your screen (e.g., 1024 × 768). Because the GIMP is in the screen shot you take, you may want to minimize it before capturing the image. To make that possible, select an appropriate time delay—let's say five seconds—from the Screen Shot dialog that appears. Minimize the windows you don't want to see, and then wait. After the capture completes, a GIMP image window appears where you can make your modifications.

The Acquire function doesn't limit you to the whole screen. When the Screen Shot dialog appears, you have the option of capturing the entire screen, or a single window. Just click the appropriate radio button. The window capture includes the borders for that window and all its decorations.

Tools, Tools, and More Tools

Now that we've had some fun and created some *true art*, it's time to find out what all those icons in the GIMP toolbox do. Before we do this, however, we should look at those two boxes at the bottom of the toolbox because what they offer affects what the icons do.

The block on the right is the color menu (see Figure 15-9). It gives you quick and easy access to foreground and background colors. The black and white squares on the left can be changed to other colors by double-clicking one or the other. If you click the arrow between the two, you switch between foreground and background colors.

Figure 15–9 The multifunction color, brushes, pattern, and gradient menu.

The box to the right is a quick dialog menu and really consists of three different tools: a brush selector, a pattern selector, and a gradient selector. Click any of them to bring up the list of choices each provides. Figure 15-10 shows the Brushes dialog. You may recall from the introduction to this section that there was a Layers, Channels, and Paths dialog in addition to the main GIMP toolbox. At the bottom of that window was the Brushes dialog (as well as Gradients and Patterns). If you left that window open, the brushes selection is still there.

If you select a different gradient, pattern, or brush from the resulting menus, you also can see them change on the dialog menu at the bottom of the GIMP toolbox. This gives you a quick visual feedback on what brush, pattern, or gradient is active at the moment.

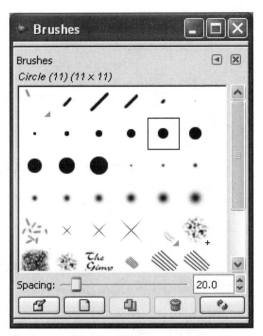

Figure 15–10   The Brushes dialog, on its own.

Now, on to the Tool Icons

In the next few pages, I'm going to cover the GIMP's tools one by one, a row at a time. Each row has six tools, except for the last, which has five. I make a point of mentioning this because this is the default layout. If you decide to resize the GIMP toolbox by dragging one of the sides out, the toolbox widens but the number of tools per row increases as well, so you could have seven tools if you want. The reverse is true should you decide to shrink the width of the GIMP toolbox.

Start by moving your mouse over the various icons, pausing over each one. Tooltips appear, telling you what tool each of the icons represents (I'll go over these in a moment). If you click any of these icons, the window below the toolbox changes to present you with that tool's option. For instance, a new window appears, providing you with that tool's options, as with the Flip tool in Figure 15-11.

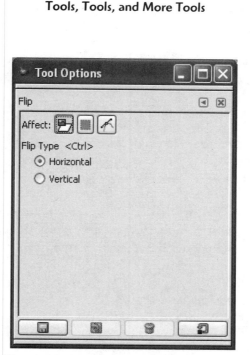

Figure 15–11　Tool Options dialog, in
this case for the Flip tool.

 Note　If you chose to separate the tool options from the GIMP
toolbox, you need to double-click (rather than single-click) the
tool to bring up its options dialog.

So what are all those icons for? An excellent question. Let's look at them
again, one row at a time, starting with—you guessed it—the first row (see
Figure 15-12).

Figure 15–12　First icon group.

The first icon, represented by a dotted rectangle, lets you select a
rectangular area. Just hold down the left mouse button at whatever point
you choose for a starting corner, and drag it across your image. A dotted line

indicates the area you've selected. If you hold down the <Shift> key at the same time as the left mouse button, your selections are always perfect squares.

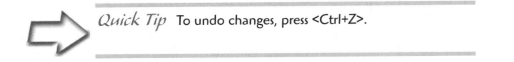

Quick Tip To undo changes, press <Ctrl+Z>.

The dotted circle icon next to it is much the same except that it selects circular or elliptical area. Similar to the rectangular selection, you can hold down the <Shift> key along with the left mouse button to select only perfect circles.

Next, we have the Lasso tool. This is another selection tool, but this one lets you select irregular or hand-drawn regions. Hold down the left mouse button and draw your selection around the object.

Quick Tip When you have selected an area on an image, you can right-click, move your mouse cursor over the Edit menu, and select Cut or Copy. You can then Paste your selection back to another part of the image.

Then comes the magic wand. This is a strange tool to get used to. It selects an area by analyzing the colored pixels wherever you click. Holding the down the <Shift> key lets you select multiple areas. This is a very useful tool but also a little tricky. Double-click the icon to change the sensitivity.

Next, it's over to the Color Selector tool. Using the color selector feels a bit like the magic wand (previously) but the functionality is based on color rather than a single area at a time. Select the color selector, click any colored area, and *all* areas matching this color are selected.

Finally, we wrap up this row with another selection tool, the so-called intelligent-scissors. You select an area by clicking around it. This tool follows curved lines around an object. It does so by concentrating on areas of similar contrast or color. Simply click around the perimeter of the area you want to select and watch the lines magically draw themselves. When you join the last dot, click inside the area to select it.

That wraps it up for the first row of tools. It's time to look at the next set (see Figure 15-13).

Figure 15–13 *Second icon group.*

The first icon in this row is the Bezier tool (also known as the Path tool), which takes some getting used to. After you get used to it, however, you'll be impressed with the flexibility it affords you in selecting both straight and curved areas. Click a point outside the area you want to select, and it creates an anchor point. Click again a little further along your outline, and you get new anchor points with a straight line connecting to the original. Click and drag an existing anchor point, and a bar appears with control boxes on either end. You can then grab those control points and drag or rotate them to modify the straight line between the points. After you have joined the final point, look at your tool options (the pane below the GIMP toolbox) and click the Create Selection from Path button. You'll see an animated dotted line, as with the other selection tools.

The second icon looks like an eyedropper. This is the color picker. Choosing an exact color can be difficult (if you need to get the tone just right), but if the color you want is on your existing image, click that spot, and you've got it (your default active color changes).

The magnifying glass does exactly what you expect it to. Click an area of the screen to zoom in. Double-click the icon to reverse the zoom. This doesn't actually scale the image; it just changes your view of things. Zoom is normally used to make it easier to work on a small area of the image.

On to the calipers, or Measuring tool. This doesn't actually change anything on your image but reports measurements. Click a starting point on the image, and then drag the mouse pointer to another part of the image. Now look at the bottom of your image window. You see the distance in pixels from your starting location to where you let go of the mouse pointer. The angle of the line also is displayed.

The fifth icon on the second row looks like a cross with arrows pointing in all directions. This is the Move tool. It is really quite simple. Click the tool, grab the selected area on the screen, and move it to where you want. If you haven't selected an area, you can move the entire image in the window.

Next, take a look at the knife icon—the Crop tool. If you start working with digital photography in a big way, this is one tool you truly want to get to know. I use the Crop tool all the time when I am trying to get a small part of a larger image. It is what I used to separate the rows of icons from the GIMP toolbox image I captured. Click a part of the screen, drag it to encompass the area you want to select. The space around your selection darkens (see Figure 15-14).

Figure 15–14   When cropping an image, the selected area is emphasized by a darkening around the rest of the image.

Now, click the Crop button when are satisfied with your selection. You can also fine-tune the settings (X and Y position, etc.) at this time.

And just like that, it's time to look at row three (see Figure 15-15).

Figure 15–15   The third icon row.

On the left, in the first position, you have the Rotate tool. Click an image (or a selection), and small square handles appear at the corners of your selection. Grab one of these handles (or points), drag the mouse, and the selection rotates. When you have it in a position you like, click Rotate on the pop-up window that appears. The image locks into place.

The second icon, the Scale tool, is very similar to the Rotate tool. Instead of rotating the selected area, you drag the points to resize the selected area. As previously, a pop-up window appears so that you can lock your changes. It's also the place to manually enter your changes if you would like finer control than dragging the mouse offers.

The Shear tool is the third on this row, and once again, it acts on a previously selected area. This one looks a lot like the last two in terms of functionality, but the effect is more like taking two sides of an object and stretching them diagonally in opposite directions. A square becomes a parallelogram, which gets longer and thinner as you continue to stretch the image. When you're happy with the changes, click the Shear button on the pop-up dialog.

In the fourth position, we have the Perspective tool. This is one of those that you almost have to try out to understand, but let me try to describe it. Remember your grade school art classes when you first learned about perspective? A road leading off into the distance compresses to a single point in the distance. With the Perspective tool, you can take a selected area and pull the points in whatever direction you want to create the perspective effect. Do that with a person's head and the top of her head comes together in a sharp little point. As with the last three tools, there's a pop-up where you lock in your changes. Just click Transform.

Next in line is the Flip tool. By default, it flips the image horizontally. The tool option, in the lower half of the GIMP toolbox, has a check box so that you can flip vertically instead.

Tip Remember that if you close the Tool Options below the GIMP toolbox, you can always double-click a tool to bring it up.

The next icon is the Text tool. That's what the big T signifies. Click your image, and the GIMP Text Editor appears. This is where you enter your text. In your tools option is the font selector; the same one that you used for your logo will appear. Select a font style, size, and color, and the changes are visible in the image. This makes it easy to change the look and feel on-the-fly. Type in your text in the Preview section, and click OK. Where the text appears on the screen, the Move tool is activated, allowing you to place the text accurately. The color of the text is your current foreground color.

And now . . . row 4 (see Figure 15-16)!

Figure 15–16   Row 4 icons.

We start this row with the paint can. This is the Fill tool. It can fill a selected area not only with a chosen color but with a pattern as well. To choose between color and pattern fill, double-click the icon to bring up its menu.

The second item on this line is the Gradient Fill tool. Start by selecting an area on your image, and then switch to this tool. Now click a spot inside your selected area and drag with the tool. The current gradient style fills that area. This is one of those things you almost need to try in order to understand what I mean.

Quick Tip Would you like a blank canvas right about now? Click File on the GIMP toolbox menu bar and select New. Those who like using the keyboard can just press <Ctrl+N>.

The third icon of this group looks like a pencil. In fact, this and the next three buttons all work with a brush selection (the bottom right box). This pencil, as with a real pencil, is used to draw lines with sharply defined edges. Try drawing on your image with the different types to get an idea of what each brush type offers.

The next icon is the paintbrush. The difference between it and the pencil is that the brush has softer, less starkly defined edges to the strokes. Double-click the icon to bring up the paintbrush's menu and try both the Fade Out and Gradient options for something different.

If the next icon looks like an eraser, that's no accident. The shape of the eraser is also controlled by the current brush type, size, and style. Here's something kind of fun to try. Double-click the icon to bring up its menu, and then change the Opacity to something like 50 percent. Then start erasing again.

Now, it's on to the Airbrush tool. Just like a real airbrush, you can change the pressure to achieve different results. Hold it down longer in one spot and you get a darker application of color.

And now, may I introduce the fifth and final row of icons (see Figure 15-17)?

Figure 15–17   The fifth row is primarily drawing tools.

The first tool on this line is another drawing tool: the Pen or Ink tool. Double-clicking the icon brings up a menu that lets you select the tip style and shape, as well as the virtual tilt of the pen. The idea is to mimic the effect of writing with a fountain pen.

Next to the pen is the Clone tool (the icon looks a bit like a rubber stamp). Sheep? No problem! We can even clone humans. Okay, that's a bit over the top. Where the Clone tool comes in handy is during touch-ups of photographs. Open an image, hold down the <Ctrl> key, and press the left mouse button over a portion of the image—the tool changes to a crosshair. Let go of both the mouse button and the <Ctrl> key. This is your starting area for cloning. Now, move to another part of the screen, click, and start moving your mouse button (the shape of the area uncovered is controlled by the brush type). As you paint at this new location, you'll notice that you are recreating that portion of the image where you indicated with the <Ctrl+mouse-click> combination. Start with someone's head or body, and you can have twins on the screen.

The droplet you see in the third position represents the Convolver tool. Use it to blur or sharpen parts of an image. You switch between the two operations by selecting the mode in the tool options below the toolbox, or by double-clicking the icon. Change the rate to make the effect more pronounced.

Quick GIMP Trick When you need to zoom in on an image to get some fine work done, just press the plus sign on your keyboard. If you zoom in enough though, it can get difficult to navigate the larger image. You wind up trying to adjust the scrollbars to locate the area you want. Instead, click the little crosshair icon in the bottom-right side of the image editor window. A smaller version of your image window appears with a target area outline that you can move to where you want it.

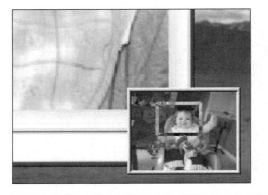

On to the Finger, or the Smudge tool. Pretend that you are painting. You press your finger on the wet paint and move it around. The Smudge tool has exactly the same effect on your virtual canvas or, at the very least, a similar effect.

Finally, the Dodge and Burn tool looks like a stick-pin, but those who have worked in a darkroom might recognize it for something different—a stick with an opaque circle on the end of it. It is used to adjust the brightness or shade of various parts of an image (a photograph might have been partly overexposed).

Touching Up Photographs

I've mentioned the idea of touching up photographs on a few occasions while I discussed the tools. The GIMP is a wonderful tool for this and more than just a little fun. One of the most common functions I use is changing the light levels on photographs, automagically and instantly. After all, light levels are rarely perfect unless you are a professional photographer and paying attention to every shot. Here's what I do.

Click Image on the Layers menu bar (or right-click the image to bring up the menu), move to the Colors submenu, then select Levels. You should see a window like the one in Figure 15-18. Notice the Auto button? That's where the magic is. I've found that more often than not, you can get a nice, dependable reset of levels just by doing this simple operation.

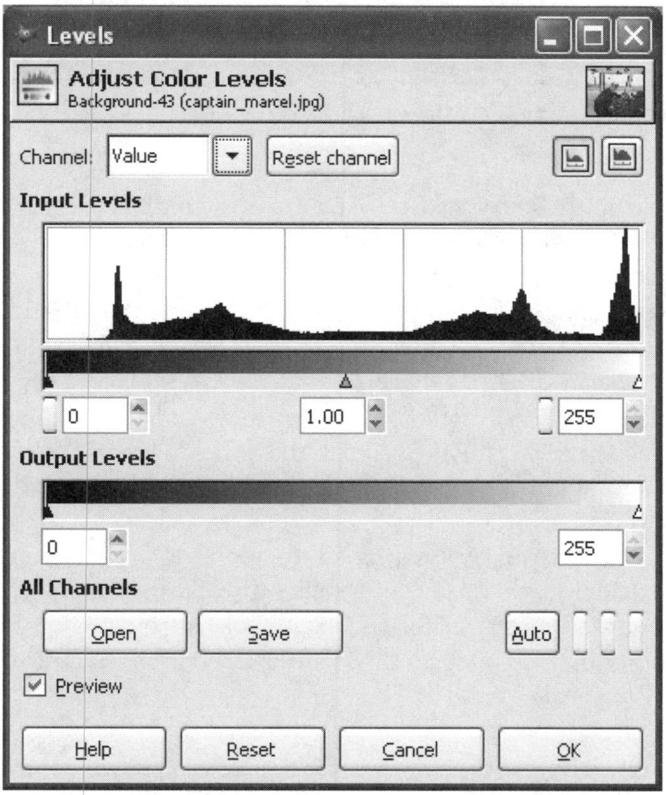

Figure 15–18   Adjusting levels with the GIMP.

Other very common adjustments you will make to your photos, particularly scanned images, are contrast and brightness. You can find this dialog in much the same place as Levels. Click Layers on the menu bar, then Colors, and finally Brightness-Contrast. To change one or the other, just pull the appropriate slider to the left or right (see Figure 15-19).

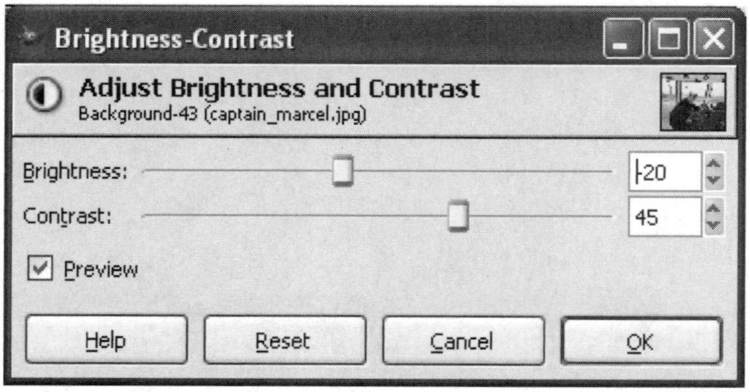

Figure 15–19   To adjust brightness or contrast, just pull the sliders.

There are also those things that are *just plain fun* to do. For instance, open an image in the GIMP, perhaps one you scanned in earlier. If you don't have something handy, grab an image from a Web site. This is just something to play with. Now, choose Filters from the image menu bar. A submenu opens with even more options. You might want to detach this menu—you'll certainly want to play with what is there.

Try FlareFX under the Light Effects menu. If you've ever taken a flash picture through a window, you'll recognize this effect. Then, try Emboss under the Distorts submenu. The effect is that of a metal-embossed picture (see Figure 15-20).

Take some time to try the various filter options. When you are finished there, right-click a fresh image and select the Script-Fu menu. There are other interesting effects available here as well, such as Clothify under the Alchemy submenu. Your image will look as though it has been transferred to a piece of cloth.

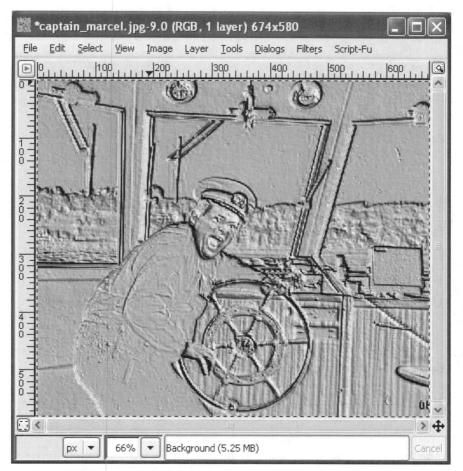

Figure 15–20 Playing with the Emboss filter.

So What Is Script-Fu?

Although it sounds like a strange form of martial arts, Script-Fu is in fact a scripting language that is part of the GIMP. With it, you can create scripts that automate a number of repetitive tasks to create desirable effects. When you created your logo, you might have noticed that a number of things were happening as it was being created. Try another logo and watch carefully what is happening. These steps are part of a Script-Fu script.

The GIMP comes with a number of Script-Fu scripts, and these are used for much more than just creating logos. Click Xtns on the GIMP toolbox, and scroll down to the Script-Fu menu. In addition to logos, you see options for creating buttons (for Web pages), custom brushes, patterns, and more. Play. Experiment. Don't be afraid.

Open an image. Then, right-click that image and scroll down to the Script-Fu part of the menu. Another menu drops down with selections such as Alchemy, Decore, Render, and so on. These are all precreated effects that ordinarily require many repetitive steps. Script-Fu is very much like a command script, where one command follows another. In this case, the commands just happen to be graphical transformations.

 Tip   Now that you are feeling more comfortable with the GIMP, you might want to check out the GUG (GIMP User Group) Web site's list of GIMP tutorials at `http://gug.sunsite.dk/ ?page=tutorials`.

You Mentioned Gimpshop?

Yes, I did. At the beginning of this chapter, I mentioned that there was a version of the GIMP that aimed to make it easier for those who are already familiar with Adobe Photoshop to work with the GIMP. Scot Moschella's Gimpshop is a *hack* of the GIMP interface so that the menus are rearranged to be more in line with those in Photoshop. That way, seasoned Photoshop users can use the menu options they are used to. Let me give an example.

If you want to rotate an image 90 degrees in the GIMP, you click Image on the menu, then Transform, then Rotate 90. In Photoshop, and in Gimpshop, you click Edit, then Transform, then Rotate 90. A few pages back, I showed you how to adjust light levels in the GIMP by clicking Layer on the menu bar, then Colors, then Levels. In Photoshop, and again in Gimpshop, you click Image, then Adjustments, then Levels. See what I mean? This is all well and good, but if you aren't already used to working with Adobe Photoshop, the benefits of running Gimpshop instead of the official GIMP are pretty much moot.

Now, before you run off and install Gimpshop, I should let you know that the Gimpshop does tend to run slightly behind the official GIMP software. Scot does a fantastic job with Gimpshop, but his modifications have to be made after the GIMP releases its product. I'm not talking about a huge delay here, but if you need features that are available only in the latest and greatest GIMP, you may have to wait a little before you can have those features included in Gimpshop.

Resources

GIMP

http://www.gimp.org

GUG (GIMP User Group) Tutorials

http://gug.sunsite.dk/?page=tutorials

Plastic Bugs, Home of Gimpshop

http://plasticbugs.com/?page_id=294

16

7-Zip Is Decompression Heaven

File compression tools go back a long way in the PC world, from the DOS-based PKZIP to the WinZip tools so common on people's computers today. Any time you've received (or downloaded) a file with a `.zip` extension, you have had to deal with compressed files. Compression utilities are also a great idea when you need to bundle up a collection of digital pictures that you want to send to your friends or family. Instead of sending a number of attached images, which can make for huge emails and create long download waits on the receiving end, you can also use compression tools to package them all up into a smaller, more compact bundle.

Although WinZip is a great tool, it's also a commercial package and there are other excellent choices that do the job very nicely. One of these is 7-Zip. This package supports the old classic ZIP compression as well as many others including Windows CAB files, RAR, ARJ, TAR, GZIP, and more. It can even uncompress Linux RPM and DEB binary packages. 7-Zip also has its own native format that increases classic ZIP compression even more.

Note Those of you who run Windows XP may know that XP already has a ZIP utility built-in and, as such, you may question the need for another tool. Nevertheless, 7-Zip should still be part of your system toolkit. The built-in ZIP file support in Windows XP is very limited in the file types it can open. It is also limited in that the compression ratio is lower than what 7-Zip can offer and it is nowhere near as flexible.

Installation and Setup

Start by visiting the 7-Zip Web site at `www.7-zip.org` and download the latest edition (or check the included disk) and you are almost ready. There isn't much to installing 7-Zip. Just double-click the executable installation file and you are almost finished. The program confirms the installation folder (accept the default unless you have good reason to do otherwise) and click Next.

The process takes a few seconds, after which the installation is complete. Click Finish and that's it.

Touring the Interface

To start 7-Zip, click Start, Programs, 7-Zip, and select 7-Zip File Manager. The program window appears with a standard menu bar across the top and a handful of quick access buttons below that (see Figure 16-1). The lower part of the program window is used for browsing to and listing files. There's a quick location bar where you can enter a pathname and a larger browser section below that. On first use, 7-Zip opens to a clean interface with just two locations listed, Computer and Network. Double-click either of these and you can navigate your local system or network-connected resources to which you have access.

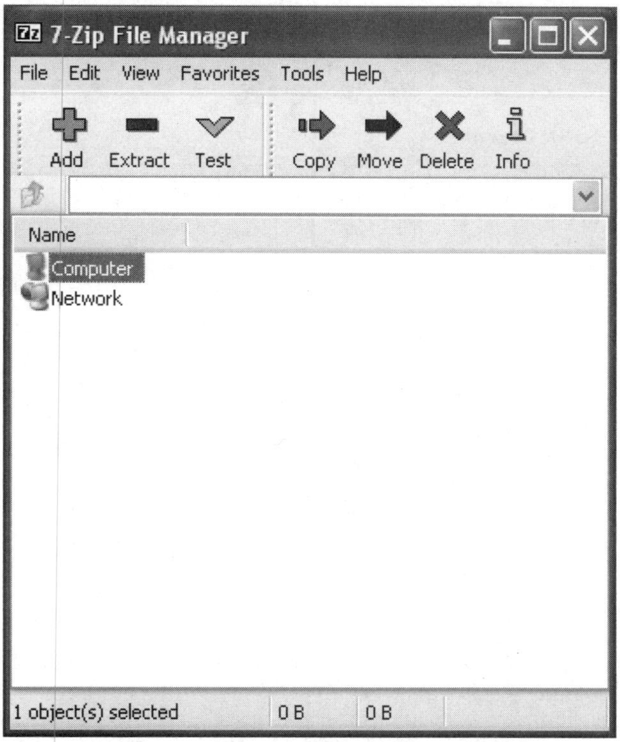

Figure 16–1   On first use, 7-Zip behaves more like a
simple file manager than a compression program.

I'll tell you about extracting and creating archives shortly, but for now I
want to take a little side trip to the Tools menu and the issue of associating file
types with 7-Zip. After installing enough Windows applications, you've probably noticed that they tend to immediately take control of whatever file formats they are built for. Not so with 7-Zip. If you want this to become your
default compression and decompression tool, you must tell it to do so. Start
by clicking Tools on the menu bar and then select Options. A five-tabbed
window appears with the System tab preselected (see Figure 16-2).

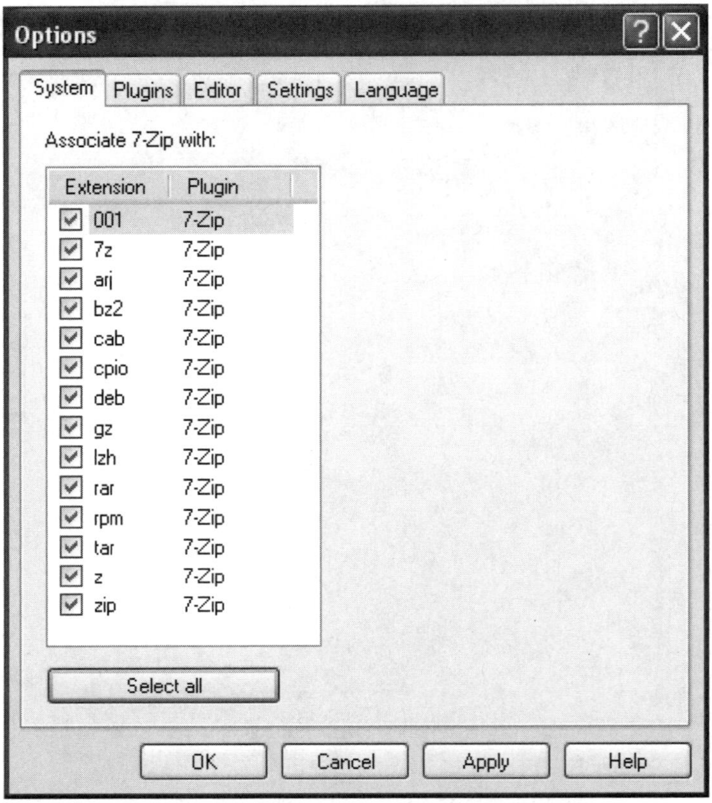

Figure 16–2   Making 7-Zip your default archive application.

You see a table labeled Associate 7-Zip With and below that, a list of archive formats with check boxes to the left of each format and extension (e.g., `zip`, `bzip2`, `rar`, etc.). Click each box to select a format or if you prefer, just click the Select All button at the bottom of the list to make 7-Zip your default application for opening and creating archives. This means that if you double-click a file that has any of these extensions, the 7-Zip application automatically starts. When you are finished, click OK to close the Options dialog.

On that note, let's take a look at what it takes to open and extract files from an archive.

Unpacking a File

There are actually two ways to do this, both somewhat similar. The first choice is to start 7-Zip and use the tool to navigate to the archive file's location. Similarly, you can use Windows Explorer to locate a file. Right-click that file and a pop-up menu appears with 7-Zip as one of the entries. Below that entry, you see several options. Click Extract Files and the Extract dialog appears (see Figure 16-3).

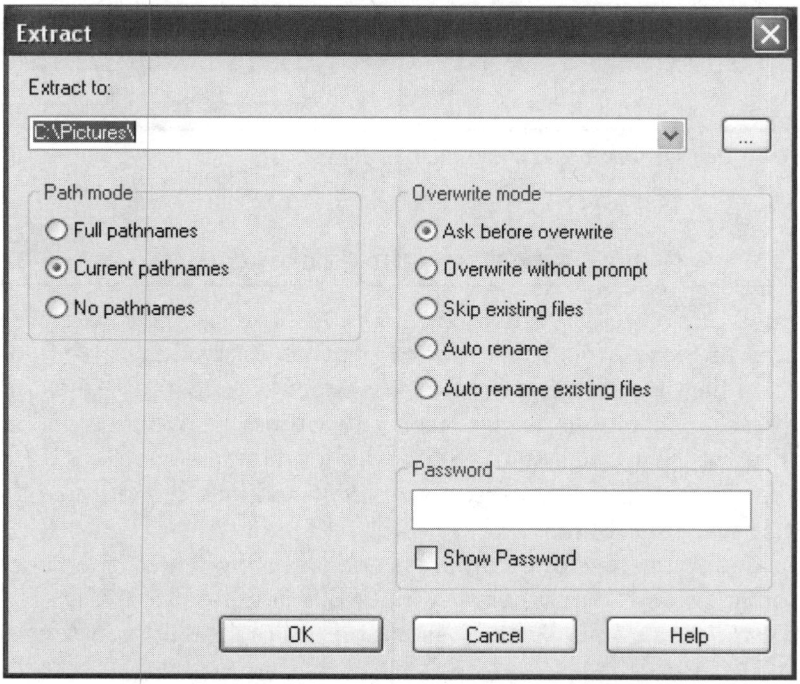

Figure 16–3 When extracting a file, select a folder into which you would like the files and folders to appear.

The second method is very similar but it does require that you have configured 7-Zip to be your default compression utility (as explained earlier). First, locate an archive with the Windows Explorer file manager or your Web browser (e.g., Firefox). Double-click the file and 7-Zip opens with a list of all the files (and folders) in the archive displayed.

At this point, you haven't yet extracted anything, so go ahead and select what you want or press <Ctrl+A> to select everything. Now, click the OK button and a small Copy dialog appears, asking for a folder name (see Figure 16-4).

Figure 16–4   Where would you like these files copied to?

Creating an Archive

Nine times out of ten, we use compression tools like this to extract files from archives that people send us or to uncompress packages we find on the Internet. The other side, however, is equally important—making compressed packages of our files to send to others. Anyone who has ever received a massive email with a large attachment or a collection of cute photos has wished that the person sending it had first compressed the photos into a nice, small bundle.

You can also use 7-Zip to compress and archive old files, then back them up by copying them to another system or burning them to a CD. The compressed data is as good as the original and it can take up substantially less room.

Pack Up Your Data

Here is the easiest way to create an archive. Navigate to the directory of your choice and select any number of files you want to add to your bundle. You do this using the classic Windows select keystrokes. To select a series of files, click the first file and then hold down the <Shift key> and click the last file. All files in between are selected. You can also hold down the <Ctrl> key to select individual files. You can even select folders full of files—sometimes this is the easiest approach.

After you have made your selection, click the Add button (it's the one with the big green plus sign) and the Add to Archive dialog appears (see Figure 16-5).

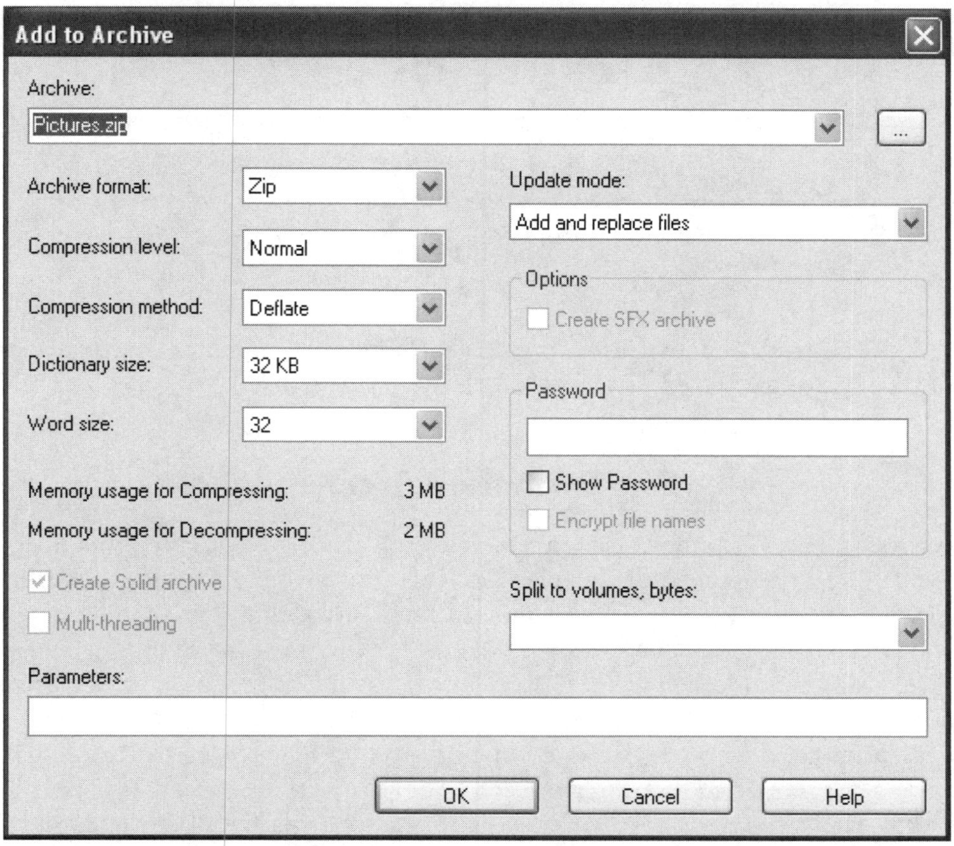

Figure 16–5   Creating an archive isn't difficult, but you do have a lot of flexibility in the result.

There are several things here worth taking note of. The first and most obvious is the name of the archive. By default, this is autogenerated based on the folder name, but you can change this to anything you want.

When you click OK, the archive is created for you. This can take a few seconds to a few minutes or more depending on the number and size of files you chose to include in your archive. As the process ticks along, a progress bar keeps you abreast of the program's work as well as time remaining (see Figure 16-6).

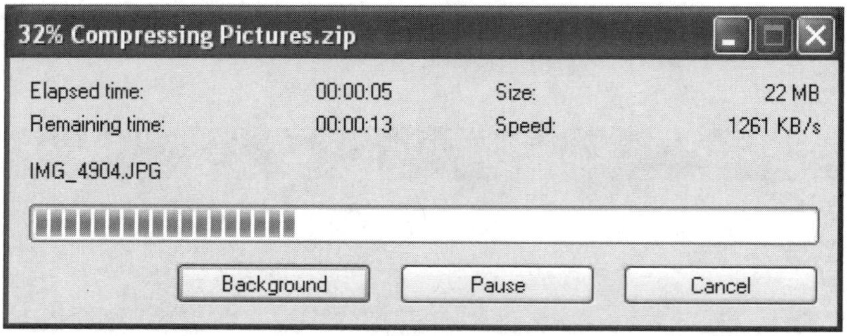

Figure 16–6   As the archive is created, a progress bar keeps you informed as to time remaining.

After a few seconds (or minutes), your archive is ready for use, whether that be backing up to a CD or emailing to a friend or colleague.

Self-Extracting Archives

As you can see, you don't have to do a lot of work to create an archive. For the most part, and for most people you deal with, a simple ZIP file is probably all you need. Nevertheless, 7-Zip can do some amazing things with archives, and we should take a moment to look at these before we move on.

Let's create another archive, something that might require a little discretion on the part of the sender and the receiver—some pictures from the office Christmas party perhaps. Start by identifying and selecting the pictures you want as described in the previous section. Then, click the green Add button to get things rolling. Look at Figure 16-7 and you see that I've done things quite differently this time. Some of those changes need a little explanation.

I suppose the most obvious thing here is the name of the archive, which has an .exe extension. This archive is self-extracting and does not require that the person you are sending it to has a copy of 7-Zip (or any kind of compression/decompression program). To create a self-extracting file, you check the Create SFX Archive box. You'll find it on the right half of the Add to Archive window.

Next, and perhaps most important, is the Archive Format. 7-Zip supports a dizzying number of compression formats when it comes to opening files, but you can only create three different types of compressed files. These are 7-Zip's native file format (.7z), the well known ZIP format, and TAR. Users coming from the Linux or UNIX world are likely familiar with TAR. To create the self-extracting archive, however, you must use the native 7-Zip format, so this is a must.

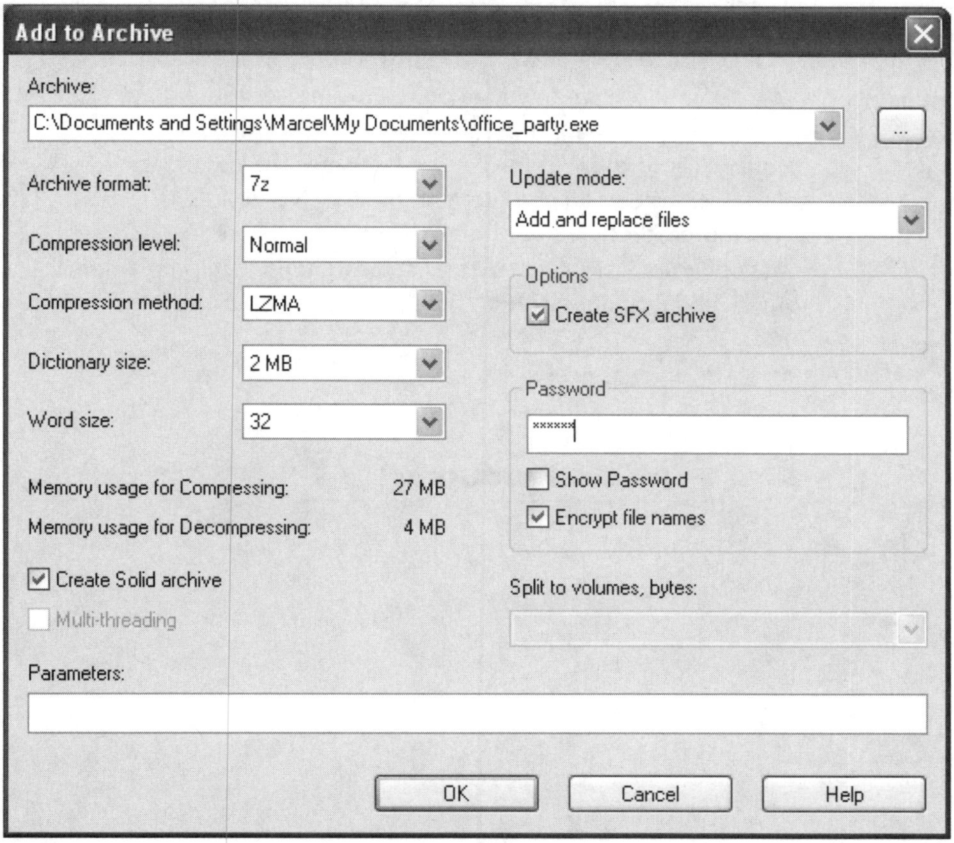

Figure 16–7   7-Zip makes it possible to create special self-extracting, encrypted archives.

Finally, you may want to encrypt the file names in your archive and password-protect the whole thing. To do that, look at the Password section on the right. Check the Encrypt File Names box and enter a password in the field provided. One interesting, and strange, setting is the Show Password check box. If you leave the box unchecked, your password is echoed as stars. If you check it, the password is visible.

Click OK and your archive is generated with a progress bar (similar to the one in Figure 16-7) listing files and displaying the time left to completion. After the process is completed, you can give the executable to whomever you choose. A copy of 7-Zip isn't required to extract the file, but your recipient does, of course, need the password to extract the file.

> *Tip* 7-Zip also comes with a command-line version. In fact, it comes with two. The first program, `7z.exe`, requires some of the components of the Windows 7-Zip package. The second program, `7za.exe`, is a completely standalone version. It supports less compression types, but does cover those you are likely to use (.7z, .zip, .gzip, .tar, .Z, and .bz2). You can find these programs in your 7-Zip installation folder, usually `C:\Program Files\7-Zip`.

Resources

7-Zip

http://www.7-zip.org

17

Spybot: Protecting You from Spyware

Ah, spyware ... it almost makes you long for the good old days when we only had to worry about viruses on our PCs. Spyware programs come in many flavors. Some are more or less benign, popping up rather annoying ads while you are trying to get your job done. These programs are generally referred to as adware. Other programs are there to cause damage, or use your PC's resources to launch attacks on other systems. This is malware. Finally, we have the real spyware, programs that literally spy on your activities, capturing private information such as your credit card numbers, bank balances, and passwords, passing it on to a remote location where your identity (and funds) can be put to criminal uses.

How did this stuff get on your PC? Some of it came through holes in your Web browser or email package. Some of the spyware programs, believe it or not, were things you asked to have installed on your computer.

"Impossible," you say. "I would never agree to something like that."

Some of the free programs you encounter while surfing the Net sound like a great deal until you discover that there are strings attached. These strings generally come in the form of an additional program that gets installed along with the free software listed. The adware usually monitors your surfing activities while building a profile on you so that the program can serve up advertising. This advertising is the free software company's way of making money. In most cases, people agree to having the adware installed when they click OK to install the package. That's why it's always good to read the license agreement before you install.

 Note None of the programs covered in this book include spyware, malware, or adware. You are getting great free software supported by the developers themselves or their companies. So, relax—you're saving money and getting fantastic free software.

Getting Started with Spybot

When you first start Spybot, you get a little message alerting you to the fact that if you remove the spyware, you don't have access to any of the positive benefits those programs may have offered you (see Figure 17-1). Because that is pretty much the idea, you can click OK to continue. You may also want to click the Don't Show This Message Again check box to avail yourself of future messages.

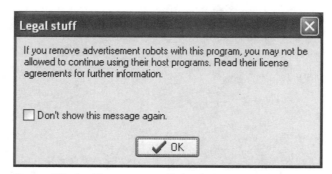

Figure 17–1   There are implications to removing spyware.

Spybot's main window is where you normally start (see Figure 17-2). The window itself is divided into two panes. To the left is a navigation bar with icons that quickly direct you to Spybot's main functions. The larger pane to the right is where you see details of the various actions selected via the navigation bar. These functions are Search and Destroy, Recovery, Immunize, Update, and Donations.

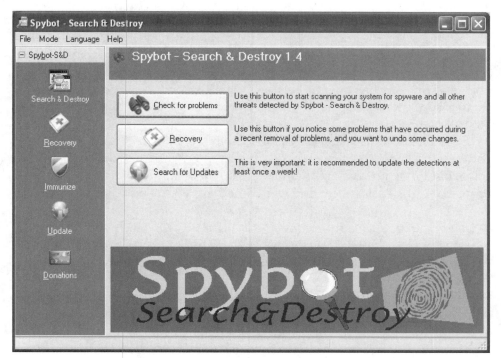

Figure 17–2   Starting in Spybot's main window.

Tip I'll cover each function as I go along, but I'll touch briefly on the Donations button. As with many projects of this type, the author makes no money selling the product, nor asks for any. If you don't want to pay for the product, that's fine too. You still get the full, uncrippled version of Spybot regardless. However, if you find the product useful and you'd like to help by sparing a few dollars, click the Donations button. The money is used to help play for Web site hosting and to further develop Spybot.

The Recovery function is there so that you can undo changes. When you started Spybot, there was a message warning you that blocking or uninstalling some of these programs would make them unavailable.

Keeping Up-to-Date

Just as computer viruses seem to evolve, presenting us with new strains on a regular basis, the same occurs with spyware. Much as we might despise these uninvited guests, it's important to understand that for the spyware developers, this is business. Those annoying pop-ups are a means of generating revenue. The disruptive reminders that you might want to look at "a black and gold vibrating dog hair vacuum!" are yet another way of generating sales. For that reason, the developers of spyware aren't going to sit idly by and let you block their product.

Because spyware doesn't stand still, Spybot provides regular updates to its database of spyware products. You could jump right in and let Spybot do its thing, but I'm going to recommend that you make sure your copy of Spybot is up-to-date. It's easy to do, and it is something you need to do on a regular basis.

From Spybot's main window (see Figure 17-2), click the Search for Updates button. You can also click the Update button on the left. Both get you to where you want to be. A moment later, the Update window appears (see Figure 17-3).

In the lower half of Spybot's main window, you see a list of items for which there is an update. Some items are checked on by default, but you may want to select others from the list. The most important one is, of course, the Detection rules (toward the top of the list). When you are ready, click the Download Updates button to start the process. A status window appears to provide you with a graphical indication of the download progress (see Figure 17-4).

After your system has the latest and greatest signatures, Spybot restarts. Armed with a recent database of spyware, it's time to say goodbye to your unwanted visitors.

Spybot - Search & Destroy

File   Mode   Language   Help

Spybot-S&D

Search & Destroy

Recovery

Immunize

Update

Donations

↑ Update
Get the newest threat recognition rules online.

🌐 Search for Updates   📷 Safer Networking #3 (Europe)   ▼

🌐 Download Updates   📄 Show Log   ❓ Help

Use this option if you want to know if there is a new version of SpyBot - Search & Destroy, and what's new about it.

This program will not send any information about your computer to me or anyone else! It will just load and display a textfile from my webserver.

(You'll need an open internet connection to do this)

Hide this information

Update	Info	Date
☐ ❓ Advanced detection library	Advanced detection routines update (87 KB)	2006-03-10
☐ ❓ Detection rules	!Updated detections (1.7 MB)	2006-07-14
☐ ❓ Detection support library	Detection support routines update (238 KB)	2006-03-10
☐ ❓ English descriptions	English target descriptions file (89 KB)	2006-07-14
☐ ❓ English help	English help file (184 KB)	2006-02-17
☐ ❓ English help for TeaTimer	English help file for TeaTimer addon (34 KB)	2005-07-25
☐ ❓ English language	Updated English language file (22 KB)	2005-12-23
☐ ❓ Immunization database	!Updated Immunization database (365 KB)	2005-09-23
☐ ❓ Main skins	New skin for colorblind people (393 B)	2005-01-28

Figure 17–3   Clicking the Search for Updates button provides you with a list of all the updates available for your copy of Spybot.

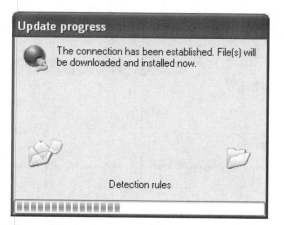

Update progress

The connection has been established. File(s) will be downloaded and installed now.

Detection rules

Figure 17–4   A progress dialog keeps you informed on the update and the various files as they are downloaded.

The Hunt for Spyware

Select Search & Destroy from the left sidebar, and then click Check for Problems from the top half of the main window. Spybot switches to another information pane in the lower half of the interface. Along the bottom, a green progress bar shows you (albeit quickly) the various types of malware or spyware that Spybot is checking for, along with its numerical position in the list of threats. Spybot now checks for several thousand different signatures, so this process may a little while.

When the process is completed, you see a list of the problems that Spybot has found. Each of these entries has a small plus sign beside the problem with additional information listed below (see Figure 17–5).

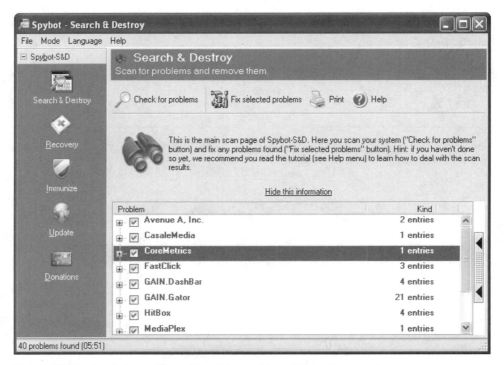

Figure 17–5   Spybot provides a list of the problems it has discovered.

The results from my scan indicate that there are 40 problems waiting to be fixed. Each is highlighted in red, indicating that the problem is considered spyware. Sometimes, Spybot has entries highlighted in green. These are considered usage tracks.

On the right, there's a wide bar with two black arrows pointing to the left. This is actually a button that opens an information window so that you can read about the problem in question. Just click the button and the information window appears to the right of the problem list (see Figure 17-6). Now, click an item and the description appears.

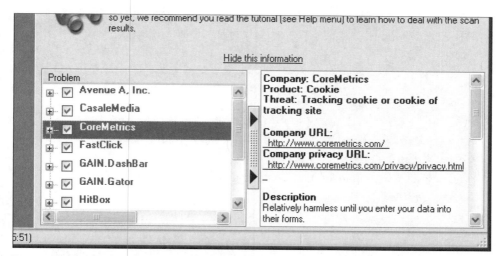

Figure 17–6 To the right of the problem window, there's a button that folds in to reveal a description of the selected problems.

Note that not every problem has a description associated with it, but it is a good idea to check the items so that you know what you are dealing with.

Important Note Not everything that Spybot discovers is *necessarily* bad. There may be software that you fully support having on your system. If you are happy with a particular piece of software, don't remove it. Furthermore, some entries aren't so much spyware as informational, so it pays to read the descriptions if you have any doubt.

Fixing Problems

After you have gone through your list of problems and assured yourself that, yes, you really do want to remove these things, click the Fix Selected Problems button. Spybot creates a backup of your registry prior to going ahead with the fix. This only takes a few seconds. A confirmation window then appears alerting you that you are about to remove the selected entries. If you want to continue, click Yes (see Figure 17-7).

Confirmation
You are about to remove these entries. Do you want to continue?
Yes
No

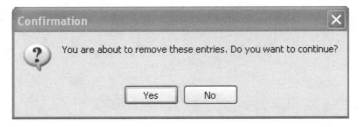

Figure 17–7 You are about to remove the selected problem software. Just make sure you don't remove something you might want to keep.

A green progress bar runs along the bottom of the results window as it fixes the various problems. In some cases, Spybot is unable to fully remove a problem program because that program is still in memory and currently running on your system. To deal with this, Spybot asks for permission to run at your next system startup (see Figure 17-8).

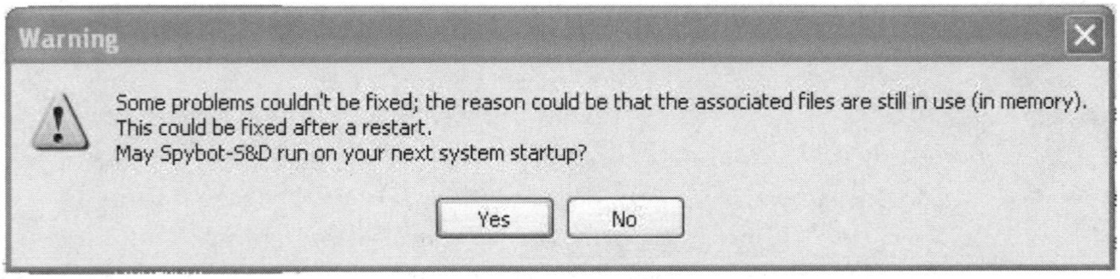

Warning
Some problems couldn't be fixed; the reason could be that the associated files are still in use (in memory).
This could be fixed after a restart.
May Spybot-S&D run on your next system startup?
Yes
No

Figure 17–8 Sometimes, problems need a reboot before they can be completely eliminated.

Click Yes and a final window appears with a summary of problems fixed, and the number of those that require a restart (see Figure 17-9).

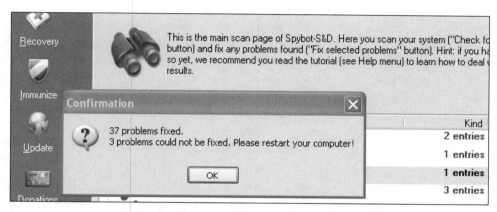

Figure 17–9 Some problems require a system restart.

Clicking OK does not automatically restart your system, so there is no need to close all of your applications in a panic. After this, you are finished. The main Spybot window returns with check marks beside all the items it was able to fix.

If you want, you can click the Print button (to the right of the Fix Selected Problems button) for a paper report of Spybot's run.

Tip This can be described as Spybot's default mode of operation. You can switch to a more advanced mode by clicking Mode on the menu bar and selecting Advanced Mode. Additional options appear in the sidebar that make it possible to fine-tune Spybot's operation. You can even change the look and color of Spybot's interface by choosing a different skin.

Immunization Prevents Further Infection

Just as it is true in the biological, human world, immunization does help to prevent future infections. After you have used Spybot to clean up the various bits of spyware on your system, consider immunizing your system against further infections by clicking the Immunize button in the left sidebar.

When you do, a small window appears telling you how many spyware products are currently blocked (most likely zero at this point) and how many it can protect against. As I write this, my copy of Spybot tells me that it can guard against 11,265 types of spyware, adware, and other malware. Click OK to banish the message. The main Spybot window then returns with a report and some further suggestions for protection before you run immunization (see Figure 17-10). When you are ready, click the Immunize button at the top.

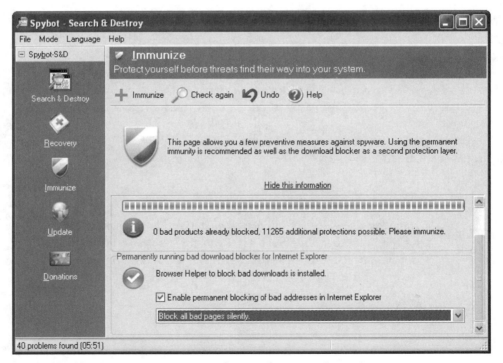

Figure 17–10   Immunization prevents future infection, at least when it comes to current, known problems.

It Never Ends . . .

After the process, which takes only a few seconds, is complete, your system is immunized. Keep in mind, however, that this is only true for things that Spybot knows about. That's why it is a good idea to keep updating the software and the spyware definitions. Clean up your system, and then immunize against new threats.

The trouble with makers of spyware is this: Just as you are taking the time to protect your system, they are looking for ways to evade, disable, and otherwise get around any protection you set up for yourself.

> *Tip* Deleted files can be undeleted with the right tools (the most basic of which is the system recycle bin), and although that can be a good thing if you inadvertently get rid of something, it can be a problem if you meant for the information to disappear permanently. To securely delete a file, switch to Spybot's advanced mode. Then, under the Tools menu in the sidebar, select Secure Shredder.

If this story has a lesson, it's that there are many lessons to be learned. Carefully read every license agreement before you click OK. Maintain a healthy skepticism and suspicion about every site you visit. Use Firefox to browse the Web and Thunderbird for email. Use an antispyware program like Spybot and keep it up-to-date. Finally, use an antivirus package.

That last piece of advice conveniently introduces the next chapter.

Resources

Spybot

http://spybot.safer-networking.de/

Chapter

18

ClamWin: Free Antivirus Protection

Welcome to the wonderful world of networked computers, where a battle rages for your machine. Every second that your computer is on and connected to the Internet, you are at risk of downloading some piece of malware that can take over your computer, cause havoc, turn your computer into a zombie attacking other computers, or worst of all, destroy your important files. The latter is sometimes done slowly and randomly so that by the time you realize what has happened, you may not have recent backups to recover from.

Viruses are nasty. The cost to business alone runs in the billions of dollars (yes, that is billion with a b). That's why an antivirus program is not only a good idea, it is essential to anyone running a Windows system. Antivirus programs work by scanning files on your system and comparing bits of code in those files to virus *signatures* in the antivirus program's database. They also come in many different forms, handling the process of locating viruses, erasing the infections, and (if possible) repairing the affected file. The cost of most antivirus packages is reasonable, but they often tie you into monthly or yearly subscription fees that keep you tied to the company forever.

In this chapter, I'm going to tell you about a free antivirus package for your Windows system. It's called ClamWin. But first, a little explanation as to how various antivirus packages work.

Always On versus Scheduled

Should your virus checker be running in the background at all times, or does it make more sense to check your system on a regular basis? This is actually a tough call. Antivirus programs that run in the background all the time may keep you more secure (or at least, make you feel more secure), but there are down sides as well.

The first is performance. I've been in many an office where certain employees discover that their PCs invariably run faster with the antivirus program deactivated. That's because the impact of running the antivirus program can be quite significant. The result is that users turn off their antivirus package so their systems can work more efficiently.

Another way of dealing with the performance issue is to do scheduled runs, some of them partial runs, making sure that the big runs happen when your system isn't required. That's the approach taken by ClamWin, the antivirus package I cover in this chapter.

 Important Note ClamWin does have some limitations that are important to mention. It doesn't do real-time checking (although this is in development). Second, ClamWin is a virus scanner, not a virus removal program. ClamWin can either delete infected files or move them to a safe location—more on this later in the chapter. ClamWin does, however, integrate with Microsoft Outlook and Mozilla Thunderbird to strip out virus-infected attachments in real time.

Scanning Your Files

Start ClamWin, either from the Programs section under the Start button or by right-clicking the ClamWin icon in the system tray. The folder selection window appears, from which you select what resources ClamWin should scan (see Figure 18-1). From the icon menu, you can choose individual files, folders, or entire drives. ClamWin also displays network drives.

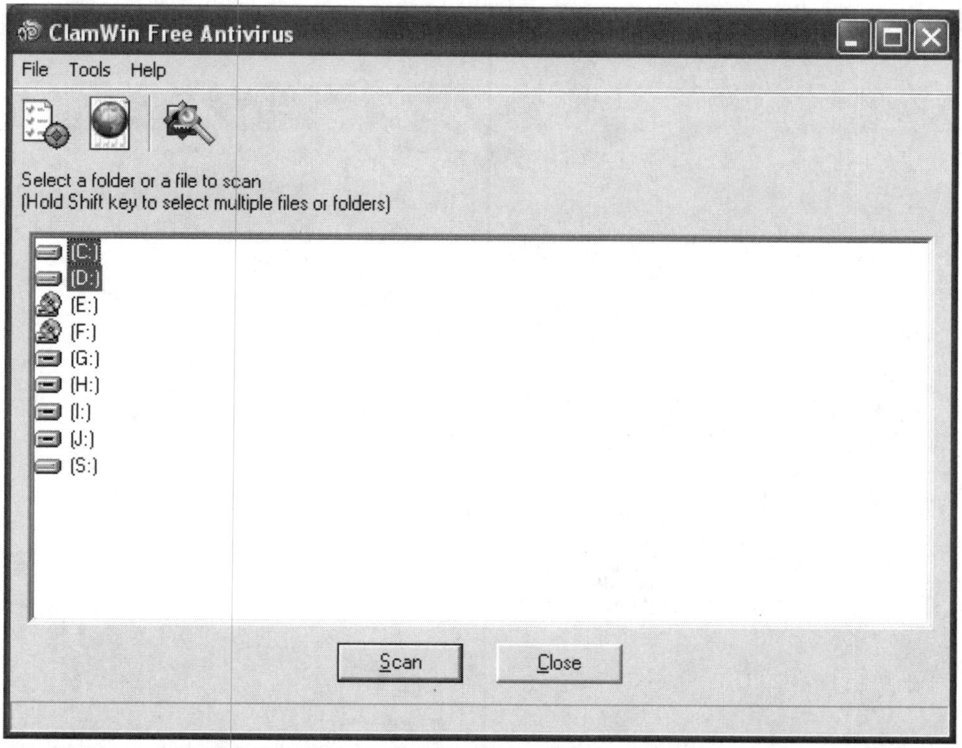

Figure 18–1 Your first step is to select a file, folder, or drive letter you want to have scanned.

The three icons (or buttons) directly below the menu bar perform very different functions. The first activates the Preferences dialog. Meanwhile, the second icon starts an Internet update of the antivirus database. Clam-Win's antivirus databases are updated several times daily, but you can get the latest at any time by clicking this second icon. The final icon starts the scan. Don't click that one yet. You need to select your drives first.

Note If you choose to scan network drives as well as your own, the process can take a long, long time.

After you have chosen the disks you want to scan, click the Scan button at the bottom of the ClamWin window (or the icon above). Files are listed in the main display window, whereas an animated scanner flashes to the left (see Figure 18-2).

```
ClamWin Scan Status                                         [X]

    C:\hp\bin\Spawn.exe: OK                                 ^
    C:\hp\bin\sroff.reg: OK
    C:\hp\bin\strcmpi.exe: OK
    C:\hp\bin\SummaryDeviceList.txt: OK
    C:\hp\bin\Thumbs.db: OK
    C:\hp\bin\TransientMessage.exe: OK
    C:\hp\bin\UIni.exe: OK
    C:\hp\bin\usbpower.reg: OK
    C:\hp\bin\USBPwrMGMT.exe: OK
    C:\hp\bin\UTILITY.DLL: OK
    C:\hp\bin\WaitAndDelete.jse: OK
    C:\hp\bin\win32all-146.exe: OK
    C:\hp\bin\winlogon.reg: OK
    C:\hp\bin\WshTools.dll: OK
    C:\hp\drivers\audio_realtek\Alcxmntr.exe: OK
    C:\hp\drivers\audio_realtek\Alcxwdm.cat: OK
    C:\hp\drivers\audio_realtek\ALCXWDM.SYS: OK
    C:\hp\drivers\audio_realtek\Alcxwdm0.inf: OK
    C:\hp\drivers\audio_realtek\Alcxwdm0.PNF: OK
    C:\hp\drivers\audio_realtek\Alcxwdm1.inf: OK
    C:\hp\drivers\audio_realtek\Alcxwdm1.PNF: OK           v

              Save Report          Stop
```

Figure 18-2   With the scan in process, ClamWin lists each file as it scans them and reports on its status.

For every file that checks out clean, the word *OK* appears at the end of the file name. If a virus is discovered during the scan, the words *VIRUS FOUND* appear along with the file name and the type of virus. When the scan is complete, ClamWin finishes with a report of several stats including the number of files and folders checked, and the number of viruses discovered (see Figure 18-3).

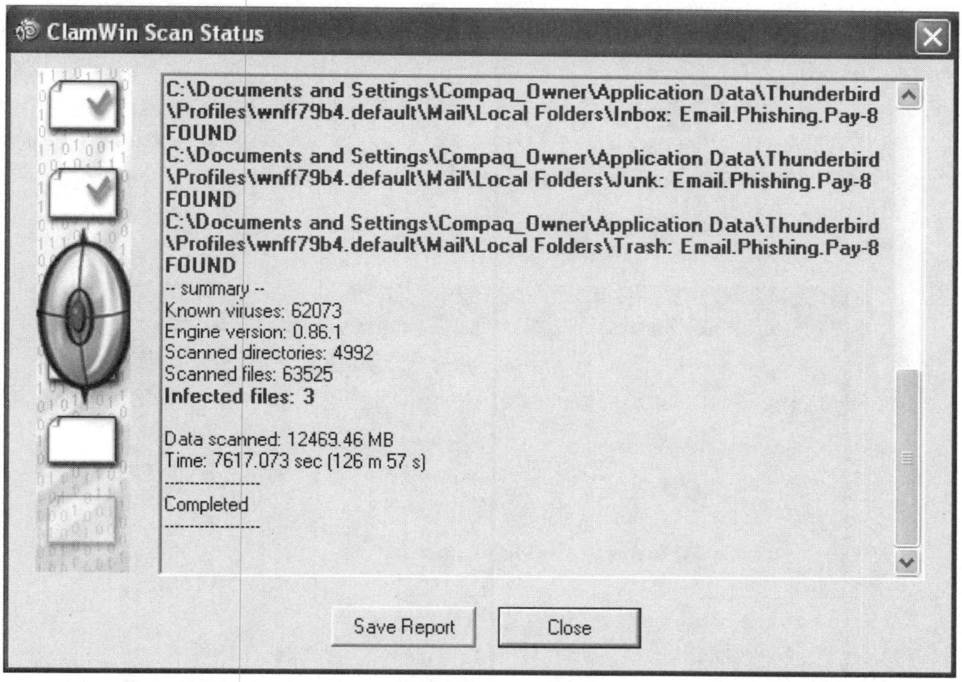

ClamWin Scan Status ☒

C:\Documents and Settings\Compaq_Owner\Application Data\Thunderbird \Profiles\wnff79b4.default\Mail\Local Folders\Inbox: Email.Phishing.Pay-8 FOUND
C:\Documents and Settings\Compaq_Owner\Application Data\Thunderbird \Profiles\wnff79b4.default\Mail\Local Folders\Junk: Email.Phishing.Pay-8 FOUND
C:\Documents and Settings\Compaq_Owner\Application Data\Thunderbird \Profiles\wnff79b4.default\Mail\Local Folders\Trash: Email.Phishing.Pay-8 FOUND
-- summary --
Known viruses: 62073
Engine version: 0.86.1
Scanned directories: 4992
Scanned files: 63525
Infected files: 3

Data scanned: 12469.46 MB
Time: 7617.073 sec (126 m 57 s)

Completed

Save Report   Close

Figure 18–3   When the scan is complete, ClamWin informs you of the results and any viruses it may have discovered.

Unless you have decided otherwise, this run strictly is a report that you can now save for later retrieval. As I mentioned earlier, under the default con-figuration, virus-infected files are not affected. You must decide how to deal with them.

Tip When you have ClamWin installed, you can check any file at any time from Windows Explorer. Any time you download a file, open Windows Explorer, and then right-click the file or folder. From the pop-up menu, select Scan with ClamWin Free Antivirus.

What to Do with the Viruses

The answer to this dilemma seems simple—*get rid of them!* Nevertheless, there may be reasons not to be too hasty in doing this. The most important is this. You may want to check so that you can make sure you have a good backup of the file before you remove it. Although your system may continue to work fine without some files, others may quickly put an end to your session.

Deciding what to do is handled through the Preferences dialog (see Figure 18-4). Right-click the ClamWin icon in the systems tray and select Preferences to bring up the dialog.

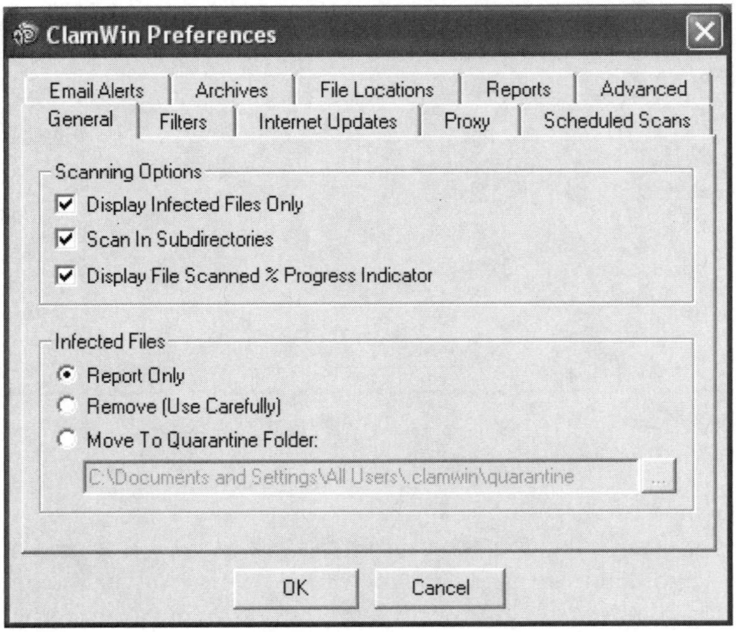

Figure 18–4   How you deal with infected files is handled through the ClamWin Preferences dialog.

There are several tabs here that allow you to customize ClamWin's operation, and I invite you to check them out in detail. For this discussion, I want to concentrate on the General tab, because this is where you decide how to deal with infected files.

As I've said, ClamWin reports on what it finds and lets you deal with it as you see fit, which is why the default is Report Only. Click the Remove (Use

Carefully) radio button and infected files are automatically removed. It might be better to have used the word Beware instead of Use Carefully. The third option, Move to Quarantine Folder, is probably the best choice of the three. Any infected files that are discovered during a scan are moved to the folder you define here.

Scheduling Virus Checks

The scheduler is quite flexible. You can create multiple schedules as well. That way, you can have your entire disk (or disks) checked once daily at a time when its impact is lessened. You could also set the program to check your personal files, perhaps once every hour or two.

Bring up the ClamWin menu by right-clicking the ClamWin icon in the system tray and selecting Configure Scheduler under the Scheduler sub-menu. The ClamWin Preferences dialog appears with the Scheduled Scans tab selected. As you might guess from this, you can also get to the scheduler by just clicking Configure ClamWin from the pop-up menu.

Initially, there are no scheduled scans. Click the Add button to the right of the main display area. The Scheduled Scan dialog appears (see Figure 18-5).

Figure 18–5 Scheduling a scan is easy. You can even create multiple scheduled runs that concentrate on different folders.

The Scanning Frequency defaults to Daily, but you can specify Hourly, Workdays, or Weekly. Enter the time at which you would like the scan to run, and the day (should you choose a weekly run). Below the schedule information, you must specify the Scan Folder, which can be a full drive or any subfolder you want. Finally, you must also enter a description for this run. Make sure you enter all the information, and then click OK to add this schedule. After you have entered this information, you can easily add more.

Keeping ClamWin Up-to-Date

Virus writers are a busy bunch, working seemingly without sleep. Regardless of which antivirus package you run, there is no such thing as 100 percent protection. The best way to protect yourself as efficiently as possible is to keep your antivirus package up-to-date. Luckily, ClamWin does most of this for you, in the background.

The program regularly checks with the ClamAV Web site, looking for updated signature files. When an updated signature becomes available, Clam-Win automatically downloads it and updates itself. You'll see a notification to that effect in the system tray (see Figure 18-6).

Figure 18–6   When the virus database is updated, ClamWin informs you with a system tray notification.

The notification bubble disappears after a few seconds. To close it immediately, click the X in the upper-right corner of the message.

Tip Remember that you can download signature files any time you want by clicking the Internet update icon on the main Clam-Win screen. You can also do this by right-clicking the ClamWin system tray icon.

From time to time, a new version of the ClamWin program itself is released. When this happens, a ClamWin update window appears (see Figure 18-7).

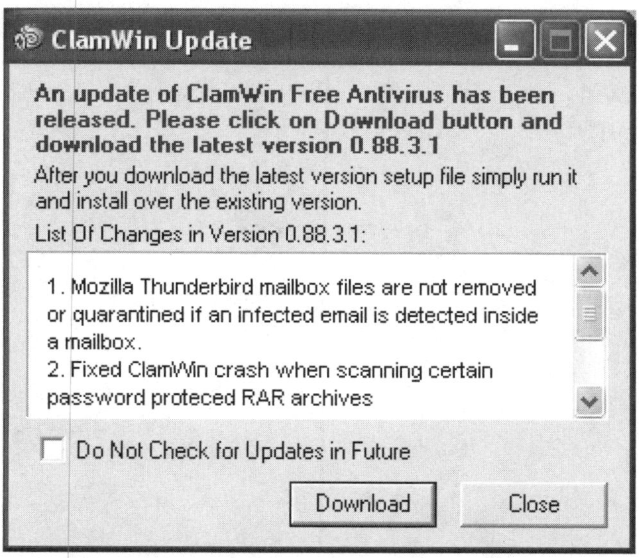

Figure 18–7 If an update of the ClamWin program itself is released, you are given the opportunity of downloading directly.

Click the Download button and a new installer is copied to your desktop. To install the ClamWin update, just double-click the icon and follow the instructions.

Limitations and Other Choices

Although ClamWin is a great virus scanner, it does suffer from two big limitations. One of them I've already told you about and that's the real-time scanning. The fact that ClamWin can automatically scan mailbox attachments in Outlook and Thunderbird may make this less of an issue. Add to that the fact that you can right-click a file and select a scan at any time from inside Windows Explorer, and this may not be an issue at all.

The second is virus removal. ClamWin doesn't disinfect files. It reports on them, deletes them, or moves them to a safe location. If you want your program to be able to disinfect files as well, consider an alternative antivirus program.

Do be aware, however, that regardless of the antivirus program, whether free or commercial, not all virus-infected files can be disinfected. In a number of cases, removing (or deleting) the infected file and restoring from a backup is your only option.

Resources

ClamWin

http://www.clamwin.com/

19

Scribus: Free Desktop Publishing

Scribus is a free, open source, desktop publishing program, or DTP. You may be familiar with other DTP software such as QuarkXpress or FrameMaker. Using Scribus, you can create advertising flyers, newsletters, books, magazines, brochures, and anything else you can envision on paper. Scribus also produces top-notch PDF documents. Although programs such as Open-Office.org Writer allow you to create great-looking documents, they aren't quite up to the requirements of a professional-level publication. That kind of precise control over the various elements that make up the page (or book, etc.) are beyond the scope of most word processors. Some things are just too difficult to do with a word processor.

Although Scribus is easy enough for a beginner to generate great-looking documents, it is also well suited to the needs of the professional. Scribus has full CMYK color support, font-embedding, interactive PDF creation (including transparency, encryption, form support, etc.), and more. The resulting product can be printed locally, exported to electronic format, or sent to a printing company for final processing. If you are looking for a professional layout program, Scribus may just be what you are looking for. Scribus, however, doesn't cost you hundreds of dollars. This is a free program.

In this chapter, I'm going to give you a friendly beginner-level introduction to Scribus. To those of you who work professionally with document design, layout, and production, I invite you to fully explore Scribus' features.

Installation Notes

Installing Scribus is easy, but there is one additional package required before you can fully use the package. That package is Ghostscript (version 8.53 as I write this). You can still use Scribus without Ghostscript, but it is required for Postscript (PS) and Encapsulated Postscript (EPS) importing and printing. As this description might suggest, Ghostscript is an interpreter for the Postscript language. If you choose to start Scribus without Ghostscript, you get a little warning message about the limitations of running without it.

You can get a copy of Ghostscript r. from the following address.

```
http://ghostscript.com/doc/AFPL/index.htm
```

After you have downloaded the file, install it, and then start Scribus.

Frames, Bristol Board, and Projects

Scribus is a page layout program, and not a word processor. If this sounds like an echo of my introductory page, please accept my apology, but this needs to be emphasized. Scribus doesn't open up to a blank page with a flashing cursor where you just start typing. Because it is a page layout program, each element on the page is part of the layout, whether that element is text, images, or even a background color. Here is another way to look at it.

When you were young, you no doubt had to do a project on bristol board. To create this project, you cut out photos, cut and pasted text from different sources, and stuck other objects on this large piece of stiff paper. Each item, including the text you wrote, was something that was attached to the page. In DTP parlance, these are frames: text frames, image frames, shape frames, and so on. That's what Scribus and other desktop publishing programs are: computerized versions of your elementary school, bristol board project.

Getting Started with Scribus

When you start Scribus, it opens up with the New Document window, from which you can select the document layout and size, along with a number of other options (see Figure 19-1). This dialog appears each time you start Scribus. If you prefer to skip the dialog and jump right in on your own, click the Do Not Show This Dialog Again check box on the lower left. You may also choose an existing document by clicking the Open Existing Document tab and using the file manager window there. Scribus also remembers what documents you were working on, so click the Open Recent Document tab if you want to select one of these. For the moment, I'm going to assume a new document.

There are several things you probably want to change here. Depending on your location, the first thing you want to do is change the default unit of measurement. Look on the far right of the window in the Options section. You can also specify the number of pages that you intend on creating here, but the important thing, depending on where you live, is probably the unit size. For instance, users in the United States may want to change this to Inches instead of the default Points size.

Closely related is the paper size. The A4 size is pretty standard across Europe. North American users will want to click the Size combo box (in the top central Page Size section) and select Letter instead. Depending on the document you are creating, you may also want to switch from Portrait to Landscape mode. If you change to letter size using inches as your measurement, your width and height now reads 8.5000 by 11.0000 inches.

Look on the right in the vertical sidebar labeled Page Layout. You can choose from a Single Page layout (which could be several single pages long), Double Sided, 3-Fold (in the classic marketing brochure style), and 4-Fold. For my upcoming demonstration, I'm going to use the 3-Fold layout to create a greeting card that fits nicely in a letter-size envelope.

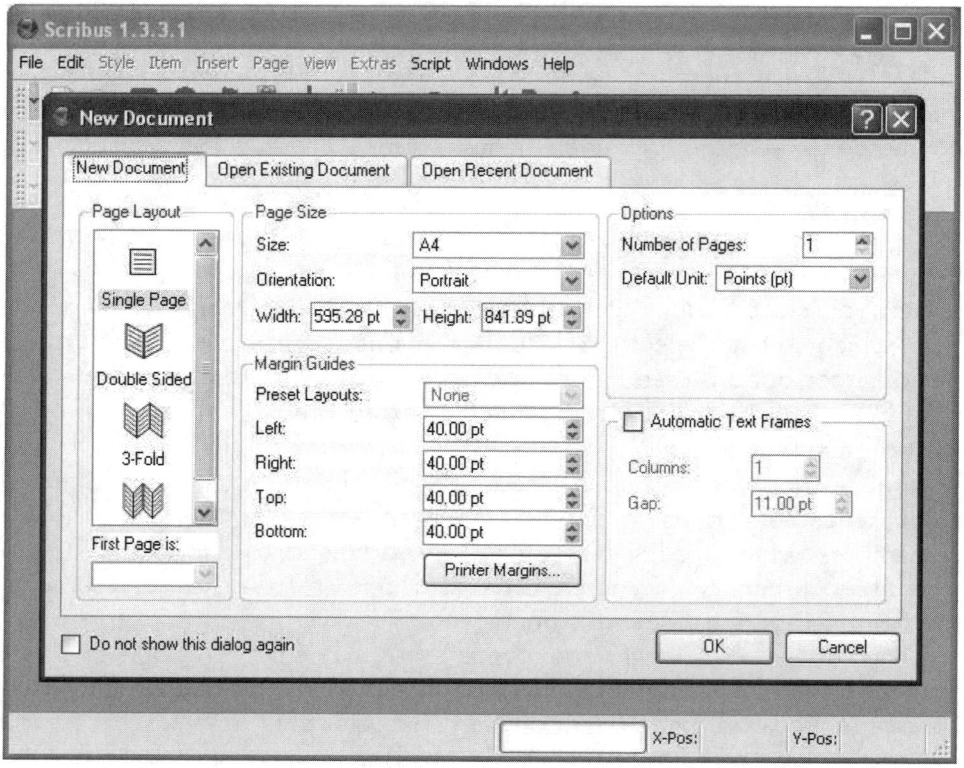

Figure 19–1   Scribus' default start dialog lets you define a new document but provides tabs to existing or recent documents.

Before we move on to our creation, I want to cover two other areas of that new Document dialog. First, there's the Margin Guides section. Several preset layouts exist including Gutenberg, Magazine, Golden Mean, and others. Directly below the individual margin measurements is a Printer Margins button. Click here and you can set your margins for your own printer's printable area, which can vary a bit from printer to printer.

Finally, on the lower right, in the Automatic Text Frames sections, is a check box that allows Scribus to automatically create text frames when new pages are added. If you are creating a book, where every page is filled with text, this is a great idea because you don't have to add that one frame to every page (I'll tell you about the various types shortly). Make sure you set the number of columns you will be using per page, if this applies to you, and click OK.

Moving Around, Tool Bar Icons, and More

By now, you are looking at a large, blank rectangle in the center of the Scribus window, just begging you to add things. At the top is the menu bar, with entries like File, Edit, Page, Extras, and so on. Each of these entries is a menu of categorized tools and, in some cases, submenus of other functions. Below the menu bar is the Scribus icon tool bar (see Figure 19-2). The left side of the tool bar is mostly concerned with file operations and more common tools such as cut, copy, and paste. The right side of the tool bar is for page elements.

Figure 19–2 A close-up of the Scribus toolbar and the various frame tools.

Move your mouse over each one and pause. A tooltip appears with a short description of the icon's function. These include inserting a text frame, an image frame, a table, or some predefined shapes, polygons, freehand lines, Bezier curves, and more. We'll look at a few of these shortly.

To the left and top of the page are your measuring guides, set out in the measurements you chose. When you move your cursor around the screen, red marker lines check your position in the guides.

The positioning itself is a little difficult to visualize, so it may make sense at this time to turn on grid lines on the page. Click View on the menu bar and select Show Grid (a check mark appears next to the menu entry).

Before you start getting creative, I'd like you to turn on a handy little window. Click Windows on the menu bar and select Properties. This brings up the Properties dialog, a floating window that you can move anywhere on the page, while continuing to work around it. The usefulness of the Properties dialog becomes apparent as time goes on. At this point, grid or no grid, you are still dealing with a blank page (see Figure 19-3). That's okay; the blank page, in all its glory, is the starting point for everything else.

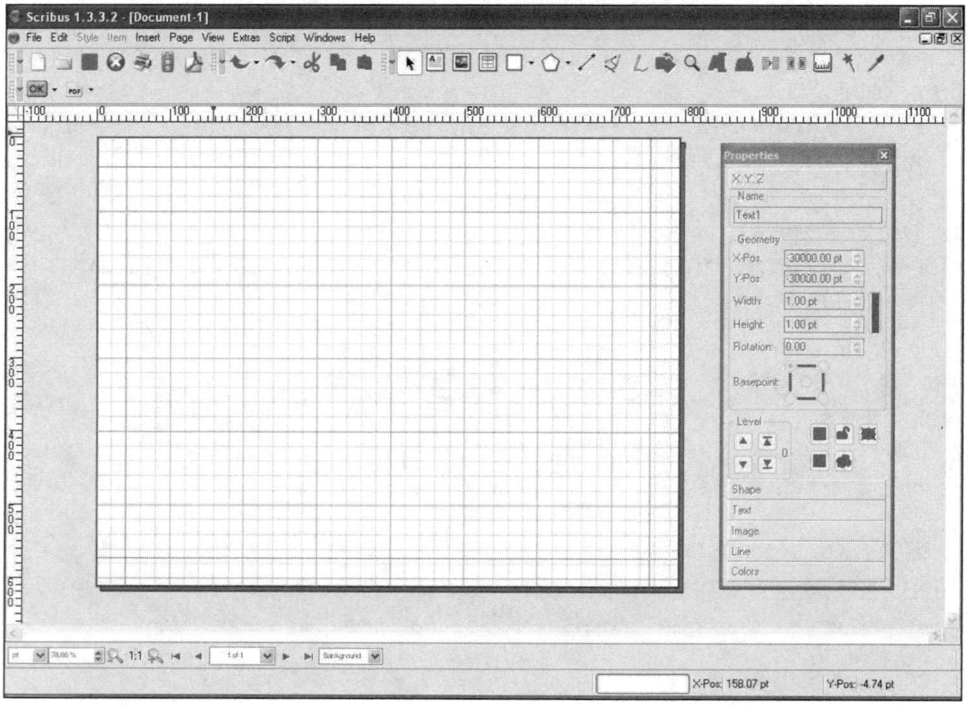

Figure 19–3   A blank Scribus page with the grid turned on and the floating Properties dialog activated.

It's important to remember that every thing in your layout (or on your page) is an object that can be manipulated, resized, moved, and so on. Objects can overlap other objects or be overlapped. Objects can also be containers for content. A text frame, for instance, is a container for text. An image frame is a container for images.

Text Frames and Properties

Text is generally the basis of any publication. Select the Insert Text Frame icon, and then click the page and drag to create a dashed rectangle and release. To do a quick adjustment on location, click and drag the frame to where you want it. Notice that the text frame contains no text at this point.

There are square handles at each corner and at the midpoint of each side. Click and drag these handles to resize the frame. Take a look at the floating

Properties window I had you turn on. The window has multiple sections labeled X, Y, Z, Shape, Text, Image (grayed out here), Line, and Colors. Each of these sections has multiple settings and clicking the name opens up those options. I want to concentrate on the X, Y, Z section first (see Figure 19-4).

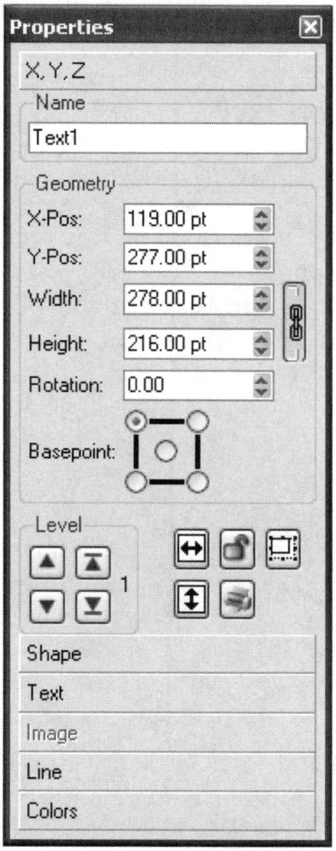

Figure 19–4 Every frame (or object) has certain attributes in common, including location, size, and rotation.

The position and size of the text frame you create is an approximate, the only possibility when you are working freehand with the mouse. To scale it appropriately, make your changes in the Properties dialog for that frame (which is automatically titled Text1). There's a little chain-link icon next to the width and height. That's to make sure that any changes you make are proportional. If you want to define width and height separately (normal with text), click the chain to break the link. You can also rotate the frame here for easy rotated text.

I will briefly touch on a couple of additional things here, and then move on. Because one object can sit above or below another object, there has to be some means of changing the level; that's what those arrows in the Level section are for. Next to the arrows, there are buttons to flip the frame vertically or horizontally, as well as lock it in place (so you don't accidentally drag it to another location).

Tip There is one other icon I want to mention. If you hold your cursor over the printer icon in the Properties dialog (next to the Level box), you see an Enable or Disable Printing of the Object tooltip. Click that icon and that object—whether text, image, or shape—will not print.

Double-click the text frame and you can edit text directly in the frame. After you have entered some text in the frame, you can always go back and edit it in place; everybody makes typos. However, this isn't always ideal because text may exist outside the frame and therefore be invisible. Unless you are talking about just a few words, you are best to use the Story Editor. Right-click your text frame and select Edit Text (or press <Ctrl+Y>) to bring up the Story Editor (see Figure 19-5).

The floating Properties dialog also changes when you click a text frame. Aside from the XYZ location settings, there is a Text section. Selecting the text properties this way does provide style, font, and color control, but unlike the Story Editor, there is no window to change the text.

Tip At this stage of the layout, the actual content of those text frames may not yet be important, as in the case of a newsletter or a magazine. You're creating a layout, not manipulating content, after all. Right-click the frame, then select Sample Text from the pop-up menu. A dialog appears, from which you can select text in different languages. Standard *Lorem Ipsum* is also available.

What on Earth *is Lorem Ipsum?* This is a standard chunk of dummy text used by the printing and typesetting industry, which has been around for hundreds of years. For the fascinating details and history of Lorem Ipsum, check the "Resources" section.

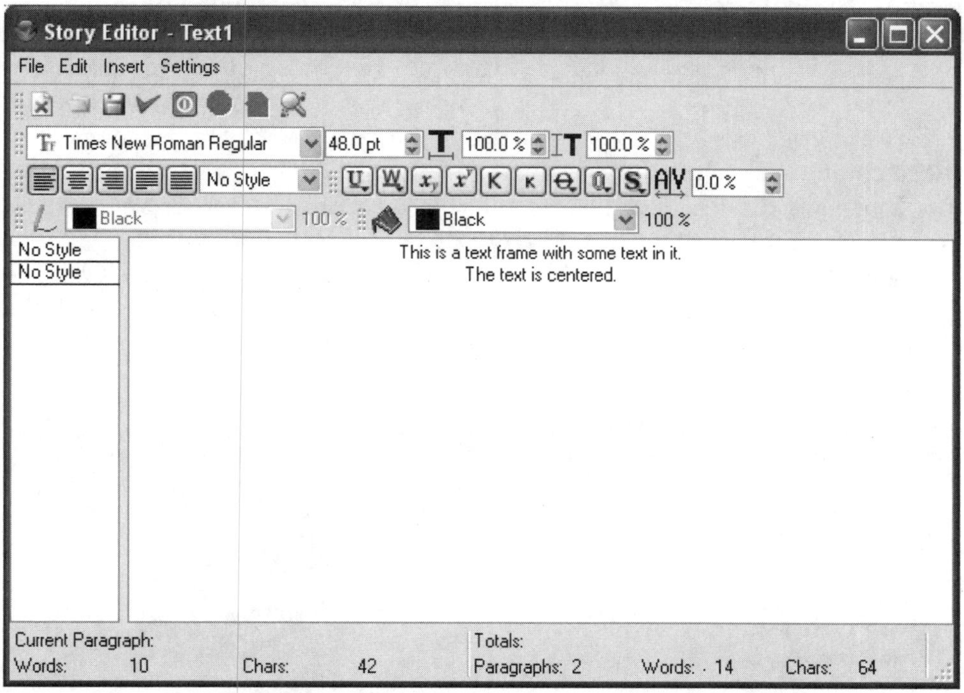

Figure 19–5 The Story Editor gives you full control over your text attributes.

You might remember that I said objects such as frames could be containers, as in the case of a text frame. Rather than typing in your text, either directly or in the Story Editor, you can get text and effectively "pour" it into the frame. Right-click an empty frame, and then select Get Text from the pop-up menu (or press <Ctrl+D>). An Open File dialog appears, from which you can select an external document. Scribus can import a number of different file formats including CSV, DOC (Microsoft Word), HTML, ODT (OpenDocument), PDB (Palm format), SXW (OpenOffice Writer), and plain text (TXT).

Working with Images

Adding an image is one of those things that will certainly throw you at first. Start by selecting the Insert Image Frame icon in the top toolbar. Click the page, and then drag the box until you have a rough approximation of the size. Don't worry too much about whether it is exactly the right size or whether it is situated exactly where you want it. You can change all that later.

When an image frame appears on the page, it looks a little different than a text frame in that there is a large X through the center of the rectangle. At this time, the frame is a placeholder for an image. There is no image in it and adding a frame does not prompt you for one. Image frames are another one of those containers waiting for content.

Right-click the frame and select Get Image from the pop-up menu (keyboard jockeys can just press <Ctrl+D>). A file manager window appears. Navigate to the folder that contains the image you want, and click OK (see Figure 19-6). If you routinely work with different image formats, it may be helpful to select the File Type and narrow the search.

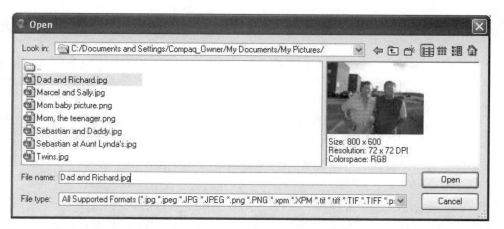

Figure 19–6 If your folder has a particularly large number of images, you can narrow it based on the file type.

As soon as you do this, you might notice that something looks a little strange. The image is still full size, somewhere beneath the image frame. Unfortunately, it's unlikely that you want just a small corner of your image in that frame. To solve that, we go back to our Properties dialog (I told you it would come in handy). Click the Image label and the attributes to scale the image appear (see Figure 19-7).

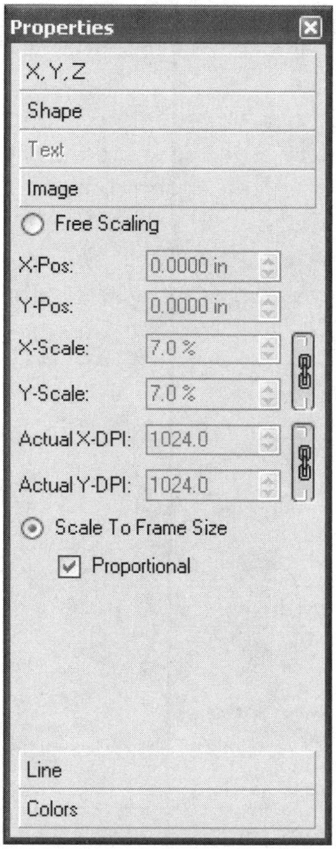

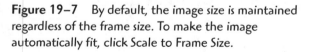

Properties

X, Y, Z

Shape

Text

Image

○ Free Scaling

X-Pos: `0.0000 in`

Y-Pos: `0.0000 in`

X-Scale: `7.0 %`

Y-Scale: `7.0 %`

Actual X-DPI: `1024.0`

Actual Y-DPI: `1024.0`

⦿ Scale To Frame Size

☑ Proportional

Line

Colors

Figure 19–7   By default, the image size is maintained regardless of the frame size. To make the image automatically fit, click Scale to Frame Size.

You can manually define the position and size (scale) of the image within the frame or you can let the computer do it for you. Click the Scale to Frame Size radio button and your image automatically scales to fit. Unless you are specifically looking for a distorted image, make sure you leave the Proportional check box checked.

Images of the Second and Third Kind

Pictures, as the preceding heading implies, are just one type of image. If you are creating an organizational chart, you are going to use boxes with links identifying the structures in an organization. Arrows may be added to a document to draw attention to a particular chunk of text or something of interest in a photograph.

Scribus provides a number of predefined shapes that can, as with any other type of object, be sized, rotated, made to sit above other objects, and so on. Click the Insert Shape icon in the toolbar to select the current shape (or click Insert on the menu bar and select Shape). To choose other shapes, click the small black arrow to the right of the icon (see Figure 19-8). That way, you can select a variety of shapes including the aforementioned arrow.

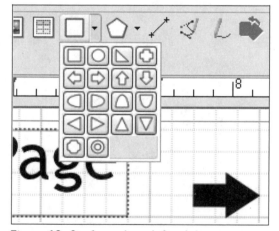

Figure 19–8   *Several predefined shapes are available for inclusion in your page design.*

The Properties dialog is your key to modifying any shape you put on the page. Click the Shape bar under the Properties dialog and you see an interesting button labeled Edit Shape (or click Item on the menu bar and select Edit Shape from the Shape submenu). The Nodes window appears as do the various control nodes and points that make up your shape (see Figure 19-9). Pause your mouse over the various icons in the Nodes dialog to discover the various options there.

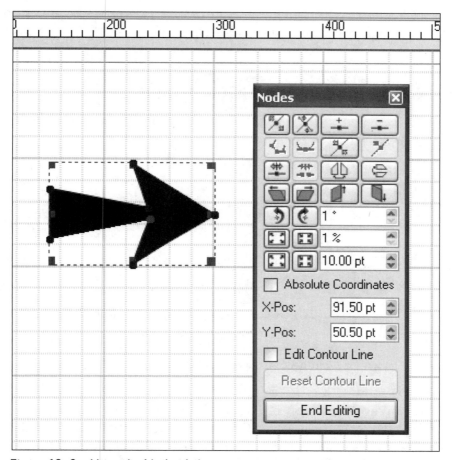

Figure 19–9 Using the Nodes dialog, you can now move the nodes that make up an image to shape it in any way you desire.

In Figure 19-9, I clicked the first icon on the upper-left of the Nodes dialog. It allows me to move the nodes that make up the arrow so that I can bring the points on the inside of the arrowhead closer in. The sides on the shape were perfectly horizontal at first.

Similarly, you can add another type of shape using the Insert Polygon icon (or click Insert on the menu bar and select Polygon). When creating polygons, you have an almost unlimited set of options. With enough sides, a polygon eventually looks like a circle. Still, you can do some interesting things when you consider that a star is a polygon with its corners inverted. Click the small black arrow to the right of the Insert Polygon icon and select Properties to bring up the Polygon Properties dialog (see Figure 19-10).

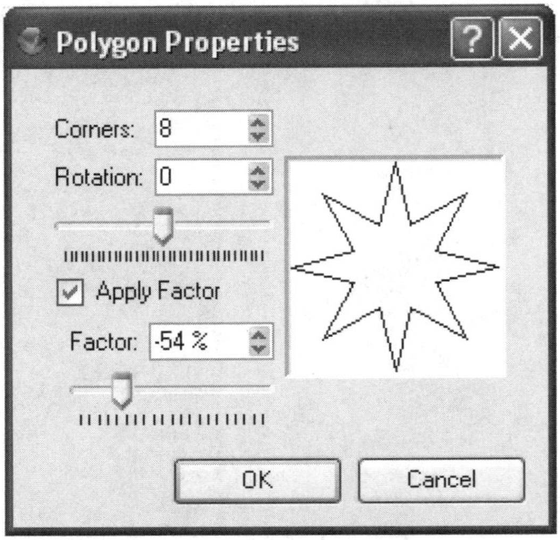

Figure 19–10   Change the number of points to create a standard polygon. Add a negative factor to invert the points and create a star.

To turn a regular polygon into a star, click the Apply Factor check box and add a negative factor. The larger the negative factor, the more star-like the polygon becomes. Just as with the shapes discussion of earlier, you can also edit a polygon, drag its nodes around to customize the shape, and more.

As you add more and more items to the page, the beginnings of a layout start to appear (see Figure 19-11). Consider the work in progress my elementary school Scribus project.

Tip   When you are working on multiple documents, Scribus keeps track of each document under the Windows heading on the menu bar. Click the menu and you see all your open documents at the bottom of the list.

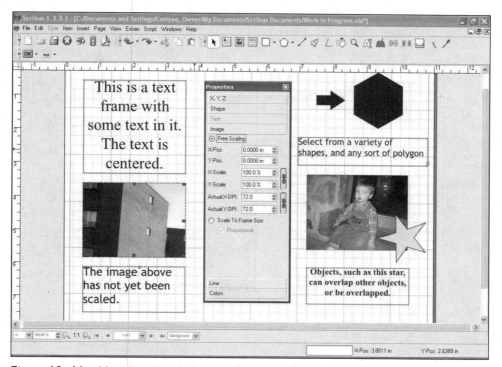

Figure 19–11 My project is starting to take shape. Notice that the floating Properties window reflects whatever frame is selected.

Printing Your Document

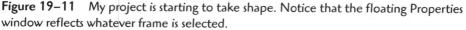

Scribus produces print-ready documents. Great! So let's print.

When you click the printer icon on the icon bar (or click File, then Print), fascinating things happen in the background. Your document is checked for errors that might affect what you can expect to see when printing starts. If there are no errors in your document and what you've created fits nicely within margins, text within frames, you go immediately to the Print dialog. However, if there are problems, the Preflight Verifier appears (see Figure 19-12) with a list of problems it has encountered with the various elements on your page.

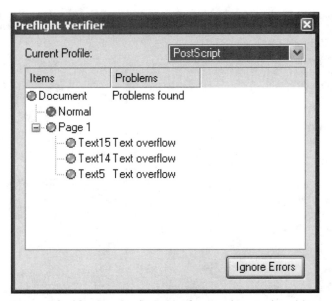

Figure 19–12   The Preflight Verifier has detected problems in the document and stops you before you decide to print.

You can go back and deal with the errors that you see there (more than likely, you will want to do that) until there are only green lights or you can simply click the Ignore Errors button and continue. You can, after all, run the Preflight Verifier at any time to see if there are any problems with your page (the icon is directly to the left of the print icon). It isn't necessary to wait until print time to discover if there are problems with your page.

If no errors occur, or you choose to ignore the errors generated and forge ahead, the Setup Printer dialog appears (see Figure 19-13). Select your print destination (you may have more than one printer defined), what pages you want, whether you want to print in color or grayscale, selected pages, and so on.

Under the Advanced Options tab, you can choose additional printing options such as mirroring pages. At the bottom of the window, there's a print Preview button so you can see what the output looks like before printing.

When you are ready, click the Print button and your print file is generated.

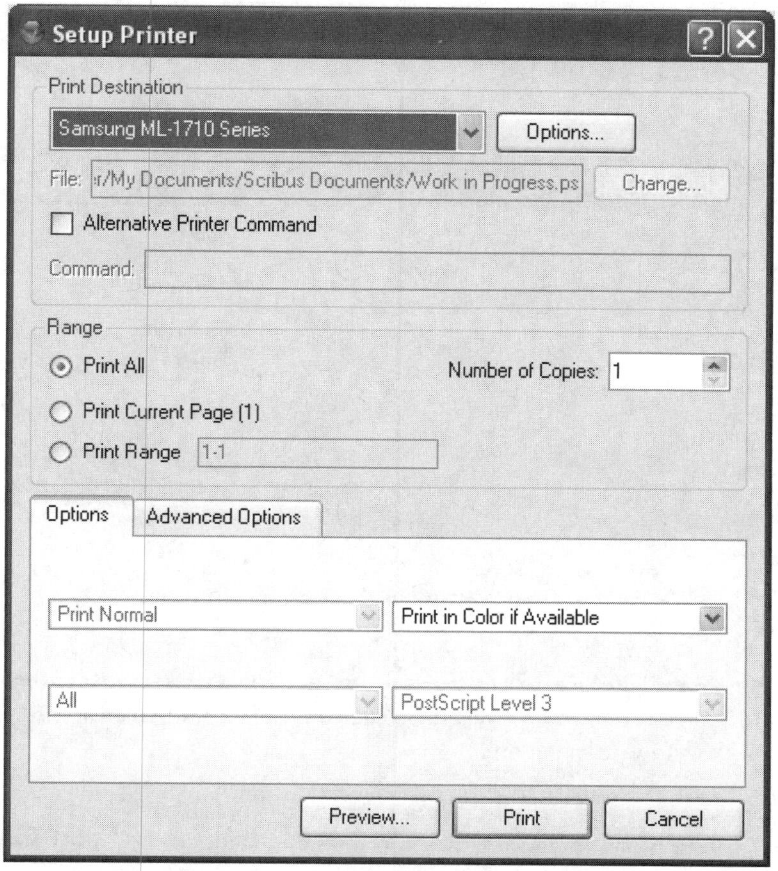

Figure 19–13   It's time to print that beautiful creation of yours.

A Scribus Calendar

Before I wrap up this chapter on Scribus, I'm going to have you create something useful and quick: a calendar, complete with a nice picture of your choosing. We're going to do this using Scribus scripts. Scripts are basically a series of steps to creating a document, stored in sequence, so that the document in question can be recreated time and again. Scripts are particularly interesting because they are also flexible, allowing the next person to customize his project.

Click Script on the menu bar, navigate to the Scribus Scripts menu, and then select CalendarWizard from the submenu. The Scribus Calendar Wizard appears (see Figure 19-14).

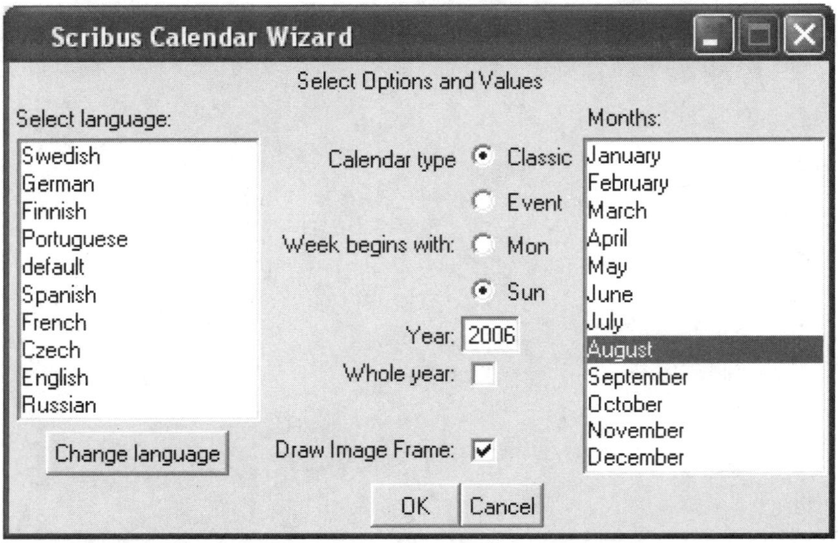

Figure 19–14   The wizard offers you a choice of languages, as well as the type and layout of the calendar itself.

Select the language you want to use, the calendar type (choose Classic for now), the year, and so on. You have the option to print a single month or a whole year. At the bottom of that window, there's a Draw Image Frame check box. At the top of the calendar page, there's an area for a picture. The default is to include a place for a picture of some sort (a family photograph or a travel snapshot perhaps), but no image.

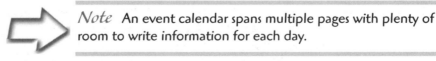

Note   An event calendar spans multiple pages with plenty of room to write information for each day.

Click OK and the Edit Style dialog appears (see Figure 19-15). This is a paragraph style assigned to the text that makes up the calendar—in other words, the month name, days of the week, and numbers. Styles are a means of describing text in detail so that you can apply a style to different sections of text. For instance, a standard first paragraph might use a Trebuchet font, with an initial drop cap twice the size of a normal letter, 5 points from the rest of the text. We tend to think of text as black, but it might be an entirely different color. Paragraphs also have set tab locations, a certain distance between lines of text and another between paragraphs. You might even want a special background color.

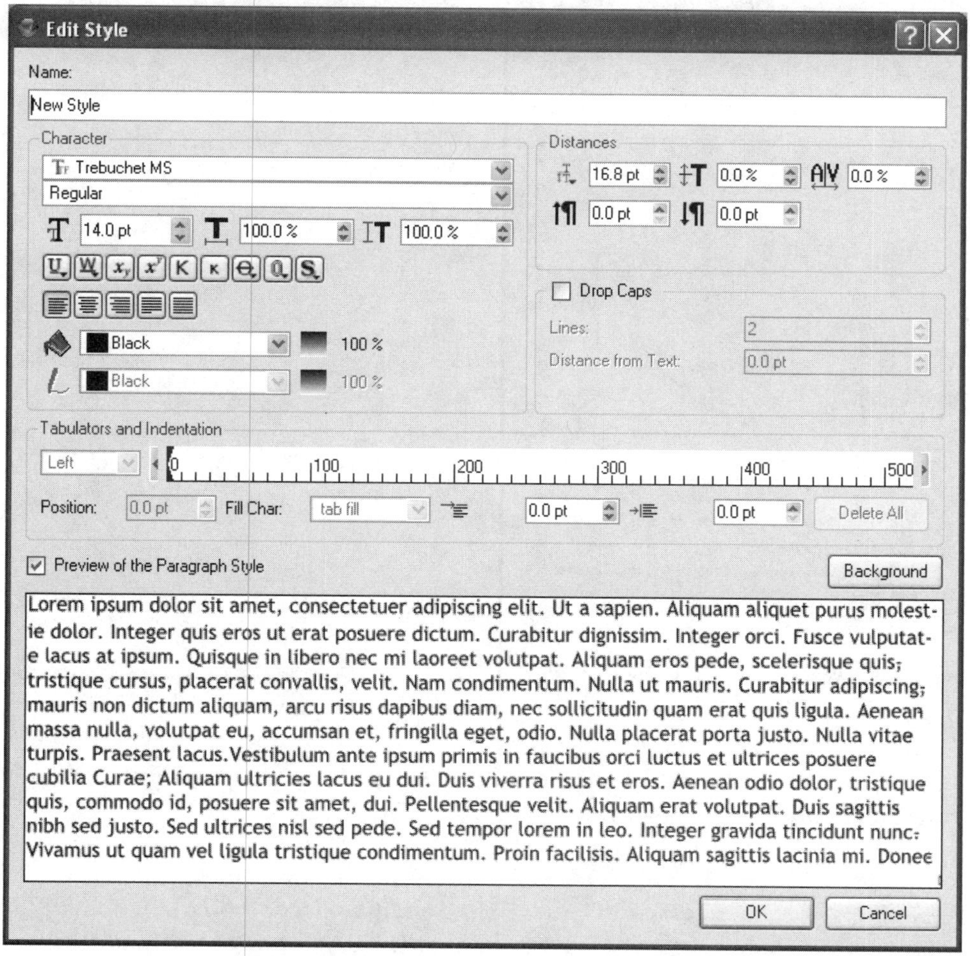

Figure 19–15 Creating a paragraph style for the calendar text.

On the top left, there's a Name field with the name New Style currently assigned. You can enter a name that makes sense to you, like Calendar Style. Select a font, font size, and even color, if you want. The bottom part of this dialog has a large preview window. There is a check box here where you can banish the preview pane. This is entirely up to you, but I personally like having the preview there. When you are happy with your changes, click OK and the calendar is generated (see Figure 19-16).

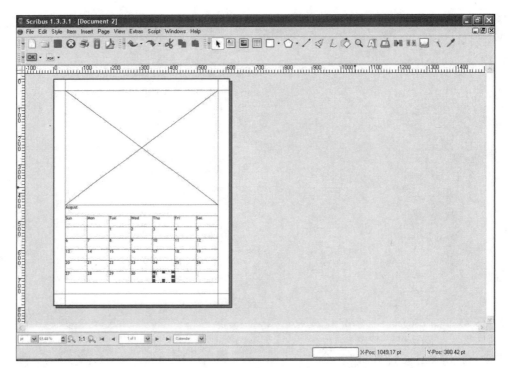

Figure 19–16   Your new calendar, ready and waiting for a nice photo to dress it up.

The calendar is now all laid out. Add an image frame to the upper part and insert an image.

Tip   Besides scripts (you can find additional scripts on the Scribus Web site), there are also document templates available. These offer great starting points for generating some beautiful documents. If you are just starting out with Scribus (as I assume you are), pay a visit to the KDE-Files Web site (see the "Resources" section) and select Scribus Templates from the menu.

Personalizing Scribus

I'm going to finish this chapter by giving you the opportunity to make your Scribus world your own.

When you first launched Scribus, there was a document selection screen where you chose paper size and orientation. I suggested that you might want to change the measurements from pixels to millimeters or inches, depending on your location. The next time you start Scribus, you have to go through all those changes again, unless you make a few changes in the program's configuration.

Click File on the menu bar and select Preferences. When the Preferences window appears (see Figure 19-17), you'll see that there are quite a number of options that you can personalize. There is a vertical sidebar running down the left side with a list of categories related to every aspect of Scribus' operation.

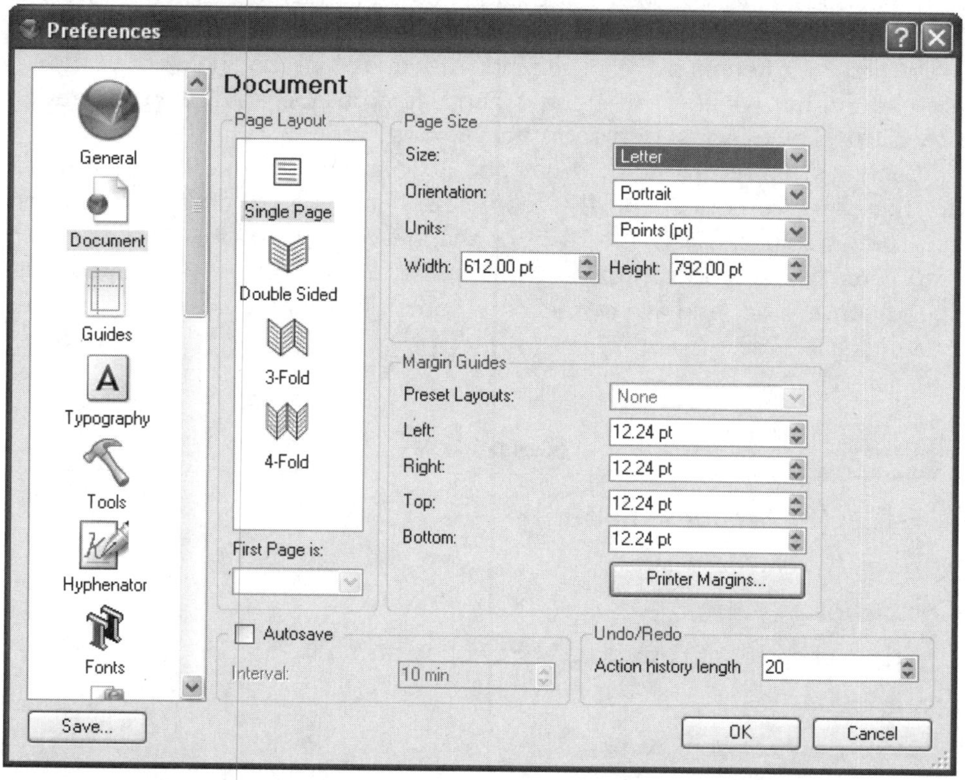

Figure 19–17 The Preferences dialog has tons of options for customizing your work environment.

The obvious item, from the perspective of my introduction here, is the Document category. If you are always working with a particular document type, it makes sense to change it here. Take the time to check out the various categories and decide how they affect you.

Scribus is a powerful, highly capable, and potentially complex package. This chapter provides a great introduction, but an introduction is what it is. The best way to learn about the package is to experiment so that you can stretch those creative muscles to their maximum. When you find yourself needing help, never fear; I have a few tips for you.

Getting More Help

In your quest to become a Scribus guru, you no doubt have some questions. Luckily, there are plenty of places to turn for that help. For starters, you can go to the Scribus Web site where you can find direct links to the Scribus mailing list and the Scribus Wiki. The mailing list is an opt-in mailing list with searchable online archives. People share information, ask questions, and help each other.

The Scribus Wiki, on the other hand, is a collaborative documentation site, created by Scribus users for other Scribus users.

Back in Chapter 4, I told you all about Gaim and discussed how you can use the client to connect to IRC networks. This is a good time to put this information to use. There is a 24-hour channel on `irc.freenode.net` called `#scribus` where you can always find someone to answer your questions. Spend some time, and when the time comes, perhaps you can share your knowledge as well.

Resources

KDE-Files (for Scribus Templates)

http://www.kde-files.org

Ghostscript

http://ghostscript.com/doc/AFPL/index.htm

Lorem Ipsum

http://www.lipsum.com/

Scribus

http://www.scribus.net

Chapter

20

Endless Free Fun and Games

There's plenty to smile about when it comes to taking a little down time with your increasingly free computer system. Expand your mind with a great puzzle. Do a little target practice in the arcade. Race down a dizzying mountain slope. Play golf. Try to keep your balance on a moving, rocking platform miles above the ground. Save a princess. Board a space fighter and take on somebody halfway around the world. Become a wizard in a faraway land. Fly an airliner.

There are tons of games out there, great games that don't require you to shell out hundreds of dollars on a regular basis. To get you started, I've included a handful of great games on the DVD included with this book. I'll tell you all about these in this chapter, and leave you with a list of others that you may want to look into on your own. Then, check out some of the great free games out there on the Internet and you'll find yourself set for weeks, possibly months.

Sit back, relax, and get ready to enjoy a little free fun.

Warning! Some of these games feature penguins. However, no penguins were hurt in the writing of this chapter.

PlanetPenguin Racer

This is one of my favorite, arcade-style games, so I'll start with it.

The idea is simple. Tux, the Linux penguin, races down snow- or ice-covered mountains on his belly (see Figure 20-1). As the speed increases, you try to dodge obstacles while picking up herring along the way. The action is fast-paced and exciting, with Tux taking flight off the occasional cliff or ramp. All this happens as you race against the clock.

Figure 20–1   Fast, frozen fun with PlanetPenguin Racer.

To make things interesting, there are several courses included with PlanetPenguin Racer. When the program starts, it runs in full screen mode by default. You can choose Configuration from the starting menu to choose a different resolution, or to run windowed.

There are two play modes. One is to enter an event and the other is to practice. The difference between the two is that in competition (enter an event), you must complete a level before advancing. In practice mode, it doesn't matter whether you complete a level; you can try whatever courses are available, regardless of your skill. If this is your first experience with PlanetPenguin Racer, I highly recommend that you start with a practice race. Each race in this mode includes a description of the course (see Figure 20-2).

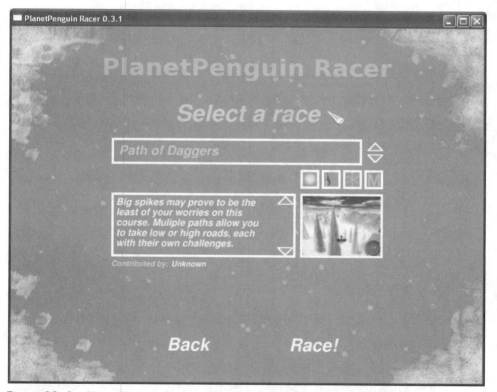

Figure 20–2   PlanetPenguin Racer is the perfect arcade ride for anybody needing a belly rub.

Before you click *Race!*, look directly below the course name at the four icons you see there. Each of these lets you add other interesting *twists* to your race, such as weather conditions, time of day, and whether or not you have to deal with wind on the way down.

When you think you've mastered all of the courses PlanetPenguin Racer has to offer, head on over to the TuxRacer Belly Rub Web site at `http://tuxracer.cjb.net/`. There are tons of additional contributed courses that you can install on your system.

Freedroid RPG

Johannes Prix and Reinhard Prix's Freedroid RPG is a beautiful 3D role playing game with superb graphics, a cool soundtrack and sound effects, and a well-developed world (see Figure 20-3). Here's the back story. Sometime, in

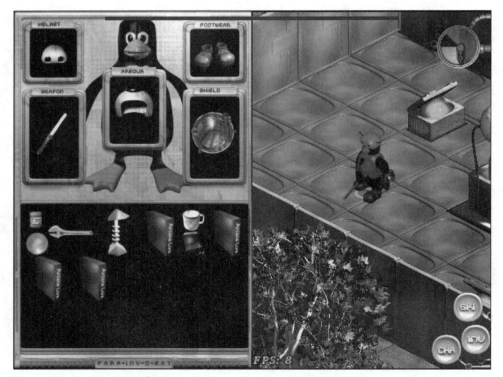

Figure 20–3 Freedroid RPG is a great combination of classic adventure with a post-industrial science-fiction theme.

the not too distant future, a mega-corporation known as *Megasoft* (or MS for short) has effectively taken over the galaxy. It managed to do this by using its vast corporate power to install trojan horses in every computer-equipped machine on the planet, including those of government and police. As a result, all of humanity was enslaved. Due to some terrible programming error, however, the machines rebelled and took over, thus making things worse than they already were.

The only hope for mankind now is a cyborg version of Tux, a so-called *lunarian*. Equipped with high-tech armor, low-tech magic, and a laser sword, our hero is ready to take on the machines and bring freedom to the galaxy.

When the game first loads, you are asked to choose a single- or multi-player game and then to load a particular hero or to start with a new one. If this is your first game, you obviously want to start with a new hero (see Figure 20-4). Type in the name you want for your hero . . . your name, perhaps? When you press <Enter>, the game loads and the adventure begins.

Figure 20–4 Freedroid RPG pits your penguin hero against the evil forces of MS (Megasoft).

If this is your first game, it's a good idea to read the introductory information scrolling across the screen. You'll learn the story behind the games, what the various keystrokes do, and lots of other useful information. When you have all this down pat (it only takes a few seconds), click anywhere on the screen to begin.

Along the way, you'll battle all sorts of villains and monsters, pick up items, money, and weapons, and meet up with all sorts of interesting characters.

Freedroid RPG is available at `http://freedroid.sourceforge.net`.

Armagetron Advanced

Remember the 1982 Disney movie *Tron*? Inside the computer, programs engaged in gladiatorial battles, fighting for their *users*. One of the deadly sports in this virtual world was a *lightcycle* race. Contestants rode a kind of motorcycle that left a wall of light in its wake. The cycles themselves can't stop. The only thing you can do is ride, avoiding your opponents' walls while trying to get them to crash into yours. The last program standing wins. The popularity of the lightcycle concept has created a number of variations on the theme, including one of my favorites. It's called Armagetron (see Figure 20-5)—think *armageddon*.

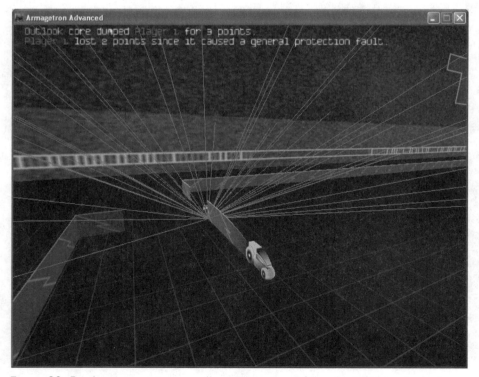

Figure 20–5   Armagetron is an excellent re-creation of the classic lightcycle duel.

Armagetron is available at `http://armagetron.sourceforge.net`.

SuperTux

If this sounds familiar, there may be a reason. And, yes, there is another penguin in this game. SuperTux is a classic jump and run platform game in the style of, you guessed it, Super Mario Bros. Under Tobias (Tobgle) Glaesser's lead (but originally created by Bill Kendrick), this game is guaranteed to provide you with hours of fun.

The story goes like this; Tux and Penny (Tux's love interest) are out for a nice date together when Tux gets knocked out and his lovely Penny gets penguin-napped by the evil Nolok. Held prisoner in Nolok's equally evil fortress, Tux must brave all sorts of perils to save his lovely lady. It is your job to help Tux succeed in his quest (see Figure 20-6).

SuperTux is available at `http://super-tux.sourceforge.net`.

Figure 20–6   Help Tux rescue his beloved Penny from the evil Nolok.

The game can be played entirely from your cursor keys, but joysticks and gamepads are also supported. The program starts with a handful of choices, such as jumping right into the game, loading a couple of bonus levels, or creating your own (a little something for later). You can also set various options like OpenGL support, turn the sound or music on and off, and so on.

The play is fast and fun. Jump over the many enemies to avoid them or jump on top of them to disable them. Be careful with the bomb character—if you squash him he'll explode, so get out of there fast. Many objects are at different levels, so you must climb or jump onto platforms to get from one obstacle to another. Collect gold coins as you go. Smash ice blocks with Tux's head to discover power flowers or ice balls that transform him into SuperTux, a being of enhanced strength and power! When you complete a level, you are transported to the next, more complicated level.

Oh, no! Knocked out by that sliding ice block again. I think it's definitely time to move on to the next game.

Tanks for the Memories: BZFlag

BZFlag is a multiplayer 3D tank battle game you can play with others across the Internet. (Tim Riker is the current maintainer of BZFlag, but the original author is Chris Schoeneman.) The name BZFlag actually stands for *Battle Zone capture Flag*. In essence, it is a capture-the-flag game. To get in on the action, I suggest you look no further than your included DVD for starters. Should you want to run the latest and greatest, however, visit the BZFlag site at `bzflag.org`.

Unless you specify otherwise, BZFlag starts in full screen mode but you can override this by changing the settings when the game starts. You start the game at the Join Game screen. Before finding a server (the first option on the screen), you may want to change your callsign (or nickname). We'll look at some of these other options after we've selected a server. For now, cursor to the Find Server label and press <Enter>.

You won't have any trouble finding people to play with—you'll get a list of dozens of servers currently hosting games (see Figure 20-7). Scroll down the list of names to find one that suits you. Your criteria might be the number of players, how busy a server is, or how many teams are involved. When you look at the server list, make sure you pay attention to the type of game being hosted on the server. Some have a team-oriented capture-the-flag play, whereas others host freestyle action. You may also be limited by the number of shots at your disposal, so aim carefully.

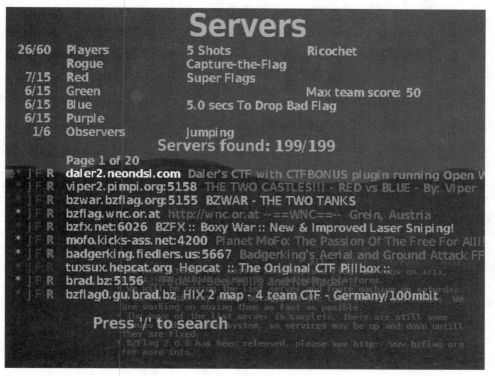

Figure 20–7 At any given time, there are dozens of BZFlag servers running worldwide and hundreds of players.

When you have made your choice, press <Enter> and you find yourself back at the Join screen with a server selected (see Figure 20-8). You could just start the game, but there are a couple of additional things you may want to fine-tune before you start up your tank. Cursor down to the Team label and press your left or right arrow keys. By default, you are automatically assigned to a team but you can change that role here if you prefer. One of the roles you can play instead of joining a team is that of Observer. This is not a bad idea if you are new to the game because it lets you watch how others are handling themselves.

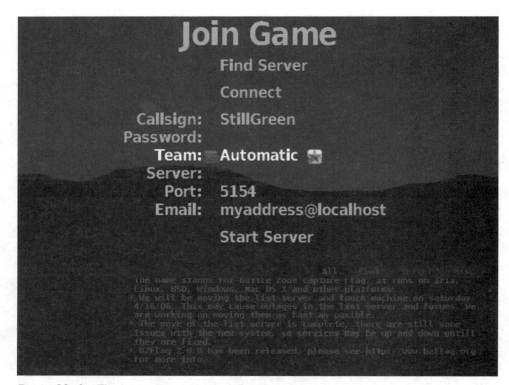

Figure 20–8   The Join screen lets you define your callsign as well as your team.

The Join screen also lets you manually enter the name of a server rather than search for it. This is useful for hosting private games on a local LAN. Speaking of hosting games, I'm sure you noticed the Start Server option at the bottom of that list. Let's go ahead and join the game. Scroll back up to Connect and press <Enter>.

I hope you are ready, because the action starts immediately, and some of these players are, well, let's just call them *seasoned*. Move your tank using your mouse and fire by clicking with the left mouse button. These tanks are highly maneuverable and can even jump in some games (you do this by pressing the <Tab> key). To find out all those keystrokes, hit <Esc> at any time and select Help. During play, BZFlag provides an extensive heads-up display with stats on players, kills, personal scores, team scores, and more (see Figure 20-9). Keep an eye on the map to your lower left as it can alert you to enemy tanks. If you can drive, fire, and type at the same time, press N to send a chat message to the group, or M to just your teammates. If you see the boss coming, press <F12> to exit the game in a hurry. Just kidding, of course. I would never suggest that you play this at work.

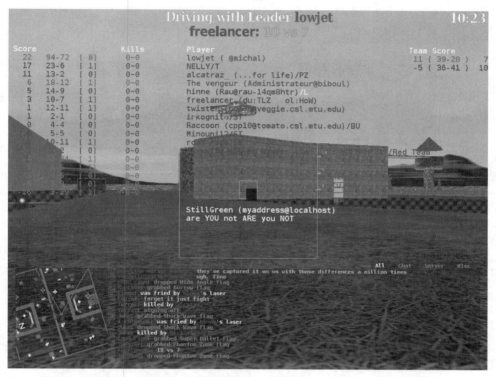

Figure 20–9 The action is fast and tense, with tanks blowing up everywhere you turn. Be careful not to be one of them.

Fish Fillets Next Generation

There is something I like about playing games that is, strangely enough, much the same as what I enjoy about reading science fiction or fantasy. The medium lends itself beautifully to creating other times, places, and even worlds. Some of these worlds can be familiar—what we call simulations—whereas others are a bit more *out there*. Fish Fillets Next Generation definitely fits into the *out there* category. Perhaps a little description would be good to start with . . .

Ivo Danihelka's Fish Fillets Next Generation is an updated rewrite of a game originally called (simply) *Fish Fillets*. The game starts with our friendly fish protagonists sitting around the table discussing whatever it is fish discuss, when suddenly, a heavy metal cylinder drops on the table in front of them—a talking cylinder, no less. Something is obviously afoot (or afin) in their world, and the intrepid duo decide to go out and investigate. There's only one problem: The cylinder has separated the pair and made it impossible for them to get out (see Figure 20-10).

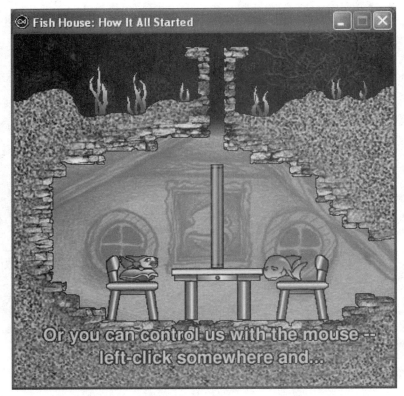

Figure 20–10   A simple puzzle, perhaps, but this is just the beginning.

Not impossible, just puzzling. This first puzzle is just a teaser, enough to get you into the second level where the information in a mysterious briefcase informs them of a diabolical plot (see Figure 20-11). The briefcase snaps open and we learn that agents from the FDTO (Fish Detective Training Organization) have intercepted snapshots of a UFO's crash landing. In that spacecraft are the secrets of interstellar flight, which might prove valuable to fishdom. Coincidentally, a mythical city sank nearby, somewhere in the vicinity of the Bermuda Triangle. This may or may not be related to the UFO crash. Oh, and if, after unraveling these mysteries, you could look into a sunken pirate ship, a treasure map, an evil organization bent on world conquest, a telepathic turtle, and . . . (well, you get the idea), it would really be useful.

Figure 20–11 The mysterious briefcase, with a message of utmost importance for our intrepid fish agents.

Your first stop is a treasure map of sorts. Down the middle is a string of pearls indicating your levels. Initially, the chain consists of eight pearls, but that number increases as you progress. Each corner provides some simple functions including an introduction (basically a link to a video on the Fish Fillets Next Generation Web site), an author credits screen, and, of course, an exit. There's also an options screen where you can adjust sound effects and music volume, subtitle language, and an option to turn off those subtitles. If you are new to the game, I suggest leaving them on for now. Incidentally, you can get back to this options screen at any time during the game by pressing <F10>.

During game play, a relaxing soundtrack accompanies your efforts (assuming you haven't turned it off in the options screen) with bubbling water and other sound effects filling in as you move objects around. All this rearranging of things is important because each level is essentially a prison and getting out requires that you solve a sometimes complex puzzle. Take your time and *make sure* you read the tips as you play. Throughout, your fish agents chatter, offer clues, or banter about their adventure. If you don't move or do anything for a while, the fish may try to get your attention with suggestions or a little gentle nudging. Because each level can require many steps, you might want to save your position from time to time by pressing <F2>. Should either of your fish agents meet their demise, you can return to your last position by pressing <F3>. Just because it looks like everything is going *swimmingly*, it doesn't mean that you should feel too comfortable. In Figure 20-12, I was patting myself on

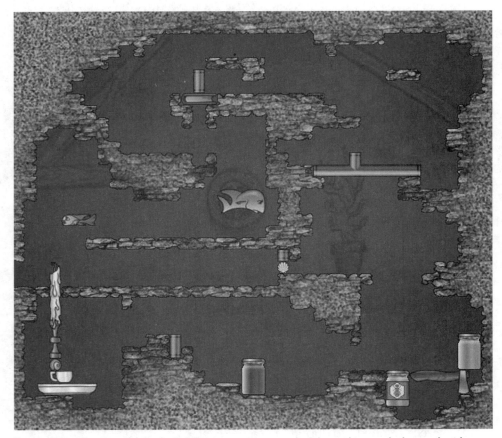

Figure 20–12   Don't get cocky! Every move you make along the way helps to decide whether you succeed, or whether you wind up stuck.

the back at having reached the end until I realized that a silly move right at the beginning of that level had me totally stuck. Oh, well, time to start over.

With each successful level, pearls light up on the main map identifying your location. Clicking previous levels brings up a best score screen for that level. Take a close look at the counter box that displays the high score. Directly below the counter, there are three icons: a brain, an eye, and an X. Should you wish to play a level again, click the brain. Clicking the eye plays back the level while you watch. The X does pretty much what you expect. If you can't remember where you are or what you are supposed to do, press <F1> for a Help menu at any time during game play.

Fish Fillets Next Generation will keep you busy for hours as you try to find your way out of the various puzzles that you encounter, haunted ships, abandoned libraries, sunken submarines (see Figure 20-13), and more. At this moment, there are 70 levels, each offering up a unique mindbender. Fish Fillets Next Generation is a must.

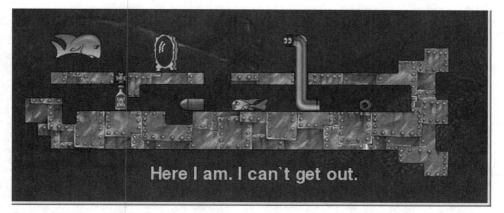

Here I am. I can't get out.

Figure 20–13 In every puzzle, you must work together to move on to the next level. You can't leave your partner behind.

Neverball and Neverputt

Suspended in 3D virtual space is a game called Neverball. The idea behind Neverball (created by Robert Kooima) seems extremely easy. You navigate a rolling ball across a variety of playing fields, collecting coins as you make your way to the goal on the other side—except that it's much harder than that. Advancing to the next level requires a minimum number of coins. To make this coin-gathering just a tad harder, the platform rocks back and forth as you try to stabilize it with your mouse. Your point of view shifts dynamically with each tip of the playing surface, and the movements can get downright dizzying.

Meanwhile, the barriers that keep the ball on the playing surface don't stop it from flying over the edge if you tip things too energetically, and every once in a while the barriers just aren't there. That goes for the floor, too, which can shift, leaving you with empty space where there was reassuring ground (see Figure 20-14). Add moving walls and obstacles that can send your ball in any direction except the one you choose and a ticking clock that eats away at your time, and you've got a fast-paced, challenging game that requires nerves of steel. Just when you think you've got this thing licked, be aware that this is just Neverball's beginner level. The difficulty of the higher levels border on the impossible.

Figure 20–14   Neverball is great, nerve-wracking fun!

Neverball makes use of 3D accelerated graphics, which means you'll need an appropriate 3D video card to play the game.

Neverball comes with a second game that draws on the same theme. It's called Neverputt and, for people who like mini golf courses, this is another winner. Like the mazes and puzzles of Neverball, Neverputt's course floats in 3D space thereby adding an interesting dimension to the classic mini golf theme (see Figure 20-15). Unlike Neverball, the courses don't rock back and forth in a dizzying way, but Neverputt isn't without its own ingenious obstacles. Neverputt comes with three different courses, the first being fairly easy and the second and third courses getting progressively harder. The amount of energy you choose to put behind your putt is controlled by the mouse— forward reduces the force and backward increases it (think rubber band).

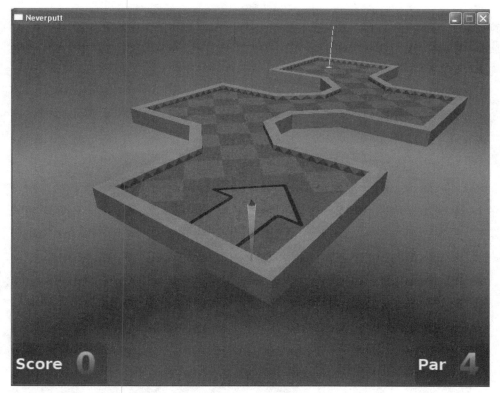

Figure 20–15   Mini golf was never like this.

Neverputt doesn't have the frenetic energy of Neverball, but you may need a break after a few rounds. Both games are great fun and just the thing to keep you away from otherwise productive pursuits.

SolarWolf

Harken back with me, faithful reader, to the days of yore. Yea and verily, I speak of the days of video arcades, when a quarter of a dollar would buy you frantic minutes whereupon you, as humanity's only hope, were called upon to protect the earth from invading, marauding aliens. Why were the aliens attacking? If one could enter the alien psyche, perhaps we might catch a glimmer. Alas, time and survival are of the essence. And if you manage to avoid the aliens and their erratic firing patterns, there are also asteroids and other assorted space hazards to contend with. Keep moving, keep firing, and Godspeed, mighty warrior of Earth!

In the spirit of those great arcade games comes SolarWolf, a superb arcade game inspired by the old Atari game, SolarFox. The days of arcade games costing a mere quarter are long gone, but so are the old Atari graphics. SolarWolf is a modern, beautiful, fast-paced reincarnation built for today's computer (see Figure 20-16).

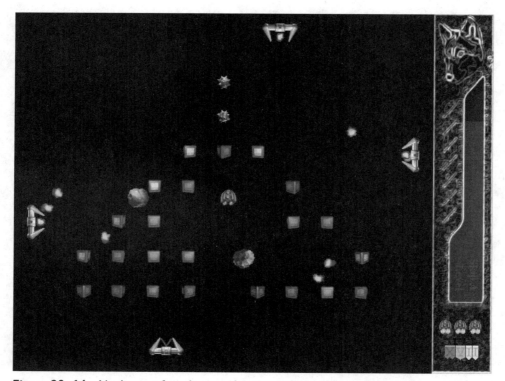

Figure 20–16   You've just found yourself in the middle of the SolarWolf action, with no weapons.

To ease you into the game, SolarWolf offers helpful tips in the first few levels (see Figure 20-17), so make sure you read these. To start with, you are introduced to your ship, the SolarWolf. You discover that despite its total lack of armament, it does have the best navigation, maneuverability, and propulsion system in the galaxy! Later screens introduce you to new threats and objects you can collect, including methods of increasing your score. The first few levels are fairly easy, but that changes rapidly; and the game's soundtrack, while somewhat repetitive (complete with wolf howls), pushes your heart rate higher with every level you finish.

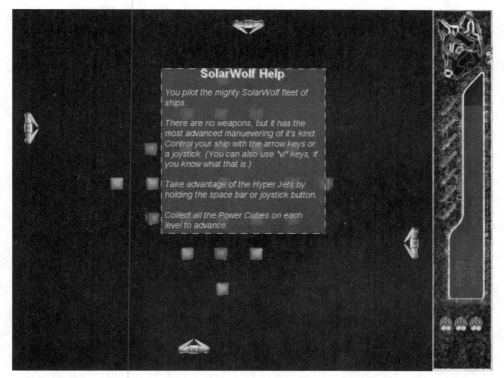

Figure 20–17 In the early stages of the game, you are given important tips for when things really get nasty.

Your job is simple. Collect the rotating power cubes to finish the level. Racing back and forth, collecting power cubes, is only so easy. You must also avoid the alien Guardian ships as they try to blow you out of the sky. Watch for the power cubes that alternate colors. To collect these cubes, which you must do to complete a level, you must fly over them multiple times.

A variety of *power-ups*—circular, pulsating objects that float through the game grid—are pretty much universally good. *Shot blocker power-ups* destroy all the alien bullets heading toward you, giving you a few seconds of clear space in which you collect your power cubes. Speaking of time, down on the right side of the screen you can find the *skip level timer,* a red, vertical bar dropping away as you play. Finish a level before the red bar drops away to nothing and you skip the next level entirely. *Time skip power-ups* occasionally fly through the game grid. Fly over them and time is added to your skip level timer.

As you master more and more levels, the Guardians become increasingly dangerous, firing repeatedly. In case I haven't mentioned it, those Guardian ships aren't the only things you need to worry about. Spike mines start to appear in later levels and these things do what mines everywhere do, cause real damage. Avoid these at all costs. Keep an eye out for asteroids as well. Work fast because eventually the sky is filled with mines, asteroids, and bullets. Although it's true that most things you encounter in the game are there to destroy you (power cubes notwithstanding), there are occasional prizes in the game. For instance, *shield power-ups* float through the game grid. Fly over one of these and you are rewarded with a few seconds of invincibility and a well-deserved speed boost.

Maybe I'm being too easy on myself, but one of the things I really love about SolarWolf is that it lets me start a new game from where I left off (see Figure 20-18). This means that you don't have to start at the very beginning of the game before getting back into the dangerous situation that caused your earlier demise. If you want to erase a particularly bad performance (or a friend's particularly good one), this screen provides a way to delete player names from the roster.

The game starts in full screen mode. There are a handful of configuration options you can tweak. Instead of selecting Start from the initial screen, choose Setup instead. From the setup screen that follows, you can adjust the sound and music volume, change the resolution and windowed mode, and so on.

SolarWolf's game play is fast, exciting, colorful, and wonderfully addictive. The graphics look fantastic, and the game controls are intuitive and hair-trigger. Sure, it's only a game, but it's easy to forget yourself in this space-age shoot-'em-up where all the shooting is directed at you and you can't fire back.

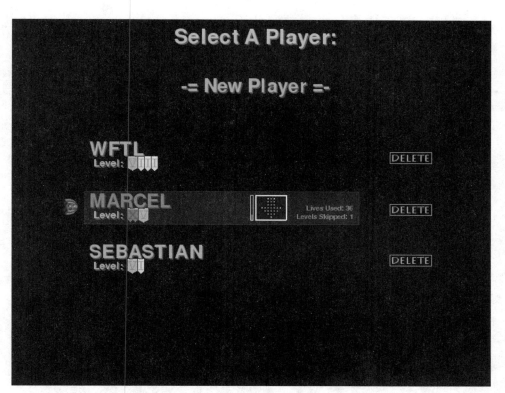

Figure 20-18 SolarWolf lets you start a game from where you left off, a nice feature if you don't want to start over each time.

FlightGear

From flying in outer space to flying a little closer from home . . .

I'm going to end this chapter by telling you about one of my favorite games, and one of the most challenging free packages out there. It's not just the play that is challenging. The demands made on your system are also considerable, so a decent 3D, accelerated video card is essential. Calling this program a game would be just plain wrong if it wasn't so much fun. Let me introduce you to FlightGear.

You may not know this (well, you do now), but your humble author is also a pilot. Consequently, I have a warm spot in my heart for FlightGear, an extremely impressive open source flight simulator (see Figure 20-19). The developers of this incredible package have produced a beautiful thing. The scenery itself is breathtaking, and the coloration of land and sky is verging on photorealistic. You can also download scenery packs for every bit of land mass in the world, allowing you to fly and explore distant lands from the comfort of your own room.

Figure 20–19   FlightGear, a truly fantastic flight simulator.

FlightGear comes with a number of different aircraft models, from a single-engine Cessna 172 (like the ones I've flown on many occasions; see Figure 20-19) to a Boeing 747, an F16 fighter, or even a Sopwith Camel. There are helicopters as well for those who have a preference for the whirlybirds. When you first start the program, a wizard appears asking you to select the aircraft of your choice.

Click Next and the wizard asks you to select a location (see Figure 20-20). The basic package comes with several locations to fly from. Care to tour the Sonoma Valley or glide lazily around Half Moon Bay? How about taking off from a busy airport with multiple runways, such as San Francisco International, The Grand Canyon maybe. With FlightGear, it's not a problem. Make a selection, click Next, and it's time to activate your display settings and make a few last-minute selections.

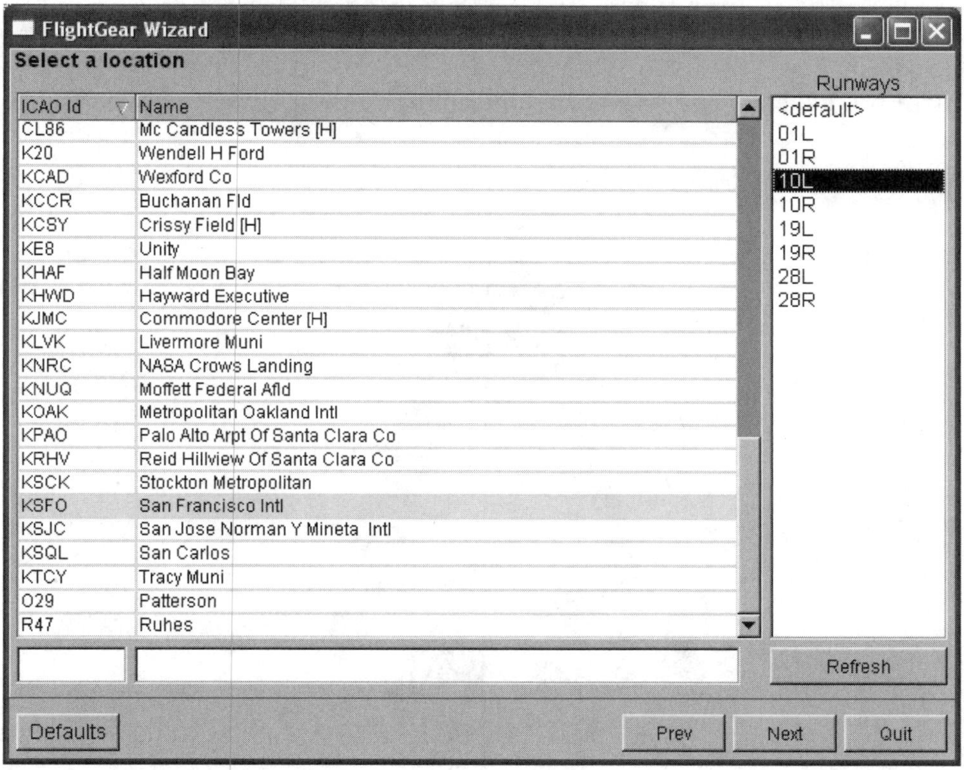

Figure 20–20 FlightGear comes with a great selection of places to fly. If you want some place else, the FlightGear Web site has the rest of the planet to download.

To appreciate FlightGear, you need a 3D accelerated video card, but the better the card, the more features you can turn on. Choose your resolution, whether you want to run in full screen mode, and what kind of detail you want in the world around you. You can set time of day, lighting, fog, weather (there's a real-time weather fetch mode); you can even play with others over a network.

FlightGear is more than just a game. This is a superb and truly realistic flight simulator. The extra work and the rewards for this one are well worth it.

Penguins . . .

So what was all that about penguins, anyhow?

The star of three of the games covered in this chapter was a penguin. Not just any penguin though, but Tux, the Linux penguin (see Figure 20-21). Tux is the mascot of the Linux operating system. By using the free software in this book, you could save yourself hundreds, even thousands of dollars. You'll be more productive, have more fun, and run more securely with fewer viruses and less spyware. Your Windows system may feel that much more stable as a result.

Figure 20–21   Tux, the Linux mascot.

To get the most out of free software, however, consider running Linux. It is truly free. It is stable. It is more secure. That last statement should catch your attention. Linux is extremely secure, and virtually immune to viruses. If you are tired of having to deal with viruses, spyware, adware, and other malware, take a look at an operating system that allows you to do all the things you normally do with your PC, safely.

In the next chapter, I'm going to show you how you can take Linux for a spin without having to install it or uninstall Windows.

Resources

Armagetron Advanced

http://armagetron.sourceforge.net

BZFlag

http://BZFlag.org

Fish Fillets Next Generation

http://fillets.sourceforge.net

FlightGear

http://www.flightgear.org

Freedroid RPG

http://freedroid.sourceforge.net

Neverball (and Neverputt)

http://icculus.org/neverball

PlanetPenguin Racer

http://projects.planetpenguin.de/racer/

SolarWolf

http://pygame.org/shredwheat/solarwolf/

SuperTux

http://supertux.berlios.de/

Chapter

21

The Ultimate Free Software: Linux

Now we come to the end of the book and the last chapter. By now, I'm sure you've discovered that there are plenty of exceptional free software packages available for your system, and that by using those packages you are on your way to saving yourself a small fortune. Having convinced you of the value of these programs, I'm going to make a pitch for the ultimate and best free software, Linux—specifically, Ubuntu Linux.

Included on the DVD that came with this book is a full-featured Ubuntu Linux distribution that runs entirely from the CD-ROM drive. That's right. You can run Linux on your system without having to change your system or uninstall Windows. Then, when you are ready to make the jump official, the live CD comes with a friendly installer that makes the process virtually painless.

Note Because it is running from the CD drive, Ubuntu Linux live CD runs slower than if you actually install Linux and run it from the hard disk. Keep in mind that the performance you experience from the CD is not indicative of the performance you can experience from a Linux hard-disk install. At their fastest, CD-ROM drives are no match for even the slowest hard disk drive.

Running Ubuntu Linux is as easy as putting the CD in the drive and booting. A couple of minutes later, you are working with a great-looking, modern desktop (see Figure 21-1). This CD is full of great software, much of which you have already explored in this book. Some of these include

OpenOffice.org Writer (including Calc, Base, and Impress)

Gaim Internet Messenger

Firefox

The GIMP

The bootable CD is a fantastic introduction to Ubuntu Linux, providing you with a no-commitment way to take Linux out for a spin—but there are limitations.

I've already covered one issue related to CDs, that of performance. The other limitation is also CD related. Because this bootable Linux does not install itself on your hard drive, you are limited to the packages on the CD. In other words, you can't add or install any new software. After you install Ubuntu Linux to your hard drive, this limitation vanishes and you can choose to install from thousands of great packages. In fact, you can install and run many other packages you learned about in this book:

Thunderbird

Skype

CastPodder (the Linux version of Juice)

Inkscape

Scribus

. . . and, of course, all those great games.

Figure 21–1 Meet your new Ubuntu Linux live desktop!

> ⇒ *Tip* To learn about installing software with Ubuntu Linux, visit my Web site and read the article, "Installing Packages Using Ubuntu." You can find it in the support section for this book (just click the book cover image on my Web site at www.marcelgagne.com).

Burning the CD Image

If your system has a CD or DVD burner, it came with some kind of package that lets you burn the Ubuntu image to a blank CD. If you don't have a program to burn a CD image, or you simply can't find one with your system, I'm going to recommend that you check out Alex Feinman's ISO Recorder program. The program is available from the following address.

```
http://isorecorder.alexfeinman.com/isorecorder.htm
```

The program is simplicity itself. After you've downloaded and installed the program, ISO images appear in your Windows Explorer file manager (or on your desktop) as a CD icon with the letters ISO across it. Simply right-click the image and select Copy Image to CD from the pop-up menu. A CD Recording Wizard appears to guide you through the remaining steps (see Figure 21-2).

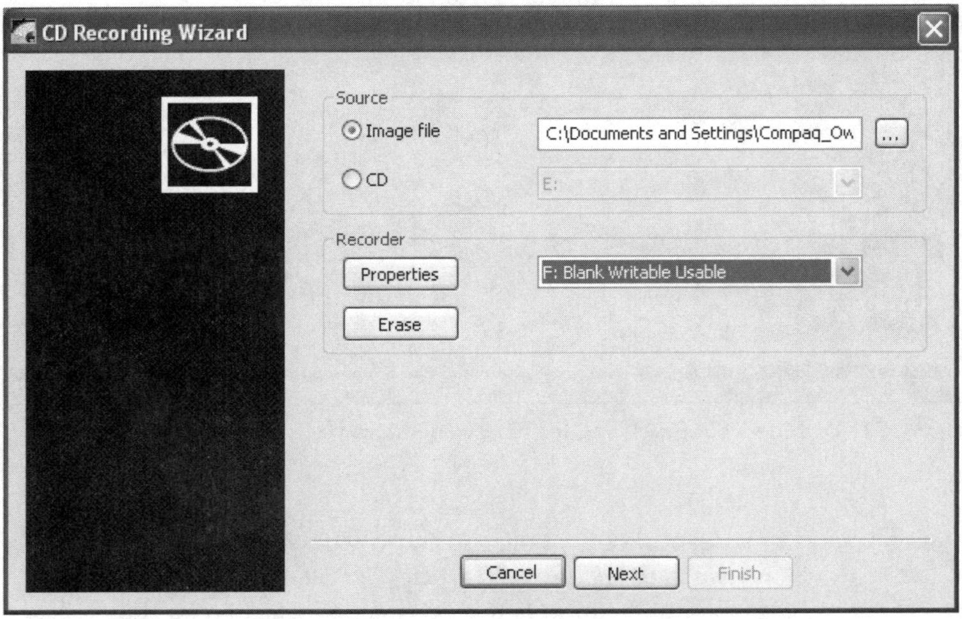

Figure 21–2   ISO Recorder makes it incredibly easy to burn ISO images to CD-ROM or DVD-ROM.

Despite having a couple of other CD-burning programs on my Windows system, I nevertheless always use Alex's program to burn ISO images. I do it because it's easy, it's fast, and it's free.

Ready to Try Ubuntu Linux?

Loading the Ubuntu Linux live CD is easy because there is no installation required.

Take your CD and insert it into your CD-ROM drive. Shut down Windows and select Restart. Make sure your PC is set to boot from the CD. Ubuntu Linux boots up to a nice, graphical screen with a simple menu (see Figure 21-3). Booting from the disk is the first option; just press <Enter> or wait. After a few seconds, the system boots automatically. Before you do that, however, notice the menu option labeled Check CD for Defects. This is a very good idea if you plan on installing Ubuntu to your hard drive, and I highly recommend that you run this step.

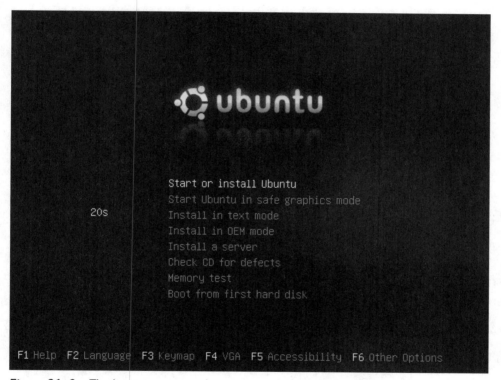

Figure 21–3   The boot menu provides a means of checking the CD for defects.

 Note Most modern systems are set to boot directly from the CD-ROM drive if a bootable CD is found there. If your system does not, you may have to change the BIOS settings on your PC to allow this. This is generally done by pressing <Delete> or <F2> to enter Setup as the system is booting. (You usually see such a message before the operating system starts to load.) Because the menus vary, it is impossible for me to cover them all, but look for a menu option that specifies the boot order. You'll see something like A: first, then C: (i.e., your floppy drive, then the hard disk). Change the boot order so that it looks to the CD first, save your changes, and then restart your system.

The boot process takes a few minutes as Ubuntu identifies devices, disks, network connections, sound cards, and so on. At some point, the screen goes dark as your video card is configured and X, the Linux graphical user interface, is started.

If the screen doesn't respond instantly, don't panic. Give it a few seconds. If nothing has happened even after you've waited awhile, it is possible that your video card is one of the rare ones not included in the distribution. Never fear, most (if not all) modern cards support VESA, and Ubuntu should fall back to this setting.

HELP!

Problems, problems . . .

The CD is amazingly good at automatically booting and running on a huge number of systems, but it isn't perfect. There is only so much software that you can pack on one CD, and that includes drivers for hardware. That said, most problems with booting the Ubuntu live CD can be resolved.

You might have noticed when the boot screen came up that there were a number of options at the bottom of the screen: F1 Help, F2 Language, and so on (refer to Figure 21-3). Some of these are fairly obvious. Pressing <F1> gives you further assistance. If you don't want to run Ubuntu with English as the default language, press <F2> and select an alternate from the list. Closely related is <F3>, which lets you select an alternate keyboard for the language of your choice.

Getting a proper graphical display is not generally a problem, but if all else fails and you still can't get a good, clear screen, try pressing <F4> and selecting VGA as your video type. Ordinarily, Ubuntu scans for and assigns the proper video driver based on your card. Several accessibility options are also built in to the boot screen that allow users with visual impairments of varying degrees to choose a more suitable environment. There are also settings for users with minor motor difficulties who may have trouble with a mouse or other pointing device. You can access these at boot time by pressing <F5>.

As the system boots, most everything is done for you. This is what is referred to as *Normal mode* and it is the best choice 99.9 percent of the time. For those who might want total control over every aspect of the boot, device detection, hardware configuration, and so on, it is possible to switch to *Expert mode* by pressing <F6>.

Boot-Level Options

The biggest set of boot changes are those that can be added to the boot command prompt itself, directly beside the `Boot Options` label. For instance, it is possible that you might experience lockups on boot or strange hardware glitches that stop the system from booting, a not uncommon problem with buggy APIC controllers (Advanced Programmable Interrupt Controller). To disable the APIC, press <F6> to bring up the boot prompt, then add this line to the end of the existing options:

```
noapic
```

Press <Enter> and the machine boots normally, but with the APIC disabled. Some of the prompts do not deal with actual problems, they just speed things along. An example of this has to do with network configuration. Normally, the Ubuntu live CD configures its network card for DHCP with the idea that an address will automatically be provided by another machine on the network. You can always change this after the system is up, but it is possible to force a static IP address at boot time.

```
disable_dhcp=true
```

To see a much more comprehensive list of boot parameters, press <F1> to enter the help screen, press <F5> for an overview of boot parameters, <F6> for parameters dealing with specific machine hardware, <F7> for parameters related to disk controllers, and <F8> for those related to the boot process itself.

Taking a Tour of Ubuntu Linux

After the system has booted, you can start playing with Ubuntu Linux. From here, you can follow along in the book and try the various programs covered. To get you feeling at home quickly, however, let me give you a quick tour of the menus and I'll show you what your system has to offer.

Looking at your Ubuntu desktop (refer to Figure 21-1), you can see that there is a gray panel running along the bottom and along the top of your screen. I want you to look at the labels along the top panel and to the left. One says Applications, followed by Places, and finally, System. Each of these represents a menu of possibilities, granting you access to the great programs included with your Ubuntu Linux system, your computer's hardware, storage devices, peripherals, and the tools you need to customize every aspect of your Ubuntu Linux experience.

Start by clicking the Applications button. Then, pause your mouse cursor over the Accessories menu, where you see some handy system tools (see Figure 21-4).

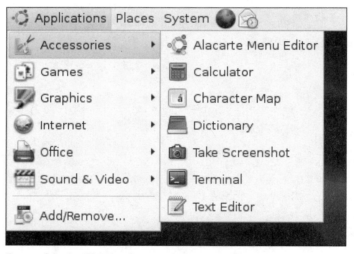

Figure 21-4   *The Accessories submenu includes a number of useful tools.*

The Alacarte Menu Editor (sounds yummy, doesn't it?) is a program designed to let you add or remove, or even modify, menu items. Sometimes a program doesn't appear where you would like it or another program that you use regularly isn't available there. Alacarte is how you change things. Calculator is a simple calculator when it starts, but it also provides advanced functions, including business, financial, and scientific functionality. Character Map is a program that makes it easy to insert international and special characters not directly available from your keyboard (useful when your last name has an é at the end).

The Dictionary looks up words using Internet-accessible resources from dict.org. You can, of course, change the appearance of your desktop. If you feel like sharing your desktop's new look with friends, Take Screenshot is the tool for you. Terminal is a means to access your system's text command line. It's not that scary . . . really. Finally, the Text Editor provides a simple, yet powerful, means of editing and manipulating text files.

Move that mouse cursor down one and let's have a look at the Games sub-menu (see Figure 21-5).

Figure 21–5 An operating system without games is like a day without sunshine—or something like that.

At some point, everybody needs a break, some time to relax and enjoy a little down time. How about trying one of the many solitaire games included in AisleRiot, or spending some time at the Blackjack table? A little Mahjongg, perhaps?

The collection of games included with your system is just the beginning. If you do decide to make Ubuntu a permanent resident on your hard drive, you can install and run all the games I told you about in this chapter, and hundreds more, from dungeon crawlers to first-person shooters, high-end 3D action, puzzles, and strategy. Your Ubuntu Linux system could be the game machine you've been looking for.

Next, we are on to the Graphics submenu (see Figure 21-6).

Figure 21–6   *Graphics applications distributed with Ubuntu include the amazing GIMP.*

The GIMP Image Editor is an almost legendary piece of software, a powerful graphic manipulation package with dozens of built-in filters, special effects, and every tool you need to produce high-quality images. I covered the GIMP in detail in Chapter 15. The gThumb Image Viewer provides an easy-to-use way to navigate your folders and view your collection of digital art. Finally, if you have a scanner, the XSane Image scanning program will scan, copy, and fax.

The Internet submenu (see Figure 21-7) starts off with the Ekiga Softphone, a VoIP communication program that provides both audio and video.

Those of you keeping track of such things will know that Ekiga started out as GnomeMeeting. For email, contact management, and a great way to stay organized, Evolution Mail handles these beautifully. I told you about the Thunderbird email client in Chapter 3, but if you were a fan of the integrated look and feel of Microsoft Outlook, you'll love Evolution.

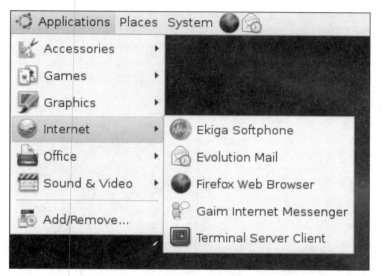

Figure 21–7 The Internet menu has everything you need to surf, email, chat, and connect to the world

The hottest Web browser in cyberspace doesn't come out of Redmond. No, it's the Firefox Web browser, and after its introduction in Chapter 2, it may well be your new best friend. An instant messaging client for AOL, another for MSN, and yet another for Jabber? Never! After learning about the Gaim Internet Messenger in Chapter 4, you are probably wondering how you ever used anything else. The Terminal Server Client is a great program that makes it possible to take control of another computer using VNC (Virtual Network Computing) or Microsoft Terminal Server.

Let's move down and have a look at the Office submenu (see Figure 21-8).

First on the menu is Evolution, which you saw back in the Internet menu with Evolution Mail. Because Evolution is so much more than just an email package, it qualifies as an invaluable office application. OpenOffice.org version 2 is a superb, and free, alternative to Microsoft Office, compatible with Microsoft Word, Excel, and PowerPoint files. It also does a whole lot more.

OpenOffice.org Base is a powerful, integrated database application, which you learned about in Chapter 9. OpenOffice.org Calc (see Chapter 7) is your spreadsheet program, similar to Microsoft Excel, whereas OpenOffice.org Draw is a flexible drawing program you can use to create all sorts of images including flow charts, organizational charts, logos, and so on. Impress, covered in Chapter 8, is a presentation package, compatible with Microsoft Powerpoint. Think of OpenOffice.org Math as a word processor for creating complex scientific formulas and equations, handy for the students out there. Finally, we come to what is perhaps the most important office tool of all, at least to this writer: OpenOffice.org Writer, a truly excellent word processing package (covered in Chapter 5).

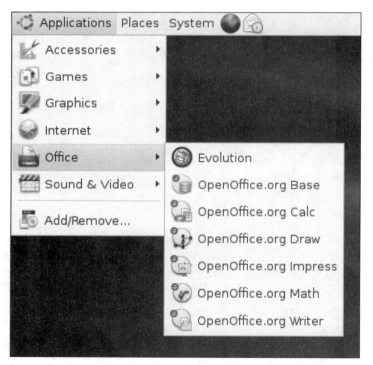

Figure 21–8   Ubuntu's collection of office applications has you covered with Evolution and the feature-packed OpenOffice.org suite.

Let's look at the last of these submenus, Sound & Video (see Figure 21-9).

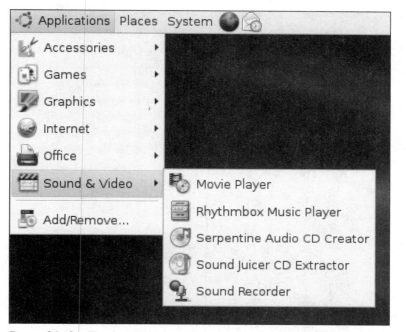

Figure 21–9 The Sound & Video submenu. Watch videos, listen to your favorite songs, and create your own music collections.

At the top of the list is the Movie Player, and its purpose is self-explanatory. With the Rhythmbox Music Player, you've got a great little juke-box program to organize your digital music, keep your ears entertained, and your spirit dancing. When you need to take your music with you, use the Serpentine Audio-CD Creator to build music CDs with collections of your favorite songs. Most of us have tons of music CDs in our collections. Getting them transferred to your PC is the job of the Sound Juicer CD Extractor. Sound Juicer is also an easy-to-use CD player. We wrap up this tour of multimedia applications, and applications in general, with the Sound Recorder, a simple program for recording sound clips.

What? I'm not done yet?

You are right; I'm not done. There is an Add/Remove menu item in that list. If you want to find out how incredibly easy it is to install software in Ubuntu Linux, this is a great place to start. Select a package from the menu, click Install, and that's pretty much it.

Tip Remember to check out the article, "Installing Packages Using Ubuntu," on my Web site at www.marcelgagne.com. You'll find it in the support section for this book (just click the Moving to Free Software book cover on the Web site).

Famous Places on the Menu

Next to the rather rich landscape of the Applications menu and its submenus, we find the Places menu (see Figure 21-10). Places primarily is a menu of physical storage locations, most of them disks or folders on your own system.

Figure 21–10   The Places menu provides quick access to your system's local and network storage locations.

From here, you can quickly jump to your home folder, navigate the computer's disks, create a CD or DVD using your writer, and search for files on your system. These storage resources don't need to always be connected to your system. For instance, if you plug in a USB storage key, it appears in the Places menu and you can access it without additional fuss.

Places can also show resources a network jump away, either on your local area network or on the Internet. If you have Windows machines with shared drives on your network, Network Servers get you there with a click.

Administering and Personalizing Your System

The final set of menus is listed under the System label on the top panel. Before I tell you about these menus, I would also like to let you know that the GNOME help system is available from the System menu. You can also lock your screen with a password (when you run off for coffee or a muffin) or log out of your current Ubuntu Linux session.

Now, let's take a look at the Preferences submenu (see Figure 21-11).

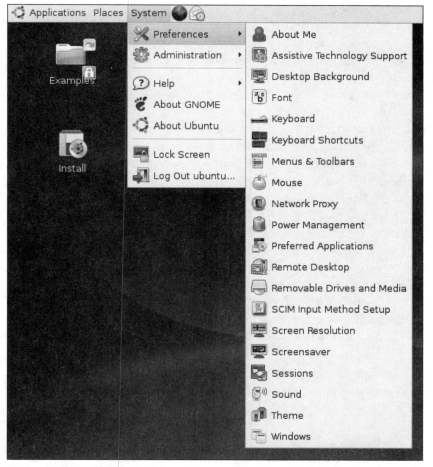

Figure 21–11   The Preferences submenu allows you to change your personal settings.

Tip Near the top left of your screen are two very interesting icons. The Examples folder contains a number of sample documents, spreadsheets, images, and multimedia files to try with your Ubuntu Linux system. The Install icon, meanwhile, is your starting point for installing the Ubuntu Linux live CD permanently onto your hard disk. I'll discuss those steps shortly.

The Preferences menu is all about personalizing the user experience. Because these are personal options, none of them require administrative privileges. You can set a screensaver, change the background, apply window decorations, or play with the colors. Pick one of the included themes and give your system a whole new look.

If the fonts look a little small, there's a simple option for changing the size of what you see on the screen. And speaking of your screen, changing the screen resolution is easy and doesn't require that you restart your graphical environment.

Okay, let's wrap up this tour of your system menu with the Administration submenu (see Figure 21-12).

System administration may sound like something most people would rather stay away from, but it's not all that scary. From time to time, you want to do things on your system that affects everyone who logs in equally. Changes made under Preferences don't affect anyone but the current user, and if your niece, Stephanie, chooses some garish desktop colors, it won't affect you when you log in.

Administration functions cover the gamut from setting up a printer to configuring your Internet access. You can share folders (so others on your home or office network can use them), look at system logs, change the look and feel of the login screen, and add users.

Perhaps one of the most important functions here involves updating and maintaining the packages on your system. Keeping up-to-date is one of the best ways to keep your system humming along nicely, and securely.

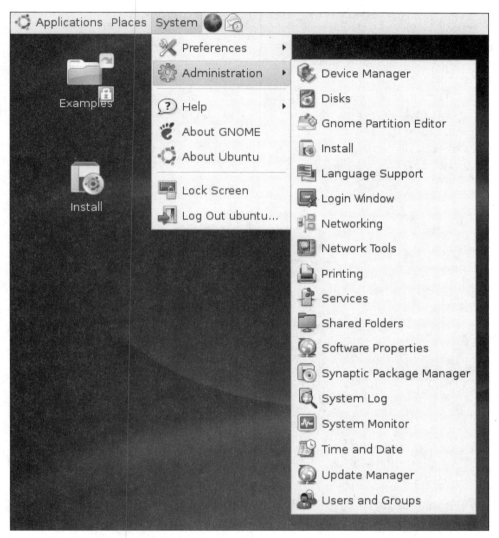

Figure 21–12 Ubuntu's Administration submenu is your starting point to configure your network, check logs, install software, and more.

Installing the Ubuntu Live CD

After you have played with your Ubuntu Linux live CD for awhile, I'm confident that you are going to want to make the experience permanent. Linux is far superior to your old OS in many ways, and after you install it to your hard drive, Ubuntu Linux will run much faster. Luckily, the process of installing Ubuntu Linux is practically pain free with Ubiquity. Answer a few simple questions and in a few minutes you have Ubuntu installed on your hard disk.

On your desktop, directly below the Examples folder, is an Install icon (see Figure 21-13). Double-click the icon to start the Ubiquity Installer.

Figure 21–13   Double-click the Install icon to start the Ubiquity installer.

When you do this, the Ubiquity Installer window appears. The first screen is a welcome screen, but it does have another important function relating to the installation process. This is the language selection screen (see Figure 21-14).

 Note This is where I repeat my warnings about making sure you have made a backup of your data. This warning cannot be repeated too many times. Make a backup, and then make another backup.

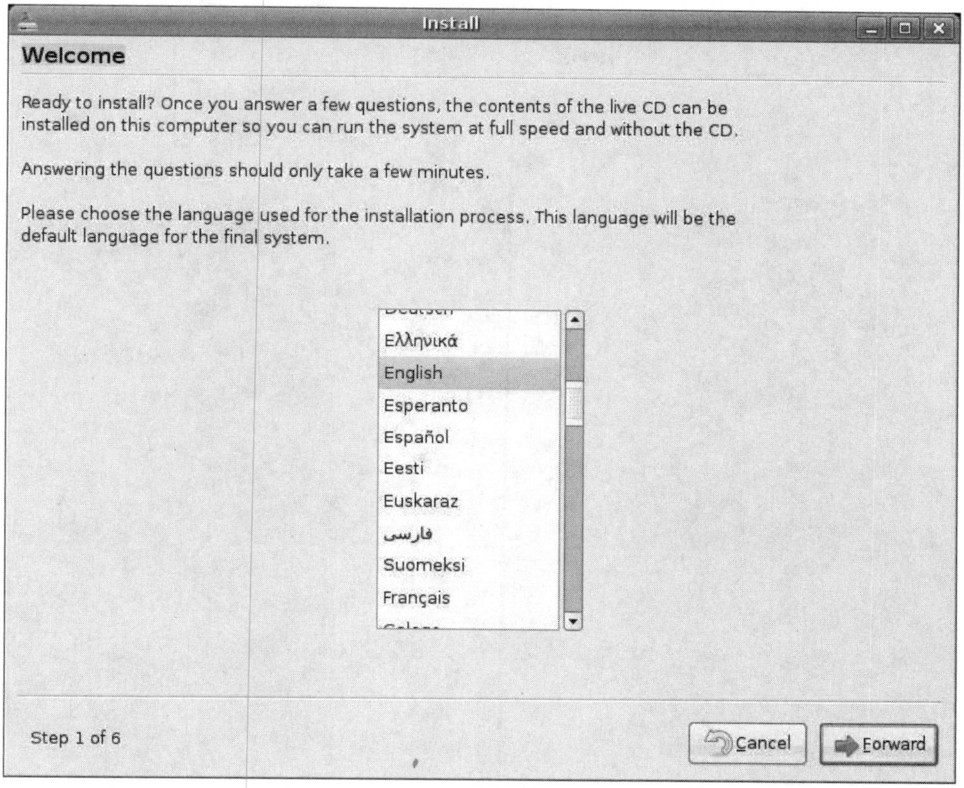

Figure 21–14   Ubiquity's first screen is partly a welcome screen and partly a language selection screen.

The language, in this case, is also the default language when the system is fully installed. English is selected by default, but Ubuntu has been internationalized for dozens of languages. There's no Klingon here, but Esperanto is available.

Make your choice, and click Forward to continue. The next screen is the Where Are You? page (see Figure 21-15). This is where you set your location and time zone. Select your location by clicking the map. One click zooms you into an area from which you can fine-tune your selection. There's also a Selected City drop-down box that you can use to the same effect, but clicking the map is more fun. Click Forward to continue.

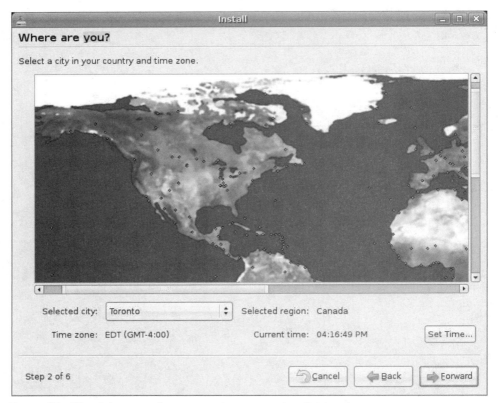

Figure 21–15   *Select your location and time zone by clicking the map.*

The next screen, Keyboard Layout, sounds very much like the language selection screen (see Figure 21-16). Nevertheless, your keyboard layout may not necessarily reflect your language of choice. As a bilingual Canadian, I still use a keyboard with an American English layout because that selection most closely reflects my notebook's keyboard. If you have an alternative keyboard, make your selection, then use the input box at the bottom of the screen to test your selection.

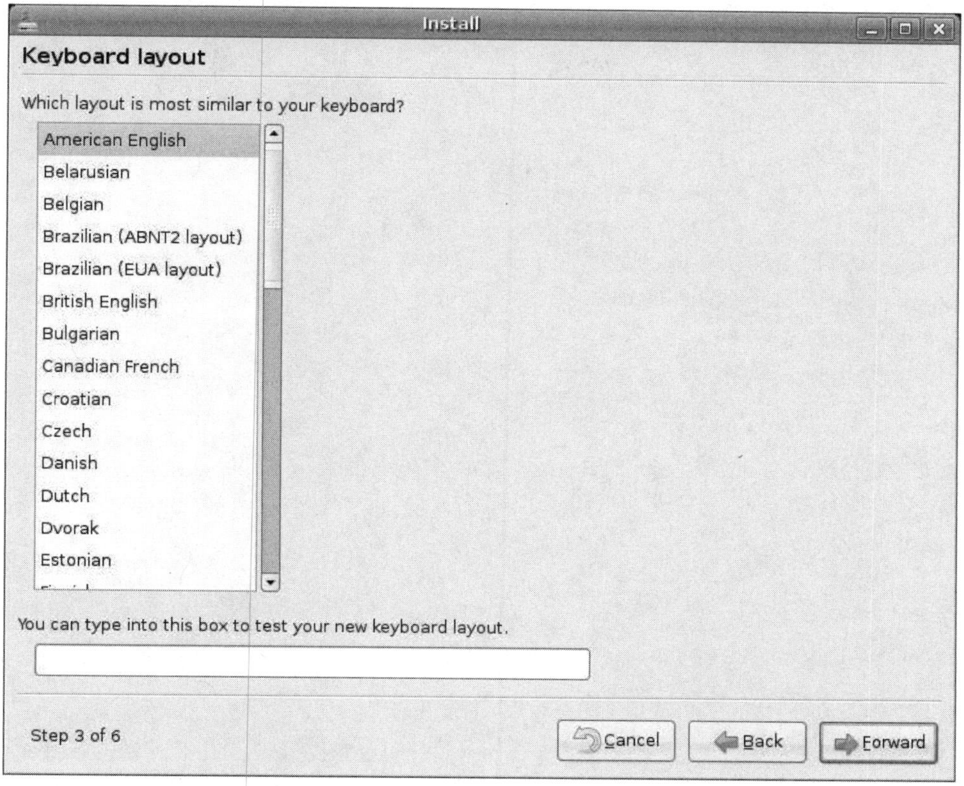

Figure 21–16 The keyboard selection screen provides a text box so you can test your hardware.

When you are satisfied, click Forward. A new window, the "Who are you?" page, appears. This is the personal identification window from which your initial user login is created (see Figure 21-17).

Enter your full name in the What Is Your Name? field. In the second field, What Name Do You Want to Use to Log In?, select a username, preferably eight characters or less (although this isn't a hard and fast rule), and tab to the Password field. When you enter the password, it is echoed back as stars (or asterisks), so don't worry if you can't see what you are typing. After this, you must enter the password again. This is to make sure that you typed what you thought you typed in the first Password field. Finally, under What Is the Name of This Computer?, enter a hostname for your system. By default, the installer appends -desktop to your username, but you are free to select something else.

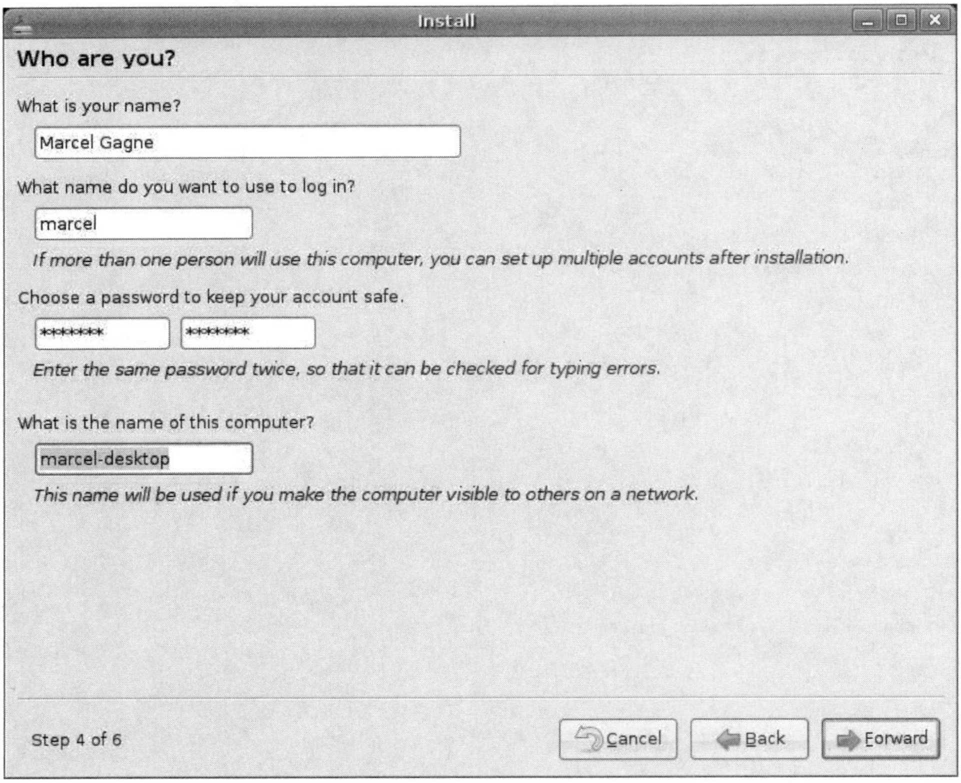

Figure 21–17   Both you and your computer need a name. The username you specify here is that of the primary user. You can add users later.

Click Forward and Ubiquity's partitioning tool starts. A small Starting up the Partitioner window appears. A progress bar keeps you posted as your disks are scanned and analyzed. A few seconds later, the main partitioning window, Select a Disk, appears. Most people have just one disk, but if you have multiple disks, select one here and click Forward. The next window, Prepare Disk Space, lets you select the amount of space you are willing to allocate (see Figure 21-18).

The information you see on the partitioning screen varies from system to system. My test system has two hard drives to choose from. Yours may have a single drive with a Windows partition that you are happy to overwrite. Notice the first option in the list. It provides an option for resizing the current partition. This is particularly useful for those who are running Windows on their system and would like to have Ubuntu and Windows coexist (yes, it is possible). If you select this option, the slider at the bottom of the list activates, and you can use it to select the percentage of space you would like to have freed up.

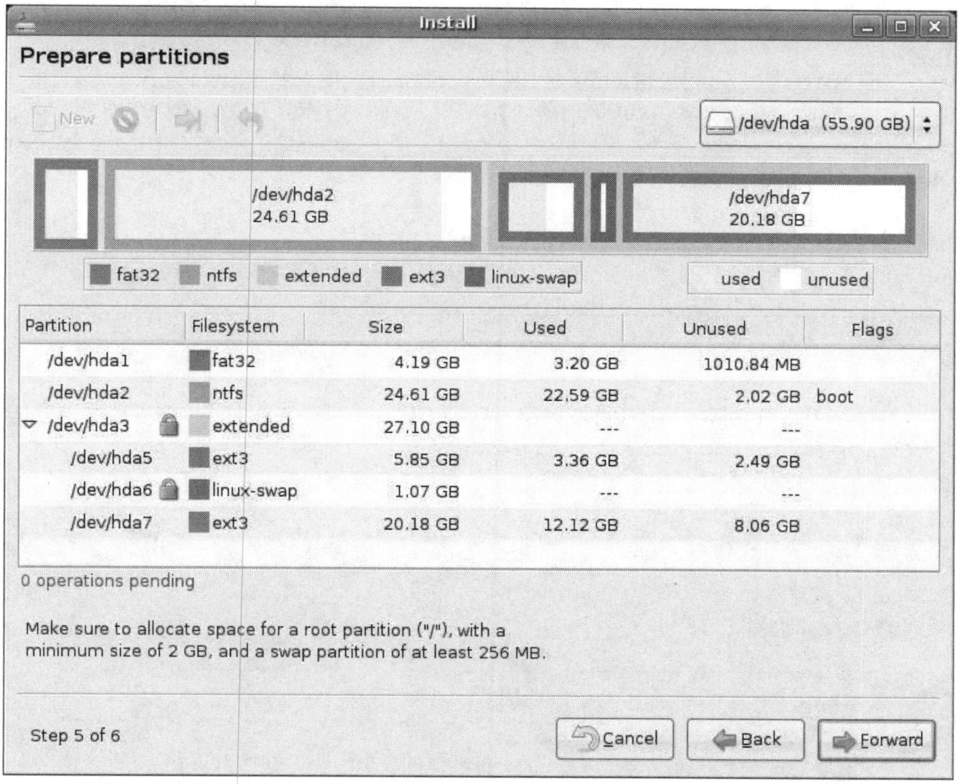

Install					
Prepare partitions					

New | /dev/hda (55.90 GB)

/dev/hda2
24.61 GB

/dev/hda7
20.18 GB

fat32　ntfs　extended　ext3　linux-swap　used　unused

Partition	Filesystem	Size	Used	Unused	Flags
/dev/hda1	fat32	4.19 GB	3.20 GB	1010.84 MB	
/dev/hda2	ntfs	24.61 GB	22.59 GB	2.02 GB	boot
▽ /dev/hda3 🔒	extended	27.10 GB	---	---	
/dev/hda5	ext3	5.85 GB	3.36 GB	2.49 GB	
/dev/hda6 🔒	linux-swap	1.07 GB	---	---	
/dev/hda7	ext3	20.18 GB	12.12 GB	8.06 GB	

0 operations pending

Make sure to allocate space for a root partition ("/"), with a minimum size of 2 GB, and a swap partition of at least 256 MB.

Step 5 of 6　　　　　　　　Cancel　　Back　　Forward

Figure 21–18　The partitioner's job is to help you create a place on your disk (or disks) to install your Ubuntu system.

Tip Unfortunately, Windows is just as likely to be taking up the entire partition table. The trick is to *shrink* the existing Windows partition, thereby creating some space on which to install Linux. To do this, you must defragment your disk in Windows before going ahead and resizing your partitions. You do this by clicking the Start button and then selecting Programs, Accessories, System Tools, Disk Defragmenter.

For this example, I've chosen to use the entire first disk (the biggest on this old computer).

After clicking forward past this point, a warning window appears asking if you are ready to install. The choices you have made up to this point, including language, username, and so on, are all repeated for you here. If you chose to use the entire disk, like me, this is your last chance to stop before your hard drive is erased in preparation for installation. Read the dialog carefully as it also confirms the partitions to be created—this is particularly important if you chose to use the available free space or you opted for custom partitioning. If you are ready, have a good backup, or you simply don't care about what's on the PC, click Install to continue.

 Tip Have I mentioned that you should have a good backup of your system, in particular, your personal data?

A dialog appears informing you of the progress as your disks are partitioned and formatted (see Figure 21-19).

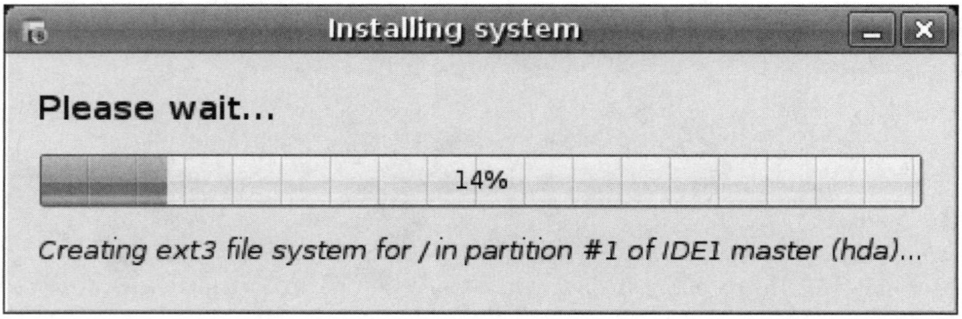

Installing system
Please wait...
14%
Creating ext3 file system for / in partition #1 of IDE1 master (hda)...

Figure 21–19 A status bar informs you of the progress as your disks are partitioned and formatted.

Although the excitement may be running high at this point, what happens next is only so exciting and the amount of time it takes depends largely on how fast your processor is, how much memory your system has, and how fast your disk drives are. This is usually a good place to walk away and get a snack and something to drink. If you feel so inclined, you can watch the progress bar as your system is prepared and installed (see Figure 21-20).

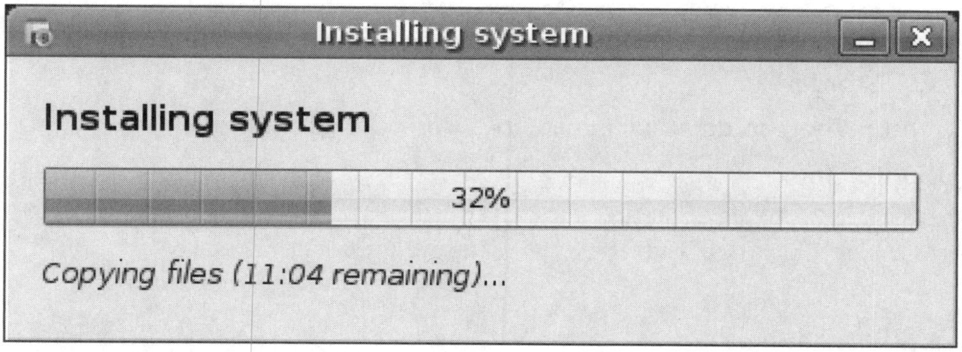

Figure 21–20 Besides providing a graphical status on the install process, the window also provides a time estimate to completion.

Some time before that bar hits 100 percent, you see a message at the bottom of the progress window informing you that it is configuring the system, creating the user, and configuring hardware, network, bootloader, and so on. These are the final steps in creating your new Ubuntu Linux system from the live CD.

When the installation completes, a final dialog appears. Click Reboot the Computer to finish the process. The system shuts down and the CD is ejected. Make sure you remove the CD, and press <Enter> to reboot your system.

With your PC system running free software, you are ready to experience computing without borders, without restrictions, and without limits.

Remember to Share

Now that you have installed your system from the Ubuntu Linux live CD, feel free to make and burn additional copies of this disk and share it with friends, family, and even business associates. The license under which Ubuntu Linux is covered makes this perfectly legal.

Resources

ISO Recorder

http://isorecorder.alexfeinman.com/isorecorder.htm

Ubuntu Linux

http://www.ubuntu.com

Index

BOOKS ONLINE

ENABLED

THIS BOOK IS SAFARI ENABLED

INCLUDES FREE 45-DAY ACCESS TO THE ONLINE EDITION

The Safari® Enabled icon on the cover of your favorite technology book means the book is available through Safari Bookshelf. When you buy this book, you get free access to the online edition for 45 days.

Safari Bookshelf is an electronic reference library that lets you easily search thousands of technical books, find code samples, download chapters, and access technical information whenever and wherever you need it.

TO GAIN 45-DAY SAFARI ENABLED ACCESS TO THIS BOOK:

- Go to **http://www.awprofessional.com/safarienabled**

- Complete the brief registration form

- Enter the coupon code found in the front of this book on the "Copyright" page

Addison
Wesley

If you have difficulty registering on Safari Bookshelf or accessing the online edition, please e-mail customer-service@safaribooksonline.com.

DVD Warranty

Addison-Wesley Professional warrants the enclosed DVD to be defects in materials and faulty workmanship under normal use for a p ninety days after purchase (when purchased new). If a defect is discovered in the DVD during this warranty period, a replacement DVD can be obtained at no charge by sending the defective DVD, postage prepaid, with proof of purchase to:

Disc Exchange
Addison-Wesley Professional
Pearson Technology Group
75 Arlington Street, Suite 300
Boston, MA 02116
Email: AWPro@aw.com

Addison-Wesley Professional makes no warranty or representation, either expressed or implied, with respect to this software, its quality, performance, merchantability, or fitness for a particular purpose. In no event will Addison-Wesley Professional, its distributors, or dealers be liable for direct, indirect, special, incidental, or consequential damages arising out of the use or inability to use the software. The exclusion of implied warranties is not permitted in some states. Therefore, the above exclusion may not apply to you. This warranty provides you with specific legal rights. There may be other rights that you may have that vary from state to state.

More information and updates are available at:
http://www.awprofessional.com/